The Watercooler Effect

The Watercooler Effect

*An Indispensable Guide
to Understanding
and Harnessing the
Power of Rumors*

NICHOLAS DiFONZO, PH.D.

AVERY
a member of Penguin Group (USA) Inc.
New York

AVERY

Published by the Penguin Group
Penguin Group (USA) Inc., 375 Hudson Street, New York, New York 10014, USA ·
Penguin Group (Canada), 90 Eglinton Avenue East, Suite 700, Toronto, Ontario M4P 2Y3,
Canada (a division of Pearson Canada Inc.) · Penguin Books Ltd, 80 Strand, London WC2R 0RL,
England · Penguin Ireland, 25 St Stephen's Green, Dublin 2, Ireland (a division of Penguin Books Ltd) ·
Penguin Group (Australia), 250 Camberwell Road, Camberwell, Victoria 3124, Australia (a division of
Pearson Australia Group Pty Ltd) · Penguin Books India Pvt Ltd, 11 Community Centre, Panchsheel
Park, New Delhi—110 017, India · Penguin Group (NZ), 67 Apollo Drive, Rosedale, North Shore 0632,
New Zealand (a division of Pearson New Zealand Ltd) · Penguin Books (South Africa) (Pty) Ltd,
24 Sturdee Avenue, Rosebank, Johannesburg 2196, South Africa

Penguin Books Ltd, Registered Offices: 80 Strand, London WC2R 0RL, England

First paperback edition 2009
Copyright © 2008 by Nicholas DiFonzo

Scripture taken from the Holy Bible, New International Version®. Copyright © 1973, 1978, 1984
International Bible Society. Used by permission of Zondervan. All rights reserved. The "NIV" and "New
International Version" trademarks are registered in the United States Patent and Trademark Office by
International Bible Society. Use of either trademark requires the permission of International Bible Society.

Most Avery books are available at special quantity discounts for bulk purchase for sales promotions, premiums,
fund-raising, and educational needs. Special books or book excerpts also can be created to fit specific needs.
For details, write Penguin Group (USA) Inc. Special Markets, 375 Hudson Street, New York, NY 10014.

The Library of Congress catalogued the hardcover edition as follows:

DiFonzo, Nicholas.
The watercooler effect : a psychologist explores the extraordinary power of rumors / Nicholas DiFonzo.
p.   cm.
Includes bibliographical references and index.
ISBN 978-1-58333-325-9
1. Rumor.   2. Social psychology.   I. Title.
HM1241.D55   2008   2008023645
302.2'4—dc22

ISBN 978-1-58333-359-4 (paperback edition)

Printed in the United States of America
1 3 5 7 9 10 8 6 4 2

BOOK DESIGN BY TANYA MAIBORODA

While the author has made every effort to provide accurate telephone numbers and Internet addresses at the
time of publication, neither the publisher nor the author assumes any responsibility for errors, or for changes
that occur after publication. Further, the publisher does not have any control over and does not assume any
responsibility for author or third-party websites or their content.

For Panfilo DiFonzo

Contents

The
Watercooler
Effect

To Rumor Is Human

Now we see but a poor reflection as in a mirror.

—PAUL OF TARSUS, FIRST LETTER
TO THE CORINTHIANS

I ASKED MY WIFE THE OTHER DAY if she had a watercooler in her office. "It's called a coffeepot," she replied.

She had correctly understood my question. I was wondering about the spot where people happened to gather, where hearsay tends to get passed along. Wherever people live, work, or play in community, the watercooler effect springs up. It transpires around a watercooler, near a coffeepot, at a pub, in a piazza, on the quad, in a chat room, on the street, at a barbershop, in a blog, or over a backyard fence. The watercooler effect occurs wherever rumors flow.

Herman Melville wrote about the watercooler aboard a Navy

frigate he sailed as a common seaman in his 1850 novel, *White-Jacket*. It was called the scuttle-butt:

> The scuttle-butt is a goodly, round, painted cask, standing on end, and with its upper head removed, showing a narrow, circular shelf within, where rest a number of tin cups for the accommodation of drinkers. Central, within the scuttle-butt itself, stands an iron pump, which, connecting with the immense water-tanks in the hold, furnishes an unfailing supply of the much-admired Pale Ale.

Melville described it as a crowded spot where five hundred sailors, servants, and cooks from all parts of the ship gathered throughout the day to get water. The scuttle-butt was *the* place where informal communication and rumor flourished: "There is no part of a frigate where you will see more going and coming of strangers, and overhear more greetings and gossipings of acquaintances, than in the immediate vicinity of the scuttle-butt. . . ." Slaking his thirst, a sailor might announce to anyone in earshot: "We're bound for Boston straightway—I overheard the Captain's man." Or whisper: "The Secretary of the Navy is a corrupt old buzzard!" Or complain: "In Norfolk, I hear there are signs saying: 'Dogs and sailors keep off the grass!'" Word would often spread rapidly through the ship's crew by way of the scuttle-butt. And so over the years, the term has come to mean any sort of rumor, hearsay, word-of-mouth, or gossip.

This book is about the psychology of what happens at the "scuttle-butts" of the world. It concerns basic mental and social processes that occur whenever people interact informally, whether face-to-face around a watercooler, over the telephone, or "virtually" on the Internet. It explores our collective intelligence in the face of uncertainty. It delves into the dynamic sensemaking that is characteristic of our human social experience. It is about the extra-ordinary power of the ordinary phenomenon we call rumor.

At the time I write this, ex-KGB spy Alexander Litvinenko has died from poisoning by the radioactive reagent polonium-210. Police first thought he was slipped the lethal substance at a sushi bar in London while meeting with an Italian, Mario Scaramella; Scaramella also tested positive for the poison though only mildly. Since then, suspicion has fallen on another ex-KGB agent, Andrei Lugovoi, who met with Litvinenko for tea the same day. In this cloak-and-dagger saga reminiscent of a good spy novel, Litvinenko issued a public deathbed indictment of Russian president Vladimir Putin as the perpetrator of this crime. Rumors about Litvinenko's demise proliferate: One portrays the poisoning as suicide; another that Scaramella would also perish; a third that British atomic scien-tists have ascertained the polonium-210 was man-made and origi-nated in a Russian nuclear reactor. Time may—or may not—ferret out the facts of this real-life political thriller.

Rumors are frequently entwined with the events of the day. In the aftermath of September 11, 2001, for example, rumors flowed freely: "Beware of Ryder, U-Haul, and Verizon trucks: in the past twenty-four hours, thirty of them (rented by persons of Arab ancestry) were not returned—doubtless to be employed in deadly terrorist bombings." "A towboat and a Coast Guard post—both in Mississippi—were showered with anthrax by crop-dusting aircraft." "Federal Emergency Management Agency personnel were dis-patched to New York City the day *before* the September 11 attacks, proving that the government knew of them in advance." These sto-ries reflect some of the human qualms, quirks, queries, and fears that filled those days.

On an intuitive level, all of us can relate to rumors; we attend to, discuss, or disseminate them—often daily. They are a funda-mental phenomenon of social beings. Every person on the planet in every period of human history has almost certainly been affected by or involved in some aspect of hearsay. It is a universal human enterprise. Rumors proliferate wherever people interact. There are computer rumors, corporate rumors, disaster rumors, medical rumors, military rumors, personnel rumors, political rumors, school rumors, and rumors about religion, race, and relationships. Workplace rumors are particularly widespread. In the fall of 1992, workers at the General Motors automotive plant in Ypsilanti, Michigan, were informed that the facility would be shut down by the end of the following summer. Standing in an employee parking lot in front of a sign proclaiming "Park your Foreign-Made Vehicles Elsewhere—NOT HERE," union boss Bob Harlow told the press that he hadn't received much else in the way of information. Rumors circulated wildly among plant workers, who were naturally worried about the future of their jobs: "The plant will be taken over by the Japanese." "NAFTA (North American Free Trade Agreement) is to blame." "The plant will stay open to produce the Saturn." It was a trying time for these employees, and in this era of mounting globalization, an oft-repeated state of affairs in the manufacturing sector.

The study of hearsay has much to say about the psychology of persons and groups. My rumor research has helped me to understand how people perceive and think of themselves, others, and the world. Rumor investigations have afforded me insight into people's anxieties. Understanding rumor has widened my knowledge of how attitudes arise and are altered, how people process data, how we collectively cultivate explanations, how prejudices and stereotypes surface and stay afloat, how conflicts spiral out of control, how person-to-person relationships and rapport are preserved in conversation, the paramount value of interpersonal trust in all human transactions, and why public relations schemes may or may not persuade. Rumor has a lot to teach us about the psyche of Homo sapiens.

Rumor is intriguing, ubiquitous, and provides a porthole into human psychology. These are all good reasons for researching rumor—but they were not *my* reasons at the time I began this line of inquiry. My work on hearsay is like the hobby of long-distance running. Joggers often commence with practical incentives—such as weight loss or social pressure—until more noble impulses begin to dominate: devotion to the sport, the rush of the "runner's high," appreciation of the "art" of movement, love of the landscape. For me, rumor was an idea that my illustrious and encouraging advisor, Ralph L. Rosnow, was interested in. Ralph—a prodigious intellect known primarily for his pioneering work on techniques in data analysis, philosophical issues in psychology, and volunteer subject effects—has contributed much to what is known about rumor. Ralph prodded me into the pursuit of hearsay.

Ralph became interested in rumor after reading Gordon W. Allport and Leo Postman's seminal work on the topic, *The Psychology of Rumor*, published in 1947. Allport and Postman had researched rumor using a system similar to the game of "whisper down the lane." In their studies, each person passed a verbal description of a picture—from memory—on to the next person down the line. No discussion was permitted. Because people can remember only so much data at any one moment, these serially transmitted "rumors" got smaller—that is, details and fine points of the message were lost with each retelling. As stated by Allport and Postman, rumors "shrunk." However, Ralph observed just the opposite in a real rumor that commenced in 1969, that Paul McCartney of the Beatles was dead. This rumor seemed to grow over time—that is, the details associated with the story increased in number. For example: McCartney's death was signified by his bare feet on the cover of the *Abbey Road* album; the band was covering up his passing; John Lennon sang "I buried Paul" at the end of "Strawberry Fields Forever"; and a *Life* magazine photo of Paul was fabricated. Additional developments about Paul's demise seemed to arise each week. This apparent contradiction—rumors grew but they were supposed to shrink—piqued Ralph's curiosity and he soon discovered a dearth of scientific study in this area. The rumor research terrain was untilled. But by the time I met Ralph in 1990, he had conducted numerous investigations on the topic and had written nearly a score of important scholarly manuscripts on rumor. Ralph's work greatly widened what we know about the psychology of rumor.

One afternoon, Ralph asked me to stop by the campus library and copy a recent article by John Pound and Richard Zeckhauser, professors at Harvard University. Pound and Zeckhauser were interested in rumors about corporate takeovers and mergers. When corporations merge, their stock values often rise dramatically. Investors pay attention to hearsay about takeovers and mergers. Theoretically, a rumored stock could be purchased and then sold later at a great profit, particularly if the rumor proved true. This leads to an intriguing question: Is trading on rumored stocks indeed profitable? Pound and Zeckhauser stated the problem more precisely: would an investor who bought stock based on rumors do better than if he had simply invested in standard blue-chip stocks? In other words, do people who trade on rumors earn more money than the market as a whole?

To answer this question, they carefully collected published rumors from the Heard on the Street column of *The Wall Street Journal* and compared the performance of these rumored stocks with the market average. Heard on the Street often prints word of mouth heard in the financial marketplace. Pound and Zeckhauser found that investors who heeded the advice of Heard on the Street hearsay did no better than the average. Contrary to the accepted wisdom of many on Wall Street, stock market rumors—at least those published in Heard on the Street—afforded no great advantage to investors. Pound and Zeckhauser were not bullish on rumors. Ralph and I thought the study was fascinating, and we wondered whether there might be a way to study rumor using the stock market. At the time, this prospect appeared rather daunting; I knew very little about securities and stock trading. But I soon discovered how I could use the "stock market" to study rumor.

One day, Ralph was seated at his desk sorting mail. I sat there pondering the stacks of paper, journals, books, theses, articles, and dissertations covering every inch of horizontal surface and stuffing the many shelves and filing cabinets of his large corner office. A young psychologist named Paul Andreassen had sent him a recent paper published in the prestigious *Journal of Personality & Social Psychology* titled "On the social psychology of the stock market." Paul's article was about how news affects stock trading. "Are you interested in this?" Ralph asked. I took the piece from his hands and packed it away for my commute home. I was skeptical if anything would come of reading it; I found equation-filled econometric articles about the stock market to be a great antidote for insomnia. But my fears were unfounded—Paul's paper proved a page-turner.

In Paul's studies, college students participated in a stock market game where they traded Goodyear stock over sixty "days." Each day lasted only twenty seconds, so the entire experience entailed approximately twenty minutes. These "investors" were given some play shares of the stock and real money at the start of the game, and could buy or sell the security each day—or do nothing. Of course prices changed each day, so the trick was to buy low and sell high— one of life's not-so-secret rules that you can't ignore if you hope to turn a profit in any business venture. Some of the investors also received several news reports, similar to what bona fide brokers experience. The news always agreed with that day's price change. For example, the headline "Goodyear Profits Up" would always be paired with a price increase that day. This is how it works in real life—it would be bizarre indeed if price downturns were accompanied by positive news, or price upturns were paired with negative news. (This happens because journalists try to explain the day's price change with news that makes sense of the change.) Other investors did not receive any news; they made their trading decisions based only on each day's price changes. So the question was: Which condition—news or no news—would be more profitable?

Paul found that no news is good news, at least when it comes to trading stock. Hearing news seemed to hinder investors from following that time-honored buy low-sell high market strategy. Traders presented with news made far less money than those who heard nothing. This result was remarkably counterintuitive; real-world investors often pay close attention to—and hard cash for—the news in hopes of making better investment decisions. But Paul had found that ignorance, at least concerning news about securities, might indeed be bliss.

Paul's investigation inspired me. I wondered if rumor—published or unpublished—would affect investor behavior in the same way as news had. I decided to research rumor in the same manner that Paul had examined news—by creating an investment game. Ralph liked the idea and I began to code my own computer game.

The name of the game was Broker. It was an engaging experience despite its simple features. College undergraduates playing Broker would regularly beat their desks in bearish agony or cheer in bullish glee as the game proceeded and their play fortunes rose or fell. In this investment game, players traded in Goodyear stock and received price and price change information over sixty "days." They also received either front-page *Wall Street Journal* news, published rumors from the Heard on the Street column, unpublished rumors from "your brother-in-law Harry," or no news or rumors. Harry was an especially dubious source. Which condition—news, Heard

on the Street rumors, Harry's rumors, or no news or rumors—
would prove most profitable?

Despite the fact that players regarded rumors—especially those
from Harry—as not credible, not plausible, not trustworthy, and
not worth risking much money on, they bought and sold stock in
the same unprofitable manner that investors who had received
news did. Consequently, participants receiving neither rumors nor
news made much more money than "informed" investors. Paul had
found that no news is good news; I had established that no rumors
is also good news.

Why are rumors such a regular part of people's experience? What
is it about being human that sets the stage for rumor activity? The
answers can be found in two fundamental features of human nature.
First, people are social and relational entities. There is something
especially "we" about our encounter with existence, even for the
solitary loners among us. John Donne's memorable poetic phrase
"No man is an island" suggests this sentiment. Like most creatures,
we seem to be designed for social interaction. We talk together, eat
together, work together; we trade, barter, and bicker. A large part
of what it means to be human is to communicate with one another.
We also view ourselves in relation to other persons—a man may be
a father, a friend, or a follower. As psychologist Susan T. Fiske put
it, we are fundamentally social beings.

Second, humans have a deeply rooted motivation to make sense
of the world. From ancient times men and women have been con-
ceived as rational embodied entities; flesh and blood creatures in
which reside the faculties of sensing, perceiving, thinking, deciding,
believing, and choosing. In other words, we are sensemaking beings.
To make sense is to give meaning to our sensations, to put a context around them so that they gain significance and fit into an
understanding that coheres. It means looking at the picture side

rather than the tangled underside of a woven tapestry. To make sense is to put our experiences into perspective so that they can be understood, known about, navigated, and predicted. Without the ability to make sense, our world would be a "blooming, buzzing confusion." Making sense of the world makes sense.

So, we are fundamentally social beings and we possess an irrepressible instinct to make sense of the world. Put these ideas together and we get *shared sensemaking*: We make sense of life together. Rumor is perhaps the quintessential shared sensemaking activity. It may indeed be the predominant means by which we make sense of the world together.

Not long ago, a promising young professor in my department died tragically after being struck by a truck on Interstate Highway 390 near Rochester, New York. It happened early one wintry morning, the day after Super Bowl Sunday. The news of this event was, of course, startling. That Monday was full of sadness, yes, but also confusion, incomplete information, speculation . . . and rumor.

We first heard that he had been in an accident but that he was all right and in the hospital recovering. Sadly, we found out later that this was not the case. We next heard that he was struck by an eighteen-wheeler in the southbound lane, but that he had been motoring northbound that morning at 5:00 a.m. How could this have happened? The weather had been very bad that morning—a blinding snow on that part of the highway. The southbound lane was separated from the northbound lane by one hundred feet of grass. We pieced together that he had skidded into the wide median "valley" between the lanes, had perhaps become disoriented because of the heavy snowfall, and had unfortunately walked across the southbound lane seeking help when the truck hit him. Questions remained however: Why had he been traveling from the south in the first place? (He lived much farther north.) Why was he traveling so early in the morning (5:00 a.m.)? We stood in huddled groups, speculating about exactly what had happened. Rumor was an integral part of that morning's experience.

Our journey together on this earth is characterized to one degree or another by uncertainty. We see only in part, not the whole. Rumor—shared sensemaking—is one element of our collective response to this component of the human condition. Indeed, rumor is the people's shared sensemaking activity par excellence. It attends all of life's activities. It has been around for as long as humans have lived with uncertainty. It reflects the fundamentally social and sense-making character of the human race. Rumor activity therefore represents something basic, central, and significant about who we are.

Well, where does that leave us? If rumor is something we do, then we may as well do it well. Given our propensity to participate in shared sensemaking, my hope is that a deeper understanding of rumors might make us in some way more fully human; that is, might help us to be just a little more discerning, prudent, humble, honest, thoughtful, secure, understanding, brotherly, and faithful. I hope that understanding rumors makes it just a little easier to render fair judgments and readier to extend the benefit of the doubt. I hope that it helps us keep our heads in times of hate, confusion, and chaos, and that it makes us just a little more committed to seeking the truth of a matter regardless of how it makes us feel. I hope that it helps make life just a bit funnier for us and makes us better people if only in a small way.

In the subsequent chapters, I'll address the following questions:

Do rumors really do anything? That is, what real-world outcomes do rumors cause or contribute to? If they lead to important changes in what people do, say, or think, then it is essential to understand how they operate.

How does rumor differ from gossip and urban legend? We should be clear on this point; it might make a difference.

Why do people spread rumors? We'll look at the circumstances that give rise to rumors and we'll explore the reasons why people pass them along. We'll also investigate where rumors spread, and how they seem to spread so quickly. It has long been recognized that rumors can travel with amazing speed.

Why do people believe rumors—especially those fantastic ones? It seems incredible that some people would believe such outlandish tales.

How accurate are rumors, and how do they become more veridical or more fallacious? Rumors have a bad reputation of being false—we'll see that this reputation is sometimes deserved, sometimes undeserved.

And, we'll look at how we can best prevent and manage harmful rumors. This last topic is of interest to anyone wishing to prevent or neutralize destructive hearsay: managers, citizens, parents, children, educators, and friends.

A final word about the term "watercooler effect." I've used this phrase to make the point that a common part of our everyday lives is, upon closer inspection, a pervasive, complex, and profound phenomenon with powerful real-world effects. A watercooler is often found in an office, but the watercooler effect occurs in countless other settings and in broader contexts. To avoid the inevitable associations and confusion that would spring up with repeated use of the term, I've resisted using it throughout the book. I also couldn't bear to put readers through innumerable references to the "watercooler effect" when, in fact, "rumor" will do just fine.

Let's begin our exploration of the extraordinary power of rumors.

2

Swimming in Rumors
THE PREVALENCE AND POWER OF HEARSAY

> *In every ear it spread, on every tongue it grew.*
>
> —ALEXANDER POPE, ENGLISH POET
> (1688–1744)
> *The Temple of Fame* (1715)

THE SNOPES FAMILY is a fictitious collection of characters from the novels of American author William Faulkner. The Snopeses are a populous and pernicious lot—in true Faulkner style, they include arsonists, bigamists, con men, extortionists, and usurers. Regularly consumed with revenge and driven by ambition, they are not a very pleasant set of relations. Snopes.com is one of the most popular rumor investigation sites on the World Wide Web. Like the Snopes family, rumors breed quickly, often fool us, and may be motivated by less than exemplary purposes. Snopes.com has kept owners Barbara and David P. Mikkelson quite busy since 1993. At the time of this writing, they estimate that the site evaluates some three thousand rumors.

Such a sizable number is not surprising. Let's consider a few of the settings where social interaction and communication occur: the Web, newspapers, the workplace, and among friends and family. Rumors thrive in all of these venues.

A Google search using the term "rumor" or "rumour" on a morning in March 2007 yielded more than 32 million Web sites. For the week previous, a Google blog search yielded 32,505 blogs posting these words. A search of Google groups during the same period turned up 771 electronic discussion groups employing these terms. Rumors are also plentiful in newspaper reports. Searching LexisNexis for the word "rumor" or "rumour" in the headlines or texts of stories reported in major newspapers in a single week produced 688 hits; a Google news search yielded 7,743 news stories. In addition, rumors proliferate in the corporate world: in 1998, a sample of seasoned public relations officers—most were senior vice presidents of communication at Fortune 500 companies—stated that harmful hearsay had reached their ears on average nearly once per week. I once conversed with a middle manager who uttered a sentiment I hear repeatedly in workplace settings undergoing any type of change: "We are *swimming* in rumors." And of course rumors flourish in our face-to-face conversations with friends and family.

This listing scratches only the surface: many rumors are not labeled as such. Often, we aren't aware that a statement is a rumor. When I identify an information claim as a "rumor" it means that I am in some doubt about its veracity. This type of speech typically begins with a cautionary prefix such as "I don't know if this is true but I heard that . . ." or even "Listen to this rumor I heard." However, hearsay is often passed along as fact, with full confidence in its veracity. "Seventy-five percent of the American public is dehydrated because they don't drink six to eight glasses of water per day." This false rumor came to me as one of the many forwarded e-mails I receive each day. There was no trace of doubt anywhere in the message, and the person who sent it to me believed it fully. (Indeed, she was simply trying to be helpful.) Rumors may even be reported as official news in a venerable newspaper. During the aftermath of Hurricane Katrina in 2005, exaggerated accounts of New Orleans residents looting, killing, raping, and shooting at rescuers were reported as fact after the city's mayor mistakenly verified them. In March 2007, talk-show callers in southeast Georgia complained that elementary school teaching positions were being given to illegal aliens from Jamaica, and that students couldn't understand them because of a thick Jamaican accent. These false rumors were passed along as fact, without any cautionary prefix. In short, not only do rumors labeled as "rumors" abound, but also rumors posing as facts make up much of our social exchange.

Knowing that some of what is passed around as fact—is in fact rumor—should be a little unsettling. Some of what we accept together as true is certainly false. This implies a gloomy conclusion about humans: Are people so credulous that they simply accept any information that crosses their path?

There *is* much evidence that people can be quite gullible. Many people pass along preposterous rumors—and believe them. However, gullibility is only part of the reason why people accept and pass rumors without question. Even when the hearer is generally skeptical, most situations don't seem to call for skepticism. Most of the time trusting what other people tell us works for us, lubricates social relationships, bolsters our existing opinions, and doesn't result in an obvious disaster—even if it is just plain wrong. Indeed, civilization generally relies on our tendency to trust others. We tend to punish those who are caught violating that trust. In any event, we don't have the resources to investigate every bit of information that comes our way. If we did greet each item of information with extensive enquiry and skepticism, we would have little remaining time or energy to live life. Generally, we find it necessary to verify only the issues that are important to us. We may accept rumors without question because of an innate gullibility, but more important, this easy acceptance works for us much of the time.

So, rumors are a frequent feature of the social terrain. What kinds of rumors roam our social interaction landscape? We can sort them into a variety of species. Researchers most often categorize rumors by the emotional tension that leads to their transmission: hope, fear, or hate.

Wish rumors concern a hoped-for outcome, such as when children and teenagers hear a rumor that school will be canceled tomorrow because of snow. Just prior to Victory in Europe (VE) and Victory in Japan (VJ) day, numerous wish rumors circulated that World War II had ended. Employees sometimes entertain wish rumors that the company will distribute a large end-of-year bonus. Wish rumors often crystallize the fantasies, hopes, dreams, and desires of a group. In contrast, dread rumors involve a feared or negative outcome, such as when rumors about the potentially deadly severe acute respiratory syndrome (SARS) virus spread in 2003. Little was known about how the virus was transmitted and what the ultimate toll would be; the information gap was filled in with rumors. In organizations, dread rumors about upcoming layoffs and changes that might adversely affect employee jobs are plentiful.

Kodak is one of many American corporations that have steadily downsized over the past twenty years; Kodak employees are no stranger to the dreaded "pink slip" rumor. In times of war, dread rumors are a cottage industry among the civilian populations most affected by the conflict. Rumors circulating in and around Baghdad are regularly collected by the U.S. Army. (These rumors can be viewed by requesting admission to the Yahoo discussion group BagSkeet.) U.S. Air Force captain Stephanie Kelley analyzed a ten-month sample of these rumors early in the conflict and found that most of them were dread rumors expressing fears about security, basic survival needs, and the stability of the newly formed government. False dread rumors spread rapidly in the tense Kashmir portion of India that answering a cell phone call from peculiar phone numbers would cause the phone to explode. Many Indians received this rumor numerous times from concerned family and friends.

Wedge-driving rumors feed on hate and serve to drive a wedge between people by derogating another group. A year and nine months before the 2008 U.S. presidential elections, false wedge-driving rumors flooded the national news that Democratic primary candidate Barack Hussein Obama attended a fundamentalist Muslim seminary that teaches terrorist tactics and ideology. The rumor was accompanied by a competitive twist—that the source of the smear was Hillary Clinton's election campaign. Both rumors were vigorously denied. These rumors undoubtedly shored up negative feelings toward the Democratic party, or senators Obama and Clinton. On the other side of the aisle, a false wedge-driving rumor that President George W. Bush and Secretary of State Condoleezza Rice were having an extramarital affair made the rounds. The story was that Secretary Rice referred to President Bush as "my husband" and that First Lady Laura Bush suddenly moved out of the White House. This rumor served to bolster negative attitudes toward the Republican party, President Bush, or his administration. Each rumor was derogatory toward a target associated with a particular party and seemed likely to play well among some members of the rival party, even though the rumors were false.

Of course, the triad of wish, dread, and wedge-driving rumors is only one way to slice the rumor pie. Other species of rumor proliferate. Often rumors are categorized by the rumor public; that is, by the group through which the rumor circulates. After interviewing several managers and communications officers at large companies about real hearsay they had experienced, it was clear that some rumors circulated primarily within the company among employees—these are called internal rumors.

Internal rumors can be further cataloged by what the rumor public is concerned about. Personnel rumors speculate about who is leaving or staying in the company. ("I heard that the CEO is leaving for greener pastures.") Rumors about who will replace who are called pecking order rumors. ("I heard that Jane is in line to replace Joe, and that Sally will take her job.") Job security rumors concern layoffs. ("This department is going to lose ten people.") Job quality rumors try to make sense of how organizational changes might affect the quality of some jobs. ("This new computer system will make our work much harder.") Other rumors circulate primarily outside the company—among customers, for example; these have been dubbed external rumors. Customers are often concerned about consumer safety. ("This soda pop contains carcinogens.") Stockholders are naturally concerned about stock price rumors. ("Continental Bank is about to file bankruptcy.") Often, external rumors affect company reputation. ("Corporation P donates to the Church of Satan.")

In today's rapidly shifting marketplace, organizations change quickly and often. Rumors abound in such situations. Upcoming changes in a large social agency in New York City produced a number of organizational change rumors: "The new procedures will not be effective in helping clients"; "The new procedures will result in more work for staff"; and "The new procedures will not be supported with additional time and resources." These rumors reflected the uncertainties and anxieties that accompany just about any change. Indeed, a reliable rule is that rumors nearly always result from change in an organization: mergers, downsizings, layoffs, sale of a company, new computer systems, new product lines, changes in job descriptions, and changes in personnel. Though positive changes such as increased profits, bonuses, and market share generate rumors, the potential negative consequences of change do so more often.

Many different species of rumor populate the social jungle. So what? Do they matter? Do rumors and rumor sensemaking affect human affairs in significant ways?

Hearsay wreaked havoc on the Sheik, a popular Middle Eastern family restaurant in an upscale Detroit suburb that was predominantly patronized by a large, nearby Jewish population. The restaurant had enjoyed a warm reception and high marks from food critics, serving such fare as crushed lentil soup, shawarmas, and falafel sandwiches; customers often waited to sit at one of its forty tables. According to owner Dean Hachem, the Sheik was doing well. Well that is until a false rumor spread via e-mail on September 12, 2001. Mr. Hachem stated: "That e-mail destroyed my life":

> My son-in-law, Dr. [name deleted], called me this morning. A nurse from [the] hospital where he works went to the Sheik on Orchard Lake Road and Pontiac Trail, to pick up lunch yesterday—and all the people in there were cheering as they watched the TV footage of our American tragedy. Do not

patronize this restaurant and please pass the word to everyone you know.

The e-mail allegedly spread at once to thousands of people through a close-knit religious "sisterhood" to which the sender belonged. The result was immediately devastating to Mr. Hachem's business: the next morning hundreds of patrons called to complain or inquire if it was true. Flyers of the e-mail were posted at a local supermarket. The Sheik's business dropped by 50 percent and remained so through 2005—despite numerous attempts to rebut the rumor. Jewish leaders in the community publicly urged patrons to return, Mr. Hachem showed footage from his security video of September 11 (no one is cheering), and former patrons were personally contacted. The power of this rumor is all the more striking when one considers Mr. Hachem's statement: "These are educated people."

Rumors are powerful. They influence attitudes, thoughts, emotions, and judgments. They alter opinions, prejudices, fears, affections, reputations, and even how much we like our job. They also affect behaviors such as who we vote for, who we choose to be friends with, what we buy, what school we go to, and whether or not we look for another job. Let's examine some life domains where rumors commonly affect us. Although rumor effects can be positive, I'll pay special attention to rumors that lead to negative outcomes.

Product rumors often reduce sales. A false rumor about AIDS-infected melons soured all types of fruit sales for two days or so in April 2007. The rumor spread quickly through cell phone text messaging in several Arab states, including Saudi Arabia and Qatar. It stated that trucks loaded with AIDS-infected melons were brought into these countries by Israel. In Saudi Arabia, the message was allegedly spread by the Interior Ministry; despite denials by that government body, the rumor spread quickly and was the subject of several top newspaper stories. As a result, many consumers hesitated to buy any type of fruit. This occurred even though Saudi government refutations included the fact that fruits are too cold to keep the AIDS virus alive.

Rumors often heighten intergroup distrust—as in the Sheik incident. Ironically, the same types of wedge-driving rumors—indeed the same rumors—frequently become popular among two rival groups. Take, for example, false rumors about a boy found mutilated in a shopping mall lavatory. The boy and his mother were shopping when the boy needed to use the bathroom. He was discovered later—in a pool of blood and castrated. This rumor circulated in the Detroit area in the winter of 1967–1968. In the white community, the boy was white and the perpetrator was black; in the black community, the boy was black and the perpetrator white. Rumors such as these lead to two different "shared realities" and heighten intergroup distrust.

In the debate-filled days of campaigning prior to the 2004 U.S. presidential election, the same false rumor sprouted about Republican candidate President George W. Bush and Democratic candidate Senator John Kerry. The rumor alleged that in a speech the candidate had said John 16:3 was his favorite Bible passage. This act demonstrated the candidate's hypocrisy, because the speechwriter hadn't known his Bible well enough to write John 3:16—"For God so loved the world that he gave his one and only Son, that whoever believes in him shall not perish but have eternal life"—a central Christian scripture. John 16:3, on the other hand, revealed the shallow faith of the politician: "They will do such things because they have not known the Father or me." Opposite versions of this rumor targeted Bush—these presumably played well among Democrats; and Kerry—these presumably played well among Republicans. Such rumors can only intensify distrust between members of already deeply divided political parties.

Intergroup rumors may even spark riots. Aboriginal youth rioted violently in Sydney, Australia, one hot summer day in 2004. Alcohol and long-standing distrust of the police fueled the violence, but the riot was sparked by a rumor. The incident began after an Aboriginal boy on a bicycle fell onto a spiked fence and was impaled. A police car happened to be in the neighborhood on another call and came to the aid of the boy, but he died. Ironically, rumors that the boy had been chased by the police quickly spread and incited a group of two hundred youths to throw homemade explosives at police— forty of whom were injured in the melee. According to one U.S. government report, more than 65 percent of the riots occurring during the civil rights era were incited by rumors.

Stock market, securities, and commodities rumors have long been known to affect market trading. World oil markets waited tensely while Iran held fifteen British sailors in custody following the capture of a British naval vessel in Iranian waters in March 2007. Prime Minister Tony Blair claimed the ship was nowhere near Iranian territory and hinted that military action would soon follow if the sailors were not released. Iran—a major producer of world oil supplies—defiantly insisted on its sovereign right to defend its borders. False rumors spread that a U.S. naval vessel clashed with an Iranian ship and that British soldiers had been sent to free the sailors. These rumors sent crude oil prices soaring to sixty-eight dollars per barrel, a five-dollar overnight spike. Stock market traders commonly hold that trading on such rumors is profitable, even if they aren't true. After all, what is important in the securities game is the price of the stock, not the veracity of the rumor. However, as I discussed in the introduction, stock market rumors may lead investors to depart from profitable trading strategies, leading to an unprofitable portfolio.

Organizational rumors—especially during times of change—affect job attitudes and heighten stress. Hearing negative rumors about company management—month after month—eventually led to greater distrust of management, less job satisfaction, less organizational commitment, and less intention to stay in one corporate division that was undergoing a radical downsizing. "I wouldn't trust anything *they* say" was a common employee sentiment in this situation. "Management has not been honest with employees" was another. And it wasn't only attitudes that were affected. During two of the four months studied in this longitudinal investigation of organizational change, negative rumors were associated with lower (self-rated) productivity.

Propaganda rumors—misinformation deliberately planted to gain political, strategic, competitive, or military advantage—also have a long history. During World War II, German agents alternately spread upbeat and downbeat rumors one after another among the French, with the intention to confuse and demoralize the French people. The infamous Nazi propagandist Joseph Goebbels also spread many different rumors about German operations so that they functioned as a "smoke screen"; the real intention of German activity was thus difficult to discern. Many of the wedge-driving rumors collected by the Massachusetts Committee of Public Safety during this time could be traced back to Axis radio broadcasts whose intentions were to divide Allied forces against themselves.

Similarly, political propaganda rumors may be driven by strong polarization and competition. Rumor researcher Jean-Noel Kapferer describes rumors circulating before municipal elections in 1983 in Grenoble, France. The rumors alleged that Hubert

Dubedout, the socialist mayor, had an Algerian mother and was related to a wealthy tycoon from Arabic North Africa, a "Mr. Boudoudou" (the names sound familiar). The rumors may have contributed to Dubedout's defeat in that election. Allport and Postman called such political propaganda rumors "whispering campaigns." More recently, the late Saddam Hussein regularly spread rumors to discourage resistance to his dictatorship. In light of this, rumors that he possessed weapons of mass destruction are likely to have first originated from Hussein himself, as well as Hussein's opponents (e.g., Ahmed Chalabi and other Iraqi defectors) who desired U.S. assistance in toppling him.

Health rumors misinform the public about health issues. One such rumor—believed by 41 percent of survey respondents—alleges that cancer spreads rapidly to the rest of the body when it comes in contact with air; thus it is wise not to treat cancer surgically. One can imagine how such a false rumor might result in cancer patients' decisions to forego surgery, especially patients who distrust official sources of health information such as doctors, specialists, and medical associations. One widespread cancer e-mail—falsely alleged to have originated from the prestigious Johns Hopkins Hospital—informs recipients that the standard cancer treatments of radiation and chemotherapy are less effective than a regimen of fresh vegetables and diet supplements.

Medical rumors have harmed people. In 2005 I appeared on NPR's *Talk of the Nation* with Jeff Stier, associate director of the American Council on Science and Health. Jeff told of how a false rumor that aspartame sweetener caused multiple sclerosis led an elderly woman to replace her beverage of choice—Diet Coke—with regular Coca-Cola. This woman drank a lot of Diet Coke and her grandchildren were concerned that she might be putting herself at risk for the disease. Unfortunately, the woman was a diabetic and the sugar contained in regular Coke adversely affected her.

One long-standing false story in circulation claims that an easy way to get rid of obnoxious patrons at a bar is to slip a few drops of Visine eye medication into their drink—they'll spend the rest of the night with an otherwise harmless case of diarrhea. In reality, however, ingesting Visine is dangerous. The main ingredient— tetrahydrozoline—causes severe depression to the central nervous system. In June 2006, five Wisconsin high school students poured some Visine in a classmate's drink as a prank. The student spent several days in the hospital recovering from the poisoning, which had severely lowered his heart rate and interfered with his breathing.

Rumors of clandestine plots hatched by powerful secret associations undoubtedly reinforce the sense of helplessness felt by those who circulate conspiracy theories. Some examples are "AIDS is a plot to wipe out minority groups"; "the government is storing information in its files to use against its citizens"; and "fluoridating drinking water will hurt people." People who believe rumors of conspiracies and secret plots tend to exhibit lower levels of trust and feel more alienated and powerless than those who are more skeptical. A man once described a rumor to me of how, during the Clinton years, he had witnessed planes crisscrossing Washington, D.C., that were leaving trails of—what he thought at the time was—white smoke. He then heard, though, that the planes were spraying contraceptive "dust" as part of a secret government plan to reduce the population. Interestingly, he professed not to believe these rumors at first, but gradually became convinced of their verity. Rumors such as these build upon—and in turn strengthen— strong attitudes of distrust, powerlessness, and anomie.

Rumors surrounding natural disasters can increase anxiety. Recently, rumors after monsoons in India caused such widespread alarm that it is now against the law to spread rumors after a natural disaster. Upon conviction, people who spread rumors "leading to panic" may end up spending one year in prison and face a stiff fine.

This 2005 statute came into being after rumors of floods and imminent dam failures led to wasted effort due to confusion and chaos.

Disaster rumors can contribute to distrust of disaster relief efforts. Following a natural disaster—such as an earthquake, hurricane, or tsunami—people may face difficult conditions: loss of home, power, utilities, and lines of communication. In such circumstances, people are in a heightened state of alert that provides a fertile breeding ground for rumors. After Hurricane Andrew devastated Dade County, Florida, in 1992, officials reported that thirty-eight people had been killed, fourteen from the storm. Yet rumors persisted that the actual count was much higher and that authorities were suppressing the real number. Stories circulated that eighty people had been found in a demolished building, a makeshift morgue had been set up at the Port of Miami, one thousand bodies were buried in a mass grave, and that scores of body bags were being hidden in freezers. Perhaps the most bizarre of these rumors was that bodies were being jettisoned as torpedoes from submarines. The official counts of death did not seem plausible to south Florida residents who had seen far higher death tolls from previous—and less devastating—storms. (Evacuation efforts for previous storms were less successful because of more primitive hurricane tracking, transportation, and communication systems.) The anger and distrust these rumors engendered was remarkable.

Clearly, rumors are influential actors in a number of life's theaters. They cause or contribute to a variety of important outcomes. How exactly does this happen? How do rumors achieve the effects we've been discussing?

In one of my courses I ask four students to stand up at the front of the class. I then put Post-it notes on their foreheads at random, each with an adjective in capital letters: LAZY, DANGEROUS, FLIRTA-

TIOUS, or MENTALLY ILL. I then carry on a conversation with them about their majors, hobbies, and clubs, how they like college thus far, and their plans for the future. It's nearly impossible to ignore the label when interpreting what each person says. One student—labeled LAZY—described his experience at college thus far to be "very challenging"; it was difficult to resist the idea that he needed to work harder. Another—labeled FLIRTATIOUS—stated that she had made lots of friends at college; I didn't wonder why.

This tendency to interpret things according to the ideas that are currently active in the mind is called the law of cognitive structure activation. Cognitive structures are ideas, stereotypes, or mental frameworks. They are "activated" by simply bringing them to mind. Hearing any idea, including a rumor, is like putting on a pair of colored glasses—it puts the scenery in a certain light. Hearing a rumor that someone has a particular personality trait, for example, makes us more likely to interpret what the person says in line with that trait.

Rumor effects undoubtedly occur in part because they activate powerful mental frameworks that lead us to classify people in particular ways. One such framework is mental illness. Despite advances in understanding mental illness, it remains a stigma. People tend to perceive mental illness as a sign of weakness, danger, or poor character. Imagine that you are a non-psychology student in college. You come to my laboratory to take part in a simple questionnaire study. You read a series of brief descriptions about a person:

Sophie is running for president of your class. She has a good reputation, and seems to have many ideas and plans for your class that you agree with. You feel she would be a beneficial president and are currently planning on voting for her in the upcoming election.

If you are in the "no rumor" condition, this is all that you read. In the "rumor" condition you "hear" hearsay that Sophie has a mental illness: "The day before the election, several of your friends tell you they heard Sophie takes medicine for bipolar disorder." You then answer several questions about how you feel about Sophie, how strongly you desire to be around her, and how likely you are to vote for her.

In a recent study, my student Juliana Lehr found that hearing the rumor of mental illness made non-psychology students rate Sophie much more negatively, reduced their desire to be around her, and decreased the likelihood that they would vote for her. Similar results occurred when Sophie was rumored to have schizophrenia, psychotic disorder, depression, anxiety, obsessive-compulsive disorder, posttraumatic stress disorder, and a general "unknown mental disease." The rumor of mental illness activated the "mental illness" cognitive structure, resulting in a more negative perception of Sophie.

In a similar way, hearing a negative rumor can activate a generally negative framework—despite disbelief in the rumor. That is, a negative rumor can lead us to appraise the target of a rumor more negatively—regardless of how believable we think the rumor is. "Mud sticks" as the old saying goes.

Despite incredulity at the false—and fantastic—rumor that McDonald's uses worm meat to make their hamburgers, subjects in one study at Northwestern University evaluated McDonald's more poorly after hearing that wormy tale. In this study, graduate marketing students completed a survey after watching television ads, one of which was for McDonald's. A fellow student—really a confederate in the study—then planted the rumor: "You know these McDonald's commercials remind me of that rumor about worms and McDonald's—you know, that McDonald's uses worm meat in their hamburgers." Later, participants were asked to evaluate eating at McDonald's. Students hearing the rumor without any rebuttal evaluated the fast-food chain more negatively than those not hearing the rumor.

In another condition, the rumor was heard, then facts were given to combat the rumor (similar to McDonald's actual national press campaign to combat this rumor). Rebuttals such as "Worms are too expensive!" and "The FDA . . . found that McDonald's uses 100 percent pure beef" didn't have much effect, though; participants still rated McDonald's more poorly compared to those who hadn't heard the rumor. The researchers theorized that the negative association had "stuck." They wondered whether a positive reframing could reverse these effects and so in one condition, subjects heard the rumor, then heard a confederate say that worm meat was an expensive French delicacy. This condition was designed to offer a positive framework by which to interpret "worm meat." It worked. Evaluations of McDonald's in the "French delicacy" condition rebounded to normal levels. The researchers had successfully reframed the worm-meat hamburgers to be a positive idea.

A second way that rumors accomplish their effects is to explain events using a cause that lasts over time; these explanations then affect our predictions of future events. Let's unpack this idea.

First of all, rumors are often explanations for events. Why is the CEO leaving? (To start his own company because he is ambitious.) Why is AIDS pandemic in Africa? (Because it was started in a Western laboratory as a means of genocide and it was tested on one hundred thousand Africans.) Why is management laying off half of the department? (Because they want to look good to investors, without regard for long-term consequences.) Allport and Postman said, "In ordinary rumor we find a marked tendency for the agent to attribute *causes* to events, *motives* to characters, a *raison d'etre* to the episode in question."

Of course, rumors often take the simple form of bits of information. "The Port Jervis dam is bursting!" is a good example. But during discussion such bits of information tend to quickly acquire an explanatory flavor: "*Why* is the dam bursting? Perhaps it is because government inspectors ignored crucial building codes. Why? Because they were paid to look the other way, or they were lazy." In short order, a causal chain of events is concocted so as to explain the current state of affairs. Rumors may start as isolated bits of information but soon evolve into cause-and-effect sequences.

As the Port Jervis example shows, these explanations often employ causes that are stable over time, such as dispositions. The dam is bursting ultimately because of the dispositional tendency of government inspectors to be lazy or corrupt. Dispositional traits such as laziness and dishonesty are causes that are likely to stay in place for long periods of time. Dispositions, temperament, and personality last over time. In psychology they are called stable causes. In contrast, unstable causes tend to change unpredictably.

Stable causes afford us prediction. When stable causes are embedded in rumors, then rumors also seem to afford us prediction. Stock market rumors provide a prime example here. Stock prices can be considered events that occur each day; they are even reported on a minute-by-minute basis. Journalists are often faced with the task of making sense of changes in stock prices. Why did Goodyear stock rise today? Journalists will often make sense of the change with an explanation such as "Goodyear stock rose today because management is doing such a good job." Good management practices are a relatively stable cause; if they are managing well today it is likely that they will continue to manage well in the future. In this example, a rumor leads investors not only to attribute today's price increase to good management, but also to expect tomorrow's price to rise for the same reason. (Stable causes, by definition, continue to act over time.)

This point becomes clear when you contrast stock prices with coin flipping. You flip a coin and it comes up heads. Will it be more likely to come up heads next time? No. The cause of the coin coming up heads—assuming a fair coin—is unstable. It includes the energy exerted by your thumb as you flip, the velocity of your thumb, the height of the toss, the exact direction of the toss, the mass of the coin, air density, humidity, and wind speed. Collectively, these variables are unpredictable, and we say they are random in character. Many economists say that whether or not a stock will rise or fall on any given day is also a random walk—like coin tossing, too many forces are at work and they are collectively unpredictable. Like the coin toss, tomorrow's stock price change—up or down—cannot be predicted.

Rumors change this perception, however. Investors exposed to stock market rumors expect the stock price to change tomorrow in accordance with the rumor. If the rumor claims that "Goodyear stock rose today because management is doing a good job," then investors tend to predict that the price of Goodyear will probably rise tomorrow as well. This leads to a pattern of buying behavior that, surprisingly, is not so profitable. Investors will buy stocks that go up and sell stocks that go down. In other words, investors will buy high and sell low—not a very profitable way of investing in securities.

This is exactly what I found in my doctoral work at Temple University. Student "investors" played a computerized stock market game in which they could buy, sell, or do nothing with Goodyear stock each "day"—each "day" lasting twenty seconds. (I first mentioned this study in the introduction.) The prices were arranged so that there was no way of predicting tomorrow's price change; like the real stock market, the direction of each day's price change was like flipping a coin. Some investors received either published or unpublished rumors, some received front-page news, and some did not receive any messages as they played the game. As predicted, the rumors and news proved very unprofitable for participants. Receiving these messages led them to depart from the time-honored rule of profit: buy low, sell high. Ignorance (of rumors) is not only blissful, it is also profitable.

A third way that rumors—particularly negative rumors—affect outcomes is that they serve as an advance warning system. Negative rumors teach people what to avoid without having to experience it themselves. This reasoning amounts to "Better to be safe than sorry!" In response to a false dread rumor—spread by cell phone and on MySpace.com—many teenagers stayed home from a high school in Arlington, Tennessee, in April 2007. The rumor stated *"DO NOT GO TO SCHOOL. I've heard there's supposed to be a shooting."* On hearing this, one parent was visibly shaken and kept her children out of school. Even though it was a rumor, it was "too risky."

The human tendency to place a higher premium on negative information than on positive information has been called the negativity bias. Decision scientists have shown that people are generally more attuned to the bad things that could happen to them than the good things. People will be more motivated, for example, to avoid losing one hundred dollars than they will be to gain one hundred dollars. It follows that there should be more dread rumors than wish rumors in circulation; and this is indeed the case.

There is simply more of a market for statements about potential dread events. Robert Knapp, for example, collected more than 1,089 rumors during World War II and classified them as either wish, dread, or wedge-driving rumors; 25.4 percent were dread rumors and only 2.0 percent were wish rumors. More recently, Air Force captain Stephanie Kelley analyzed rumors that had been collected in and around Baghdad for ten months in 2003 and 2004.

Dread rumors were the most prevalent; Baghdad residents' fears at that time concerned how well the emerging government would be able to function, supposed U.S. and Zionist plots to rule over Iraq, the possibility of civil war, quality of life, and security.

During my graduate school days, I became excited about a course in cognitive psychology. The main requirement in this class was to write a three-page, double-spaced paper each week. In my enthusiasm, I wrote a seven-page, single-spaced paper, on average. The professor commented favorably on the quality and quantity of my work. I got an A. I felt a warm glow of satisfaction and pride. After the course was over, however, I visited the professor in her office and noticed that grades for the course were posted on her door. Everyone had received an A. I was crestfallen! Why wasn't I happy that each of my fellow classmates was also rewarded with an A? Somewhere in a primitive part of my brain I had reasoned, "I worked harder than my classmates, therefore I should be getting a bigger reward than they; there should at least be some Bs on that list!"

A fourth way that rumors—particularly wedge-driving rumors—affect outcomes is by altering judgments of fairness. Whenever people are part of a community or participate in a task together, two questions eventually arise: first, how much effort is the other guy putting into this, and how much reward are they getting out of it? Second, how much effort am I putting into this and how much reward am I getting out of it?

Organizational psychologists call these mental calculations input-output ratios. My own input-output ratio is simply the time, effort, and other resources I am contributing to the group versus the rewards or compensation I receive. For example, a dedicated nurse might work long hours, take short lunches, and volunteer to help patients for free during off-hours, yet receive a small salary.

Despite appearances, this state of affairs by itself wouldn't lead to the nurse's discontent. Rather, discontent comes from comparison with others. If every other nurse in the organization is also contributing much for little external reward, our dedicated nurse will conclude "it's tough for everyone." But if other nurses are perceived to contribute little and receive much, it's difficult to resist the conclusion that this state of affairs is unfair. "I heard that Jane is always the first one to leave the office, but she got the same raise as the rest of us—how unfair!"

In academia, the rumor might go like this: "I heard that one senior faculty member who never publishes anything got a five thousand dollar raise this year; how typical! Those old professors hardly work at all, while we junior faculty work our tails off advising students, writing publications, and serving on thankless committees—how unfair!" These perceptions of inequity are most often redressed by changing the part of the equation over which one has the most control: one's own effort. That is, perceptions of unfairness often lead to a reduction of effort. "Why should I work so hard when others are taking it easy and receiving the same pay?" These ideas are collectively known as equity theory.

Within the framework of equity theory, it's easy to see how wedge-driving rumors that affect equity perceptions spring up. First, consider the types of information upon which equity judgments rely: compensation and performance, topics that are shrouded in uncertainty. Unlike my graduate school course, most organizations don't publish a list of everyone's salary. Such information is often considered private, and asking someone what they make is typically considered rude. This code of silence inevitably leads to uncertainty about other people's pay.

Similarly, the efforts, skills, and accomplishments that others—especially those who aren't directly observed—bring to the task at hand may not be accurately measured. "Those people in HR [or Engineering, or Accounting, or Marketing]—what do they do all day?" Groups that are physically separated from one another are particularly prone to this sort of speculation. Uncertainty thrives as a result of secrecy (in the case of compensation) and lack of reliable data (in the case of effort and activity).

But uncertainty isn't enough to spawn rumors. As Allport and Postman put it, rumors arise when both uncertainty *and* importance exist regarding a topic. This is the famous law of rumor: Rumors abound in proportion to the ambiguity or uncertainty inherent in a situation, and the importance of the topic. Americans may be uncertain about the price of tea in Afghanistan, but this issue typically isn't important to them, and so tea rumors are unlikely to brew.

However, the question of being treated fairly is important to most people. In order for the world to be an understandable and predictable place, we like it when humans (especially ourselves) are treated fairly. This explains the popularity of wedge-driving rumors that portray other groups as receiving favored treatment. "Why is it that when members of [a rival group] apply for a job, they receive special treatment, but when members of [our group] apply, we are rejected?" The following rumor was collected by the U.S. Army in Baghdad on July 5, 2007:

Iraqis want to know why some areas, such as Sadr City, which everyone knows is full of militias and criminals, receives four hours of electricity every night while the honest and peaceful citizens suffer with either only one hour or NO electricity every night?

Clearly, one element of interest to hearers of this rumor is that it allegedly contains information about how other people are being treated in comparison to "us." In a word, it contains information that influences perceptions of fairness.

A fifth way that rumors bring about effects is that they simply teach us how we should feel about things. Psychologists have labeled this type of education social learning: we learn attitudes from others. Rumors may indeed be the main means by which we learn these attitudes. "This is a terrible place to work!" or "This is a wonderful place to work!" teach us to feel negatively or positively toward our place of employment. Rumors support and legitimate these attitudes. These lessons have obvious implications for morale, and explain why loss of morale is cited as one of the largest effects that rumor can have in organizations.

Interestingly, rumors can lead to self-fulfilling prophecies, so that a rumor that was not initially true affects behavior in such a way that the rumor then becomes true. The famous bank runs of 1929 illustrate this point: Hearing false and widespread rumors that the banks had insufficient funds, patrons rushed to withdraw their money. This action caused many financial institutions to indeed have insufficient funds. A more recent version of this phenomenon was documented by sociologist Frederick Koenig: because of false rumors that Continental Illinois National Bank and Trust Company was about to file for bankruptcy, patrons quickly pulled their funds. This happened despite the fact that banks cannot file for bankruptcy. As a result, Continental Bank did indeed become insolvent and had to be bailed out by the Federal Reserve.

3

It's Clear That It's Unclear

How Rumors Help Us Make Sense
of an Uncertain World

> *Nostradamus predicted the terrorist
> attacks of September 11, 2001, as
> the start of World War III.*
>
> —POPULAR RUMOR IN CIRCULATION
> AFTER SEPTEMBER 11, 2001

I WAS PROOFREADING A MANUSCRIPT about the history of rumor
research on the morning of September 11, 2001, when my wife
called and told me to turn on the television. As I sat in spellbound
silence, I saw jetliners crash into the World Trade Center, erupt into
fireballs, and each of the Twin Towers collapse. The TV announcers
were silent at that moment—too stunned to even comment. That
morning in Sarasota, Florida, the president called for a moment of
silence to honor those killed in the attacks. And in the week that
followed, the sky was also eerily silent—no planes were permitted
to fly.

These spaces of silence punctuated the long expanses of conversation—and conjecture—in the aftermath of that memorable day. America had been attacked; she felt physically and psychologically threatened and a heightened sense of unity and patriotism. We spontaneously gathered in houses of worship to pray. We monitored the Internet, radio, and television news for information. We talked to one another and wondered aloud: Why? What's next? During these very unusual days rumors flourished: "The Justice Department has advised all employees to avoid using the [Washington, D.C.] Metro to get home because of a subway attack." "Arabs employed at Dunkin' Donuts and International House of Pancakes celebrated in reaction to news of the attacks." "A hijacked plane is headed for the Sears Tower in Chicago." None of these rumors were true, but they were part of how we tried to make sense of the new (to us) threat of terrorism.

These 9/11 rumors dramatically illustrate some of the key elements of rumors that I will explore in this chapter. Up to this point I've tried to show that rumors are prevalent, that various types of rumors exist, and that rumors cause or contribute to a variety of outcomes. But exactly what do we mean by the term "rumor"? In the introduction, I described rumor as shared human sensemaking par excellence, but *how* do rumors help people make sense of their worlds? I'll tackle these questions in this chapter; in the next, I'll distinguish rumor from two related genres of informal communication: gossip and urban legend.

Let's begin by defining our term. Rumors are unverified information statements that circulate about topics that people perceive as important; arise in situations of ambiguity, threat, or potential threat; and are used by people attempting to make sense or to manage risk. There are three questions that this definition addresses:

What do rumor statements consist of? What types of situations do they tend to arise from? And what are people trying to do with them?

First, rumors consist of information statements—noun and verb statements that purport to inform us. "Harry Potter is dead" proposes that J. K. Rowling, the author of the famed children's book series, "killed off" the hero in its last installment. (This rumor—uncertain at the time—lured Potter fans into clicking Web links that contained a computer worm.) "Tropical Fantasy Fruit Punch is owned by the KKK" alleges that the Brooklyn Bottling Company is controlled by the Ku Klux Klan. (False—it is owned by Eric Miller.) "As part of a grisly initiation rite, gang members in Illinois—driving with their headlights off—have killed unsuspecting motorists who blink their headlights at them." (False—the Illinois State Police call this the "headlights hoax.") These rumors are all declarative—they tell us something.

Second, rumors consist of statements that circulate among people; they are never merely a private thought held by an individual. Rumor is a group phenomenon, something that happens between at least two people (usually more). I may know that my boss is unhappy in his job, that he was recently scolded unfairly by his superiors, and that he has taken a few days off. I may speculate to myself that he has flown to another city for a job interview, but this thought is not yet a rumor until I share it with another person. Rumors are therefore not synonymous with prejudices, stereotypes, beliefs, or attitudes, although each of these may be conveyed in a rumor. Rather, rumors are fundamentally acts of communication.

Third, rumors consist of statements in circulation that people generally consider significant or of interest to tellers and hearers. They tend to be about topics that we regard as relatively more urgent, vital, consequential, or imperative. The classic rumor is often embedded in the anxiety-filled utterance "I heard that our department is being downsized; did you hear anything?" Obviously, a department layoff would be of great importance to employees because unemployment is a threat to well-being. Or, rumors about stocks that I own are important to me because they're relevant to my financial bottom line. This sense of importance can stem from our interest in anything we hold dear or cherish. For example, sports rumors reflect the intense interest of fans. Soccer player Michael Owen was beset by many rumors of his supposed intention to leave his Newcastle team, perhaps originating from his absence from play due to many injuries over two seasons. In the realm of political games, if I'm a solid Democrat or Republican, rumors about politicians from either group greatly interest me. Ralph Rosnow called these sorts of concerns "outcome relevant"—the outcome of a particular situation or issue is relevant to me, my welfare, my well-being, or my sense of self.

Fourth, and most important, these information statements in circulation are not verified—they are not supported, buttressed, checked, or authenticated. A verified statement has a stamp of approval on it: an imprimatur if you will; a person or source that will vouch for the validity of the information. A verified statement is not necessarily the same as a true statement: True means that the information corresponds with objective reality, while verified means that someone vouches for its correspondence with objective reality. News is typically—though not always—verified; rumor is not.

Some examples will help clarify what "unverified" means. Let's consider the two possibilities: statements that a person thinks are unverified, and those he or she classifies as verified. Perhaps most readily identified as unverified are statements that the sender himself classifies as unverified—that is, those he is openly unsure of: "I'm not sure that this is true, but I heard that management is now requiring that nurses in our department be 'on call' nights and weekends." The cautionary prefix "I'm not sure that this is true . . ." is a dead giveaway that the statement is unverified. It doesn't matter whether the information following the prefix is true or false; at the moment of transmission it's imparted as a rumor. Of course, this unverified rumor could be true or false.

Next, consider statements that a person classifies as verified. These could also be true or false. Verified statements that are true are certainly not rumors. What about "verified" statements that are false? That is, statements that are false, but which people—the transmitter, the receivers, or both—vouch for as true. False statements might be vouched for as true by con men and propagandists, or by the misinformed and mistaken. Verification in all such cases is necessarily weak—because the statement is false—even if it has been vouched for by the most impeccable source. The impeccable source is either lying or mistaken. Misinformation spread by propagandists is rumor. Saddam Hussein regularly spread rumors about his ability to spy on and punish ordinary Iraqi citizens to discourage potential rebels. A less intentional example are the exaggerated reports of raping, killing, and pillaging by the citizens of New Orleans following Hurricane Katrina that were reported by credible news agencies—it seemed a reasonable course of action to believe them at the time—yet they turned out to be objectively false. They were therefore rumors—the evidence that buttressed these statements crumbled. Statements that are *apparently* verified also fall into this category. Flyers and e-mails circulating in the 1980s and 1990s proclaimed that the head of Procter & Gamble (P&G) announced on the *Phil Donahue Show* that the corporation donates to the Church of Satan. The flyers urged recipients to contact the show for a transcript as proof. Anyone who took the time to do so found out, of course, that P&G's CEO has never been on this show (indeed—on any talk show). The "evidence" upon which the statement rested failed on closer examination. False statements that people believe to be verified are ultimately unverifiable—and are therefore always properly considered rumors.

So, rumors consist of unverified information statements in circulation that are perceived to be important or of interest. What types of situations give rise to these kinds of statements?

Recall the GM automotive factory workers in Ypsilanti, Michigan. These workers were told that by the end of the summer of 1993, the plant would close. Not much else was revealed, leaving employees with a lot of questions: When will it happen? How will the shutdown proceed? Who will be laid off? How will these decisions be made? Information was also missing in a large consumer loan corporation where I interviewed managers several years ago. This corporation faced an extensive restructuring involving the relocation of one large division to another city. Motivated to give only solid information to employees, managers were quite secretive about the reorganization plans. They actually gave the reorganization effort a secret code name and were instructed not to discuss it with workers. Rumors abounded.

Rumors tend to arise in situations that are ambiguous and/or pose a threat or potential threat—situations in which meanings are uncertain, questions are unsettled, information is missing, and/or lines of communication are absent.

Similarly, during natural disasters lines of communication are sometimes knocked out, often resulting in an information blackout. One wintry day in the early 1990s, I had difficulty returning home on my daily commute because a severe ice storm had disrupted transportation—including my train—throughout all of southeastern Pennsylvania and New Jersey. My fellow passengers and I were unable to gather information that would have helped us answer some key questions: How long will the storm last? Are there any other trains running in my direction? Are the roads safe enough to drive on?

Even the prevalence of cell phones doesn't necessarily disambiguate such weather-related snafus. Traveling through O'Hare airport on a recent summer day, I—along with thousands of other passengers—looked at the departing flights roster and read "FLIGHT CANCELED." No other information was given. Clearly, it was an unclear situation. I started talking with perfect strangers and, through rumor, I learned that the reason for cancellations was high winds, that the proper response was to "get in line" at the United Airlines desk, and that in these situations it was best to make hotel reservations immediately for that night. (I made it home after a couple of days in Chicago.)

Ambiguous situations also occur when one bit of information contradicts another—a common occurrence in life. Not long ago, I happened to be in Memphis, Tennessee, and I took the opportunity to visit the National Civil Rights Museum. The museum is housed in the Lorraine Motel, where Dr. Martin Luther King Jr. was assassinated on April 4, 1968. Across the street is another part of the museum: the Main Street rooming house where James Earl Ray allegedly fired the fatal shot resulting in King's death. In March 1969, Ray confessed to shooting Dr. King and was sentenced to ninety-nine years in prison. However, he recanted three days after he confessed and hinted that he had been an unwilling patsy as part of a conspiracy. He spent the rest of his life seeking a retrial and denying his alleged part in Dr. King's murder.

Lloyd Jowers, a restaurant owner in Memphis, claimed in 1993 that King's death was the result of a conspiracy involving the Mafia and the U.S. government. In 1999, a civil suit against Jowers found that a conspiracy to kill Dr. King did exist. Dr. King's family also became convinced of Ray's innocence and issued a statement to that effect that same year. Despite this, a U.S. Justice Department investigation completed in 2000 disagreed. It didn't find any of these allegations to be credible. Confused? So are many people, and as a result, rumors about what happened to Dr. King on that April day in 1968 are alive and well.

Rumors also tend to arise in situations that pose a threat or potential threat—possibly to one's welfare or even survival. This explains why rumor statements are generally considered important by rumor discussants.

At the beginning of this chapter I recounted some of the rumors that arose out of the widespread feelings of vulnerability in the weeks following September 11, 2001. Continued terrorist activity and ubiquitous security checking have refreshed this unease and fueled more rumors. In July 2007, police arrested a suspected terrorist in the port city of Santander, northern Spain, who had been found with a gun and a timer. Unsubstantiated reports then circulated that plans had been found on him to bomb a ferry line to the United Kingdom. Rumors then flourished that the *Pont-Aven,* a vessel connecting Santander and Plymouth, was the target of a terrorist bombing plot. The potential threat posed in this situation was obviously to human life.

But anything that challenges one's welfare or well-being is a potential threat. A computer consultant company owner I once interviewed recounted how his organization was the target of a negative rumor campaign. The campaign was orchestrated by employees who preyed upon fears that the new computer system would make job duties more difficult and even lead to layoffs. Rumors were spread purposely that the consultant was "incompetent."

Similar rumors circulated among staff in an organization I

helped change toward a measurement culture. Some employees feared that the proposed changes would make it much more difficult to do their jobs, and even that they might not be able to perform the new tasks at all. Negative rumors about the change surfaced: "Management will not adequately support the change." The rumors were an attempt to identify and cope with potential threats. Change of any stripe can be scary—it may lead us into situations that we can't handle.

The threat posed can be psychological in nature. A situation may challenge a belief, attitude, mind-set, or sense of identity. Strong feelings of defensiveness can be called forth when we—or groups that we identify with—are criticized or derogated; we can *feel* very threatened indeed. Rumors can neutralize such threats, for example, by denigrating the source of the challenge or by bolstering our own position, cause, or group.

In 2007, WorldPublicOpinion.org conducted an in-depth survey of citizens from four predominately Muslim countries—Egypt, Morocco, Pakistan, and Indonesia; the sample was representative of the population of each of these countries. The survey explored sentiments toward the United States and Al Qaeda, and attitudes about the use of violence on civilian populations. Very large majorities of participants opposed violence against civilians, as exemplified in the acts of September 11, 2001, perpetrated by Al Qaeda. However, because American intentions are widely believed to be hostile to Islam, respondents were motivated not to criticize any group—including Al Qaeda—antagonistic to the United States.

Among a number of interesting findings were the perceptions of who was responsible for the attacks of September 11. A very small minority—2 percent of Pakistanis, for example—thought that Al Qaeda orchestrated the attacks. When pressed in focus groups that Osama bin Laden had taken responsibility for the attacks on videotape, many participants became visibly uncomfortable and defensive, expressed disbelief, and suggested that the video was fake. A common response was that "Hollywood can create anything."

Instead, many thought that unknown persons, Israel, or even the United States was behind the events. To wit, rumors persist that four thousand Jews were told by the Israeli Secret Service on September 10, 2001, not to report to work at the World Trade Center the next day—the implication being that Israel bombed the buildings to incite anti-Arab sentiment. Rumors portraying Israel or the United States as masterminding September 11 are likely to spring up in situations where participants feel defensive about Al Qaeda's role in the attacks. Arab nations, of course, do not have a monopoly on such rumors—they circulate among all people whenever defensive sentiments arise.

So, rumors arise in situations that are ambiguous, or pose some threat or potential threat. But how do they help people deal with ambiguity and threat?

In the early summer of 2007, five happy and carefree young women died in a horrible head-on collision with a tractor-trailer on a two-lane highway near Rochester, New York. One week earlier, they had graduated from high school. They were in an SUV headed to a summer house at 10:00 p.m. along a two-lane rural road, when they passed a sedan, then inexplicably swerved into the path of the oncoming eighteen-wheeler. Fuel lines were broken and their vehicle erupted in a terrible conflagration. The force of the impact was so great that the young women were killed instantly. Why had their SUV swerved into the path of the oncoming truck?

The answer to that question will probably never be definitively known, but a grieving community tried to answer it as part of an effort to make sense of the tragedy. Out of this sensemaking, two false rumors were fashioned. One was that the driver of the sedan had sped up as he was being passed, forcing the SUV into the truck's path. This was in fact the opposite of what happened: The sedan slowed down to allow the SUV to safely pass. Another was that the oncoming eighteen-wheeler didn't reduce its speed before the collision. False again: The truck driver jammed on the brakes as soon as he saw the SUV enter his lane—he left more than 120 feet of skid marks before the impact. These rumors were put to rest weeks later at a news conference during which it was revealed that the SUV driver's cell phone had sent and received text messages just seconds before the crash. It appears likely that distraction due to cell phone usage was at the heart of this sad event. The rumors that arose served as hypotheses to people trying to make sense of what happened.

It's clear that rumors help people make some sort of sense out of unclear situations. The GM workers in Ypsilanti circulated rumors in an attempt to achieve clarity about the impending plant closing. Employees in the lending institution I interviewed passed rumors as a way of ferreting out the facts of the restructuring situation. My fellow stranded train and plane travelers and I used rumors to sift a picture of the weather, transportation routes, and appropriate courses of action. People set forth rumors about the death of Dr. King in order to resolve the contradictory statements associated with this national tragedy. Human nature abhors an explanation vacuum. People in groups use rumors to construct, evaluate, and refine explanations for the ambiguous situation.

In situations that pose a threat or potential threat, rumors also help people manage that threat by encouraging them to deal with it through positive action, or by simply making them feel better about it. Rumors about the bombing of the *Pont-Aven* alerted patrons not to travel via that ferry; passengers could avoid the possibility of a sudden death by delaying their trip or choosing another route. Rumors that a computer consultant is incompetent warned clients not to use that consultant; company officials could avoid years of computer-related troubles by simply choosing a different consultant or by not installing a computer system at all. A rumor that "the Port Jervis dam is breaking!" instructs Port Jervis residents to flee the scene immediately if they know what's good for them; they could preserve their lives by acting quickly.

A rumor in 2001 warned: "Avoid Boston on September 22 because drunken Arabs at a bar let it slip that there would be a second wave of attacks that day." By staying out of town on the twenty-second, Bostonians and others could evade the dangers encountered by people living and working in New York City on September 11. Rumors among college students about professors—"Milgram is a hard but fair grader"; "Rogers is an easy A"; "Allport is a phenomenal lecturer"—help students avoid unfavorable experiences such as unfair grades, low marks, and boring lectures. In all of these examples, the rumor implies a course of action that—if available—will supposedly aid the hearer in avoiding a negative or achieving a positive outcome.

Many negative outcomes in life are, of course, unavoidable. For these, rumors assist people by helping them emotionally cope with the dreaded event or state of affairs. Rumors can help do this by, again, simply helping people make sense of an unclear situation. Merely understanding why a bad thing is happening is a good emotional coping strategy.

Understanding that the GM plant will be closing down this summer because foreign labor is cheaper won't alter the negative outcome for employees—losing employment—but it will remove a sense of arbitrariness from the situation. The plant closing can be understood as the result of larger economic forces, globalization, or corporate greed. Understanding how the SUV with five young women crossed into the opposing lane will not bring them back to life or lessen the feelings of loss felt by family and community—but it will set the event into a larger context. The crash could have come about, for example, as part of larger patterns of cell phone distraction, aggressive driving, or time pressures faced by truck drivers. We search for explanations in part because the very presence of an explanation is comforting. Rumors often help people by providing a ready-made explanation.

Rumors can also help people cope emotionally by neutralizing a psychological threat—especially a challenge to our positive view of ourselves. In conflict situations, this is particularly so. In the study investigating sentiments toward Al Qaeda, focus group respondents presumably latched on to rumors that the United States or Israel organized the events of September 11 because they deflect the threatening idea that Al Qaeda was responsible for killing nearly three thousand civilians. Similarly, negative racial attitudes are distasteful—we don't like to think of ourselves as judgmental toward a person based solely on the color of his skin, her gender, or country of origin. We consider ourselves fair-minded people. How is it that we sometimes exhibit racial prejudice, then?

Wedge-driving rumors—negative stories about members of the rival or targeted group—can justify distasteful attitudes. In the aftermath of Hurricane Katrina, false rumors about black individuals in New Orleans engaged in looting, raping, and shooting at rescuers were widespread. False rumors that groups of unruly black persons vandalized rest stop facilities while being bussed from New Orleans at taxpayer expense were also common. Such rumors can make prejudiced individuals feel better about their negative racial attitudes toward African-Americans. Conversely, false rumors that New Jersey State troopers and their dogs chased a black child, causing the boy to fall into the Raritan Canal near Princeton and drown, spread quickly in the African-American community one hot summer in the late 1980s. Such rumors can make prejudiced persons feel better about having negative racial attitudes toward European Americans.

In a similar vein, we don't like to think of ourselves as prejudiced against even a rival group. But prejudice against any rival group can be legitimated by negative rumors about that group. Politics has always been a hot topic, but what can explain the current acrimony between Democrats and Republicans? Negative rumors about politicians from the opposing party help people justify their intense biases. I receive negative political e-rumors from both sides of the aisle. These rumors are always of "the other side is bad" variety. They are never checked for veracity, but simply forwarded to friends believed to be like-minded. These rumors serve a purpose—to justify negative prejudice toward the rival group—in this case, the opposing political party. We would normally consider such bias for what it is—unfair and distasteful; rumors, however, can make it palatable.

Central to our discussion of rumors is their role in human sensemaking. So, to better understand what rumor is, we need to understand how we make sense generally and the role of rumors in that process. More specifically, how do individuals make sense and how do rumors affect this individual sensemaking? And how do groups make sense together and how do rumors affect this group sensemaking?

Not long ago, my wife and I were exiting a movie theater just past midnight. The theater was located near a large Barnes and Noble bookstore, around which stood a huge crowd alternately cheering and clapping as they awaited their turn to purchase *Harry*

Potter and the Deathly Hallows, the seventh and last installment of J. K. Rowling's amazingly popular children's book series. I slowly drove by the fringe of the crowd; it was New Year's Eve in the middle of July. People of all ages had waited in line the entire day in order to be among the first to receive the coveted volume. Three news stations were also present, adding to the circus-like fanfare. It was a happy event. My wife and I couldn't recall such excitement over the release of a book. Many would stay up all night to read the 784-page tome and then attend a brunch to discuss it with other bleary-eyed enthusiasts. Some would go straight from the bookstore to parties where the main social activity was sitting and reading. What could *explain* the Harry Potter phenomenon?

What was it about this children's book, our culture, or media that led to this unprecedented interest and fanfare at this moment in time? Any satisfactory explanation would convey the desires, beliefs, and aims of the many people involved in Pottermania, and clarify the underlying psychological, sociological, and literary underpinnings of this muggle (ordinary human) event. Good candidate explanations might appeal to the literary quality of Rowling's epic, an increasing desire for a sense of wonder in our modern age, contagion phenomena, global interconnectedness resulting from the growth of the Internet, or the increasing media savvy of marketers.

To ask how individuals make sense of things is really to ask how they go about the task of explanation. Explanation is aimed at increasing comprehension and understanding. It can involve offering details of a situation that enable us to understand it, or the reasons—i.e., the desires, beliefs, or aims—of the actors involved. Good explanations clarify meanings, ideas, or thoughts.

Psychologists have outlined the process an individual undergoes when seeking to explain an event, situation, or feature of their experience that is unclear. The process has a common-sense flavor to it; explanation is a universal human activity. A person first becomes aware of an event—it is noticed. It is then interpreted—an initial explanation is set forth. If so motivated and able, the person can then iteratively test and revise this interpretation, or generate alternatives for testing and revision. This iterative testing may involve searching for additional information. At some point, the individual settles on a final explanation. Noticing and interpreting happen automatically; that is, they occur in an almost reflex fashion, without effort or thought. Testing, revising, generating alternatives, and selecting a final explanation, however, take effort.

Whether automatic or effortful, each of the tasks in the explanation process is guided by cognitive structures. I introduced this term in Chapter 2; it refers to associations of ideas, such as stereotypes or frameworks. Cognitive structures are activated by bringing ideas to mind. For example, if I say the word "Italian," several ideas are brought to mind or become more accessible in our awareness: pasta, large close-knit families, Roman noses, expressive gestures, espresso coffee, medieval art, Mediterranean climate, and Mafia. These elements are associated with one another around the concept "Italian"; they form a stereotype.

Cognitive structures guide the explanation process at each step. For example, they help us notice events. Upon learning that our new neighbor's name is DiFonzo, their facial features, expressive gestures, and many children become more salient to us—we notice them. When we encounter an event that puzzles us, cognitive structures help us interpret the event automatically—without thinking. We learn that Mr. DiFonzo's uncle in Sicily was found dead from a gunshot wound; we privately wonder if it was a Mafia-related killing. Cognitive structures guide us in the effortful generation of alternate explanations as well. We know that the Sicilian uncle collected guns for a hobby and——guided by the cognitive structure "gun collecting"——we inquire as to whether he accidentally shot himself while cleaning his guns.

Rumors affect this process of explanation at several points along the way, often by simply delivering the relevant cognitive structure. First of all, they help us to notice events. Many times this is a simple matter of the rumor calling attention to a particular incident, theme, characteristic, or situation. False rumors that Snapple is owned by the Ku Klux Klan brought attention to the kosher symbol—signified on the Snapple label by the letter *K* with a circle around it. In addition, rumors often also convey an initial interpretation of an event. To continue our Snapple example, the presence of the *K* symbol on the Snapple label, according to the rumor, indicated that the company was owned by the KKK.

The false rumors of Paul McCartney's death both called attention to and interpreted why he was barefoot on the cover of the *Abbey Road* album: according to the rumor, the deceased are customarily interred without shoes in Britain. (Actually, this isn't true.) Rumors activated the cognitive structures that guided the noticing and interpreting in each of these examples. This "rumor guidance" often happens automatically——without effort, intention, or thought.

Rumors may also activate the cognitive structures that motivate and guide the effortful search for new information to help us evaluate an explanation. A rumor that American Home Mortgage Investment Corporation had shut down part of its lending operation inspired information-seeking about the company's lending practices. The company had indeed engaged in risky practices; it had issued many loans to borrowers without requiring extensive documentation. The rumor resulted in a 23 percent reduction in the company's stock value in one day, despite protests by company officials that the rumor was untrue.

One particular type of cognitive structure that rumors frequently deliver to individuals is the stable cause—a cause that lasts over time. In the previous chapter, I discussed how a rumor that "Goodyear profits are up because of good management practices" activated the stable cause idea that good management will continue, thereby leading to the prediction that Goodyear stock would continue to rise. In experiments, these rumors did indeed lead to predictions that Goodyear stock would continue to rise and in this way systematically affected buying behavior—but, as it turns out, unprofitably.

In another study I discussed in Chapter 2, rumors that Sophie (a fictional character) has some form of mental illness conveyed the idea that Sophie was mentally ill, activated the stable cause idea that mental illness lasts over time, and thereby led to the conclusion that her mental illness was likely to continue. Mental illness would presumably impair her judgments and adversely affect her desirability as a friend. Students (not educated about mental illness) were then less likely to vote for Sophie as class president and to desire to be socially close with her.

The point is that rumors often affect individual sensemaking by activating a stable, lasting cause to explain events; this frequently leads to predicting that the recent events, behaviors, or conditions will continue. Put another way, rumors often lead to this kind of sensemaking simply because they often supply a lasting cause for the current state of affairs or trend of events: The way things are going now will continue into the future.

For individuals, then, rumors make us think about some events, affect how we frame these events, and affect what we continue to learn about these events. But what about collections of connected individuals? That is, what about groups? How do groups make sense together and how do rumors affect group sensemaking?

In the mid-1990s, Internet discussion groups were a new phenomenon. A small percentage of people at that time participated in e-mail Listservs. My colleague, Prashant Bordia, was one of them. He noticed that discussions of rumors on these groups were sensemaking activities and he carefully recorded and analyzed these electronic posts.

One discussion in particular intrigued him and became the subject of his master's thesis: people on one particular Usenet site were concerned that Prodigy—a large Internet service provider at the time—was spying on customers' personal files. The false rumor asserted that this profit-driven corporation was uploading private information from subscribers' hard drives without their knowledge or consent. Prodigy then allegedly sifted through this information for marketing purposes—that is, to develop a clearer demographic and psychological picture of their customers so that they might be more successful at selling them additional products and services. Demographic and psychological profiling was not new at this time, but the idea that a large company would, without permission, upload private customer files was a key part of the rumor that sparked concern and discussion.

Broadly speaking, group sensemaking resembles individual sensemaking in that particular tasks are performed by many different people rather than just one. There is a division of labor. That is, noticing, interpreting, revising, and settling on a final explanation are performed by members of the group rather than by a single person. One task, for example, is to first bring a rumor to the group. The sociologist Tamotsu Shibutani called this the messenger role. After analysis of the types of statements that people actually include in their posts, Prashant and I categorized such roles as "communicative postures." For example, the messenger role is best represented in an explanation delivering posture. In the Prodigy rumor discussion, a discussant might post "I don't know if this is true, but I heard that Prodigy is uploading our private files for use by their marketing departments"—the person delivers an explanation to the group along with a cautionary statement that it might be false.

We dubbed such tasks "postures" because they represent the temporary role that a person may play while "taking their turn" at any given point in the discussion. That is, "posture" conveys that the role that one plays in a discussion may change over time. A person might cautiously deliver an explanation at one stage of a discussion, but then later perform a different role in that same discussion. She might, for example, later express disbelief in that explanation and present an argument supporting her contention that Prodigy was not surreptitiously uploading customer data (we dubbed this an explanation falsifying posture): "I don't believe that Prodigy is uploading information because to do so would take up too much bandwidth."

Prashant's analysis detected other communicative postures displayed in these discussions. A post that was explanation evaluating would analyze and interpret the rumor explanation. For example: "Perhaps the Prodigy cache file grows over time because they are first compressing the user's personal files, then adding it into the cache file before uploading!" Explanation accepting posts would express belief in the rumor: "I believe they are doing this." Explanation verifying postures would go further and express belief in the rumor along with a supporting argument: "I believe Prodigy is doing this because they are solely interested in making a profit and would not hesitate to violate our privacy rights." Of course, when people are collectively analyzing a rumor explanation, they need to search for, find, deliver, and analyze additional information.

A directing posture would provide information and suggest a strategy for further information gathering: "Whenever I dial in to Prodigy, my modem light turns on intermittently, even if I'm not sending or receiving information; someone should find out if this is the way modems ordinarily operate." Information-seeking postures would simply state the gaps in knowledge needed in order to generate or evaluate a rumor and would often be in the form of a question: "What do we know about the Prodigy cache file?" Information-reporting postures would share information and personal experience: "Ever since I subscribed to Prodigy, my computer has been operating more slowly." Other postures performed the functions of motivating participants to continue sensemaking by either considering negative outcomes ("I'm scared about what this could mean about my privacy") or positive ones ("I wish our private files would remain private"). Still other (casual participation) postures would simply "lurk" or digress from the topic.

The point in pondering these postures is that people, when they "take their turn" in an electronic discussion by posting a message, perform a particular function in service of the group's goal of making sense of the situation. Clearly, rumor discussions are not simply telephone game transmissions, otherwise known as "whispers down the lane"—A tells B a rumor, who then tells C, who then tells D . . . and so on down the line. This common conception of rumor is simplistic and individualistic—it frames rumor as something that primarily happens with an individual rather than a group. Instead, a group sensemaking discussion around a rumor consists of a sometimes confusing interchange of news, information statements, opinions, explanations, commands, questions, motivators, and digressions.

But even though the discussion seems unwieldy, there are clear trends as it moves forward. At first, people display explanation delivering and directing postures: they cautiously bring the rumor to the group, and strategies are proposed to find out more information. Supported by information seeking and reporting, and motivated to continue by considering negative or positive outcomes, they engage in explanation evaluating postures—they are actively sifting, sorting, and making sense of the rumor. Finally, people participate more casually as a consensus is reached or interest dies down. They move on to other topics or simply stop participating. Despite the apparent chaos and confusion, these discussions are colorful and purposeful interchanges that—collectively—proceed in a fairly predictable fashion around the central task of sensemaking.

4

A Family Resemblance

Gossip and Urban Legend, Rumor's Close Cousins

> *If you can't say something good about someone, sit right here by me.*
>
> —PERSONAL MOTTO OF
> ALICE ROOSEVELT LONGWORTH
> EMBROIDERED ON A SOFA PILLOW

By all accounts, Alice Roosevelt Longworth was a favorite subject—and source—of gossip. Born in 1884, the eldest daughter of then New York Assemblyman Theodore Roosevelt was bright, beautiful, and . . . headstrong. After Roosevelt's rise to the U.S. presidency, in 1901, she became "Darling Princess Alice" to the American public because of her many antics. Alice had a flair for attracting attention by flouting convention. She smoked cigarettes publicly in a time when smoking by women was taboo; when her father forbade her to smoke in the White House, she puffed atop the roof. Unchaperoned she traveled about in roadsters with men—a daring thing at the time. While on a diplomatic cruise to the Far East, she jumped into the ship's swimming pool fully clothed. She placed bets with bookies. She was often the talk of the town in a highly conventional era. Her later marriage to Ohio Representative Nicholas Longworth was rocky—not surprising in light of his play-boy habits and heavy drinking—and she surprised the Washington socialite set with the birth of her only child, Paulina, eighteen years later. Paulina was in fact the product of a long love affair with another Republican politico, Senator William Borah of Idaho. Alice may have been the talk of the town, but she also "gave them something to talk about."

In her later years, "Mrs. L" came to be known as an influential purveyor of gossip among the Washington political elite. A 1969 article in *American Heritage* magazine recorded her habitually malicious tongue: " 'X is not only a snob,' she said recently, 'but a stupid snob: snobbish about the wrong people.' " Here is a sample of scuttlebutt from an interview with *Washington Post* reporter Sally Quinn in 1974: "I like Julie better than Tricia [daughters of then-president Richard Nixon]. I've never been able to get on with Tricia. She seems rather pathetic, doesn't she? I wonder what's wrong with her?" Longworth was ninety years old at the time of the interview and filled it with entertaining personal social commentary. "I like Jackie [Jacqueline Kennedy Onassis] very much. But I've always wondered what on earth made her marry Onassis. He's a repulsive character. He reminds me of Mr. Punch. . . . Jack was so attractive." Through her many long years as "Washington's *other* monument," Mrs. L was renowned for her delight in collecting and disseminating gossip. "Ethel [Kennedy] is behaving very badly these days. There's a certain brash quality about her I never liked. I liked Bobby though, a great deal." Princess Alice might properly have been crowned the "Queen of Washington gossip."

Gossip is idle—and typically derogatory—social chatter about an absent individual's personal or private matters. It's a juicy tidbit of information about someone. Gossip arises in situations where people are building, changing, or preserving personal relationships or social status within a group. Gossip helps people bond with, amuse, know about, exclude, and aggress against one another, and conveys social norms. Gossip is an especially "group-ish" type of informal communication.

A little-known fact among my students is that my first career was as an environmental engineer. I worked for a state agency involved in the granting and administration of public funds for water treatment projects. I would regularly travel around that state with other engineers to inspect and report on the status of these construction projects. Most of the people in our group were either recent graduates just starting off or middle-age "lifers" who had been with the agency their entire working career. One gentleman, however, had extensive expertise from many years as a practicing project engineer and consultant. "Bob" (not his real name) had a biting wit and frequently complained about the bureaucratic obstacles we often encountered—and were forced to create. On those long car rides to inspect projects, engineers (mostly male at the time) would chat about Bob: "Did you ever wonder why Bob, with all his experience, isn't listened to by the managers?" one engineer once said to another. "No, why?" was the response. "It's because he's a know-it-all." The coworker continued, "He rubs people the wrong way."

Now, this information about Bob was not self-evidently *necessary* information. Hearing about Bob's sharp edges may have been interesting, but not vital to the performance of work duties. It was not in the same category of, say, talk about the merits of a contract change order and would not be part of the daily activity report.

Rather, it was relaxed in manner and filled part of the long hours of travel from the office to the job site. It was informal, not something to be put in writing on a departmental memo. These engineers were engaging in an activity akin to boys chewing grass together on a lazy summer afternoon while gazing at the clouds. As Ralph Rosnow once commented, gossip is apparently idle—aimless and purposeless—in nature. By "idle," he did not mean that gossip is unimportant—far from it! Gossip is a very important social phenomenon. Rather, that it is *packaged* as aimless conversation, just "shooting the bull" as they say. Indeed, it may have a considered purpose. The gossiper may, for example, have been in competition with Bob for a promotion and hoped to increase his own chances by purposely spreading negative characterizations of his rival.

Think for a moment of someone you know who you would consider "a gossip." The image that comes to mind is that of a tale bearer: someone who gleefully whispers to you the failures of other people in your community. The person who, when they leave your office cubicle, you feel just a little bit soiled from the experience. The individual who seems to revel in spreading dirt about persons whom you previously had a good or neutral opinion of. The man or woman whose specialty is trafficking in personal information about others—they collect it, trade it, and perhaps use it as a commodity to enhance their prestige, advance their own agenda, or feel better about their own moral peccadilloes. In this popular image of gossip, gossip is driven by self-serving motives and is ultimately harmful to the social fabric of the community.

And indeed, there is some evidence that gossip is most often derogatory and slanderous. Social psychologist Charles Walker collected gossip on the campus of St. Bonaventure University in St. Bonaventure, New York, and then categorized it as "shame gossip" or "veneration gossip." Walker found that a much greater percentage of gossip was critical rather than laudatory. A typical middle school set of gossip statements would constitute negative social commentary such as: "Giuseppe dropped out of school and is on drugs!" "Juliet's parents are not very nice." "Anne got pregnant and had an abortion!" Some gossip is positive: "Philomena's grandparents have lots of money and are very generous!" "Dominick is a really sweet guy." Like the motto on Alice Roosevelt Longworth's pillow, however, there seems to be a greater demand in the social marketplace for tittle-tattle than for tribute. Given the characteristically negative nature of gossip, it's not surprising that it is most often told about someone who is not present.

This often slanderous aspect of gossip is one reason it has been frequently condemned in religious and ethical writings. From the book of Leviticus (19:16) in the Bible: "Do not go about spreading slander among your people." The reason is clear to anyone who has ever been the victim of slanderous gossip: a person's reputation—upon which their social standing or even their livelihood depends—is damaged. The thought that one's social community has heard that you are lazy, loose, or that you habitually lie is, after all, very hurtful. And such stories have harmful effects. After hearing that someone is addicted, abusive, unfaithful, disloyal, dishonest, hypocritical, unbalanced, unlikable, criminal, aggressive, or carries a disease, it is difficult to interact with that person with an open mind and to trust them. (Here again the law of cognitive structure activation is operating.) The Talmud speaks at length, for example, of the damage that a person can do by gossiping about another's vocation, likening it to murder. Jewish tradition also states the matter positively: because people were created good (in God's image), we are to give them the benefit of the doubt and assume the best about them. It is a matter of trusting in the goodness of other people and thinking the best of them. There is an old saying that one shouldn't try to defend oneself against slander; your enemies won't believe you anyway and your friends don't need to hear your defense. And Rabbi Dr. Asher Meir has proposed resisting office gossip by gently advocating for the target. For example: "John wouldn't have done that intentionally—he is a very hard worker," and "I'm sure that she was just trying to be helpful."

My gossip researcher friends take umbrage at this universally negative condemnation of gossip. They make the point that gossip is often simply gathering important information about the social environment. Indeed, we could not function socially without it. Nowhere is this most apparent than in gossip's function as a useful warning about harmful people. Telling a new coworker about the boss's hang-ups can help her avoid becoming embroiled in an unpleasant interaction. Telling a fellow professor about a student's habitually slacking behavior can prevent that student from taking advantage of yet another teacher. Telling a troubled couple in search of a marriage counselor about complaints filed against a particular therapist can help them avoid becoming hurt in the same way that he hurt other marriages. These objections have some merit. The free flow of such information does serve a useful social function of guarding against the harmful behavior of particular individuals. Your mother warns you about associating too closely with Lucy because she heard that Lucy does recreational drugs—this gossip is an expression of love and concern; it would be a dereliction in parental duty *not* to gossip on this occasion. It would be an abandonment of obligation to "believe the best" about Lucy. Gossip, in this case, seems a moral duty.

Dovetailing gossip's function as a warning is that gossip serves also as moral instruction and motivation to the hearer. Gossip informally regulates behavior. Hearing gossip about "Bob's know-it-all attitude" made me carefully refrain from sarcasm and adopt a humbler, more teachable attitude. Gossip informs us about how to act properly in a given social context. Wanting to avoid granting others the opportunity to gossip about us may serve as an effective deterrent for engaging in socially unacceptable acts. Even when the gossip is spread with the worst of motives as part of a tale bearer's gleeful utterances, it has the effect of educating us about what is unacceptable behavior and motivating us to avoid that behavior.

In other contexts as well, gossip may not be so nefarious. It may simply be a way of signifying friendship with another or gathering important social information. Think for a moment about the last time you participated in social chat about an individual who just happened to be absent at the time. Perhaps you were discussing this person's personal history ("Jack is divorced isn't he? Yes, he beat his wife."), her character ("Corin appears to be so sweet, but she's a real phony"), or his finances ("William made a pot of money in real estate"). Who were you engaged in conversation with? Typically it is with friends, family, or a favored acquaintance and not with someone whom you dislike, distrust, or do not feel safe with. Gossip is something you do with friends—it signals affiliation, closeness, and camaraderie. It says to the participants "This person is one of my confidantes." Anthropologist Robin Dunbar has therefore compared human gossiping to primate grooming behavior—it is something we do with another furry creature in our clan: Come, gossip with me, and we will be friends. We do not gossip with—though we may gossip about—our enemies.

Ironically, this friendship aspect of gossip explains part of why gossip has a bad reputation. What people often have in mind when thinking of tale bearing is in reality "promiscuous" gossip. Understanding the social environment is a laudable and natural desire and a key component of being a wise person, as is heeding the concerned warnings about others from friends and advisors. People who have no social sensibilities are indeed handicapped, but those who can size up a social situation we call an "astute judge of character" and "insightful." Such insight is undoubtedly enhanced by conversations in which we seek to analyze other people and understand their personal lives. This can be either good or bad, depending on the context in which it takes place and the motive behind it. Like other interpersonal activities, if we gossip with everyone we meet, it loses its special value for the relationship—it seems to work best when it is an activity we restrict to those closest to us. If one gossips with everyone, it implies that one has a special confidante relationship with everyone—a state not possible and therefore dishonest. One can't gossip with integrity with every Tom, Dick, and Harry that comes along. Doing gossip with everyone is therefore a form of false advertising. It is saying "come be my special friend" to the masses—but the masses by definition cannot be special.

Gossip does bind people together—but it also breaks them apart. In the final installment of C. S. Lewis's classic science-fiction trilogy, *That Hideous Strength,* the central characters are a young professor of sociology named Mark Studdock and his wife, Jane. Mark is emotionally insecure and perennially pines to be included in the "inner circle" of whatever social environment he finds himself part of. This occurs at the (both fictitious) Bracton College and the (secretly malevolent) National Institute of Coordinated Experiments (N.I.C.E.). The inner circles at the college and the N.I.C.E. don't actually like Mark, but woo him in order to capture Jane. This strategy is in hopes that her clairvoyance—initially unknown even to her—will aid them in finding the location where the powerful ancient wizard Merlin will awaken in Bracton Wood. To get to Jane, they ingratiate themselves to Mark using gossip about other professors. At Bracton, Mark first experiences the warm feeling of being admitted to the inner circle when Dr. Curry, a pompous administrator at the college, denigrates other professors whom he anticipates will oppose him at an upcoming meeting:

> "Yes," said Curry, "it [the College Faculty meeting] will take the hell of a time. Probably go on after dinner. We shall have all the obstructionists wasting time as hard as they can. . . ." You would never have guessed from the tone of Studdock's reply what intense pleasure he derived from Curry's use of the pronoun "we." So very recently he had been an outsider, watching the proceedings of what he then called "Curry and his gang" with awe and with little understanding, and making at College meetings short, nervous speeches which never influenced the course of events. Now he was inside and "Curry and his gang" had become "we" or "the Progressive Element in College." It had all happened quite suddenly and was still sweet in the mouth.

In a later conversation another member of the inner circle, the clever criminal Lord Feverstone, gossips in turn about Curry behind his back and Mark is (seemingly) even more centrally placed within the inner circle:

> As soon as [Curry] had got out of the room, Lord Feverstone looked steadily at Mark for some seconds with an enigmatic expression. Then he chuckled. Then the chuckle developed into a laugh. . . . "It really is rather devastating," said Feverstone when he had partially recovered, "that the people one has to use for getting things done should talk such drivel. . . ." Mark was silent. The giddy sensation of being suddenly whirled up

from one plane of secrecy to another, coupled with the grow-ing effect of Curry's excellent port, prevented him from speaking.

Mark continues to feel that his status rises as each new round of "confidential" negative gossip about colleagues and coworkers is used to inflate his ego as being a member of the Important People Group (my term for one's inner circle). This nicely illustrates the use of gossip both to include the hearer into one's clique and to exclude the person not present from the clique. Gossip is therefore intrinsically political in character in that it forges my—and may weaken the target's—alliances. Note that in Lewis's novel, the gos-sip is presented in an offhand manner, though in truth it is calcu-lated and deliberate—and effective in eventually drawing Mark into the employ of the evil N.I.C.E.

The passage gets at why gossip is often condemned—once again the motive matters. Recall the last time you went grocery shop-ping. After collecting your produce, cereal, milk, and staples, you stood in line at the checkout counter. Invariably, your eyes are drawn to the headlines of the tabloids that herald the beginning of the conveyor belt: "Alice's lover revealed!" "Angela and Bart break up over affair!" "Opheliah's dirty little secret!" Celebrity gossip is a thriving industry. Note that the content of these statements is often about matters that our culture considers private or personal. Celebrity gossip tabloid headlines appeal to perhaps a voyeuristic impulse in every person. "We want to know!" about other people's private affairs. And not just celebrities, which most people con-sider "fair game." We want to know about the personal affairs of people we are acquainted with. Coworker Jane's sordid past, the secret sexual sins of our neighbor Fred, the youthful antics of our old Aunt Mabel. And especially the undisclosed failures and foibles of those we dislike or who make us feel uncomfortable.

This last desire informs us of perhaps the nastiest motive in gossip, moral rationalization—that feeling of glee to learn that someone else is worse than we are. Relatively speaking, we must be all right then. "What? Bill smoked marijuana when he was younger, even though he rails against it now? What a hypocrite! I'm not proud of what I do but at least I'm honest. . . ." This motive explains the heightened interest in negative gossip about people in positions entrusted with moral leadership—clergy, politicians, professors, parents. The priest's encounter with a prostitute is intensely more socially "marketable" information than the prostitute's liaison with the priest. After analyzing daily diaries of student "people talk" episodes, gossip researcher Holly Hom found that they often felt empowered and more popular after telling critical gossip. Negative gossip about others is a way of boosting your view of yourself.

There is—understandably—some confusion over the difference between rumor and gossip. In class I sometimes ask students to report a recent rumor they have heard. They often record gossip. Known as an expert on rumor, I periodically receive phone calls from newspaper reporters on the topic of gossip. One synonym of the term "rumor" in the thesaurus I am using is the term "gossip." Are they the same thing?

A quick perusal of today's celebrity gossip (from usmagazine.com): "John Mayer and Cameron Diaz aren't exclusive. Just ask all of the 'non-famous girls' John has been dating." "Sean 'Diddy' Combs is defending his decision to turn Katie Lee Joel away from his White Party on Saturday for wearing cream instead of white." "Brad Pitt and Angelina Jolie are ready for another child, the actor said during a Sunday news conference for his new film, *The Assassination of Jesse James by the Coward Robert Ford*." "Actor Owen Wilson is in surprisingly good spirits after attempting to commit suicide on August 26, according to his friend, director Wes

Anderson." "A source close to the couple tells *Us* that Heath and Michelle 'quietly and amicably split a few weeks ago.' "

Compare this with rumors reported in today's Google News Alert for "rumor" or "rumour": "A recent article from *BusinessWeek* seems to confirm the rumor that LG is heavily working on a Windows Mobile smartphone. . . ." "Rumours are now going round that GD Time acquired a big plot in order to expand to a production total 3.2 million bicycles." "Great Wall Technology plans to acquire U.S. hard drive manufacturer Seagate, reports Sina quoting an unnamed insider." "Rumor—New black & red DS Lites showing up with low-quality screens." "790—The Sports Animal is reporting from 'inside sources' that have been deemed trustworthy that both manager and general manager of the Houston Astros are going to be let go today."

Clearly these two genres of informal communication differ. "I've never been able to get on with Tricia; she seems rather pathetic, doesn't she? I wonder what's wrong with her?" is qualitatively different from "I heard that our department is being downsized; what have you heard?" Rumor is never verified, but gossip may or may not be. Rumor is about larger concerns, but gossip is about private individual matters. Rumor is about collectively making sense or managing threat, but gossip is about building, changing, or preserving personal social networks. Rumor is a bread crumb in an information famine; gossip is a tasty finger food during the cocktail hour. Sometimes, however, it is hard to differentiate between the two; there are nebulous forms.

Take the case known as the "Hooksett Four." One day in March 2007, a resident of the small town of Hooksett, New Hampshire, stopped by the town building department. He wondered aloud about something he had heard: the town administrator was having an affair with a municipal employee. After the resident left, the sec-

retary shared the hearsay with three other employees in the tax asses-
sor's office. They discussed it: Could this be why the town administrator often worked late at night, and why the alleged "mistress" had
been given a promotion? The alleged mistress eventually heard
about this discussion and reported it to the town administrator. To
say that he didn't view it positively would be an understatement.
The story, by all accounts, was false. Naturally, the administrator—
married with two children—felt personally hurt, that the story had
damaged his reputation, and that the tale had humiliated his wife.
He took action that would ultimately land Hooksett in the national
spotlight: after telling the town council of the episode, the town
council launched an investigation. They questioned most of the
town's sixteen employees, then voted to fire the four employees in
April. The reason? Spreading malicious "gossip."

The Hooksett Four debacle received national media attention.
Subsequent discussions about the episode during town meetings,
in published newspaper articles, on *Good Morning America,* in opinion editorials, and in a rumor-gossip researcher electronic discussion group I host (Rumor-GossipResearch@listserver.rit.edu) have
focused on issues of free speech, the ubiquity of office gossip, and
the effectiveness (or lack thereof) of the actions taken by the town.
Each of the four former employees has sued the town for wrongful
termination. A main part of the argument hinges on whether the
episode was workplace rumor or gossip. That is, was the hearsay
event a legitimate sensemaking discussion about a work-related
issue (rumor) or was it malicious slander (gossip)? The question
quickly focuses attention on the motive for the spread. According
to the lawyer for the town, the episode was part of a long-standing
"dysfunctional" pattern of gossip and name-calling that lowered
morale and interfered with the efficiency of the town government.
In addition, the town lawyer claims the employees knew the

hearsay was untrue when they spread it and that they were trying to harm the administrator's career and marriage. The attorney for the employees denies this and characterizes the episode as a means of trying to make sense of a confusing situation. One of the employees stated: "We discussed the preferential treatment of this one person." Fairness in employee promotion is a work-related topic. They also state that they discussed the alleged affair as an open question ("I wonder if he really did have an affair?") rather than an assertion ("He had an affair").

Of course, there is no rule that says that an episode of hearsay cannot be both rumor and gossip—they are not mutually exclusive activities. After all, human actions often have multiple motives that aren't mutually exclusive. The discussion that ensued among the Hooksett Four contained some of the classic elements of both rumor and gossip. Unverified slander about bosses or leaders often has this nebulous quality. The content of the statements is slanderous, about an individual, and shared with a certain feeling of glee— these point to gossip. The statements are unverified, people are trying to make sense of an unclear situation that is important by virtue of pertaining to the boss or leader—these indicate rumor. An informal social interchange may contain elements of both.

The important point to remember is that rumor is primarily what people do together when they are trying to make sense and manage threat in an ambiguous context; gossip is what they do when they are attending to the social network: bonding with, amusing, keeping informed about, excluding, aggressing against, and conveying social norms to other people. Although what is true about rumor can also be true about gossip—both are types of informal communication, for example—pure rumor differs in important ways from pure gossip. Certain types of situations tend to give rise to rumor—those that involve ambiguity, threat, or change—

and others to gossip—when someone violates a social norm, or the group is cliquish, for example. Also, the cues that lead to belief in rumor may differ quite a bit from the cues people use in judging gossip—but whether you believe gossip to be true is not really important to the discussion. And managing rumor is probably quite different from managing gossip. Managing rumor may simply entail dispelling uncertainty, while managing gossip may entail the systematic cultivation of allies in your social network.

Then there is the tale of a twelve-year-old boy who visited an aquarium and water park with his parents on a family outing. The boy asked if he could explore the park on his own for twenty minutes and the parents, wanting to encourage his growing independence, consented. After an hour, the parents became concerned and began to search for him. After thirty more minutes he finally showed up, drenched from head to toe with water, but unharmed. They gave him a stern lecture, thanked park personnel, and headed home. During the drive they noticed a bad smell in the car. Upon arriving home they sent the boy off to bathe while they had a relaxing cup of tea. Suddenly they heard loud splashing and strange noises from the bathroom. Upon entering, they found the boy's new friend—a small penguin that he had stowed away in his backpack.

Urban legends are narratives about strange, funny, or horrible events that could have happened, the details of which change to fit particular locales and time periods, and which frequently contain a moral lesson. Urban legends arise in any context where stories are told: around a campfire, in Internet chat rooms, in casual conversation. They help people amuse themselves, transmit cultural norms and values, and express commonly held fears. The term *urban* legend is actually a misnomer because these stories often have nothing to do with cities. They are more appropriately labeled *modern* or *contemporary* legends because they contain themes related to modern life, such as automobiles, broadcasting, cell phones, contamination, corporations, intercontinental travel, mass production, shopping malls, technology, and teenage dating.

Urban legends are first of all stories: they are narratives that have a setting, plot, characters, climax, and denouement. They rope us in by weaving a clever and entertaining yarn. The tale of the kidnapped penguin is certainly amusing. In another popular anecdote, vacationers at a lake in Florida were rowing peacefully when they spotted a small dog hanging on for dear life to a piece of driftwood. They rescued the critter, took it back to their lodge, and posted a notice in the local classifieds, hoping to find the owner. No one responded, so they decided to adopt the new pet. After returning home, they went out shopping and came back to find that the dog had mauled their cat somewhat—some of the cat's fur had been torn off. When they took the dog to the veterinarian, he asked, "Have you ever heard this dog bark?" They responded, no, but he does give a funny yowl. The vet said, "That's because this is not a dog; it's a Haitian rat!" This story has many versions, including the "Mexican Rat" in which a compassionate woman brought a sick "dog" across the Mexican border, observed that it was foaming at the mouth, and took it to the veterinarian.

The details vary from story to story, but the core of the tale remains the same. A woman, walking to her car in a parking lot, noticed a man following her. She quickly jumped into the car and raced away. But the man got into his car and followed her. She drove through the downtown, past businesses, bars, and houses. He persisted in following her. Finally, she drove to the home of her brother-in-law, a policeman. Honking her horn, she quickly explained to her brother-in-law that a man was stalking her. "And there he is!" she yelled as the man drove up. The policeman quickly approached the man. "Take it easy," said the chaser. "All I wanted to do was to tell her about the guy in the backseat." And indeed there was a man huddled in the backseat of the woman's car, a knife in hand and ready to attack. This story is called "The Killer in the Backseat" and has many variations in details: the event occurs at night and the pursuer keeps his bright headlights on, the man huddled in the backseat has a meat cleaver instead of a knife.

These stories are about funny or horrible events that *could* have happened and often serve as warnings. Two boys went out for a nature hike one morning. Before long their canteens ran dry, so they stopped at a river and bent down for a drink. One of them jumped up and quickly exclaimed that he had swallowed something solid. They noticed that in the river there was a bed of snake eggs. Not paying too much attention to this, they moved on and forgot about it. About a year later, the boy who thought he had swallowed something solid became very weak but always had a voracious appetite. His mother brought him to the doctor, who examined him and then pumped his stomach—out of which came a ten-foot-long snake. This story is a version of the "Bosom-Serpent" legends; variants include the tale of the teenage girl who exhibited a swollen abdomen as in pregnancy but it turned out to be a many-tentacled octopus; the nest of spiders growing inside of an arm; the earwig extracted from the human ear opposite the one it entered; and diet pills that really make you lose weight because they contain tapeworms.

Urban legends, of course, serve to entertain, amuse, and pass the time. They are funny, horrifying, or just plain interesting. Urban legends are first of all interesting because they possess the structure of a story that I mentioned above: a setting, characters, plot, building to a climax, then denouement. These elements, properly arranged and told well, are simply irresistible. The topics of urban legends are fascinating as well: strange and unusual events. And some urban legends are interesting because they are so disgusting. Researchers Chip Heath, Chris Bell, and Emily Sternberg systematically varied how disgusting a set of urban legends were, then presented them to forty-two Duke University undergraduates and asked how likely they were to pass the story on. For example, in a story about a man finding a dead rat in a soda bottle, the low-disgust version consisted of: "Before he drank anything, he saw that there was a dead rat inside." The medium-disgust condition was: "About halfway through, he saw that there was a dead rat inside." The high-disgust condition was even more, well, disgusting: "He swallowed something lumpy, and saw that there were pieces of a dead rat inside." High-disgust stories were most likely to be passed along as compared with either low- or medium-disgust tales. A really disgusting story, at least among university undergraduates, is a really good story to pass along.

But in addition, urban legends help us manage our fears or provide a cautionary warning. Urban legends often give voice to a variety of modern fears. The Haitian (or Mexican) Rat is thought to express fear of illegal immigrants. The account of the killer in the backseat articulates a fear of the dark places in automobiles and of vulnerable females being stalked. The bosom-serpent stories convey unspoken anxieties about contamination—ingesting harmful substances, insects, or slimy animals. Giving voice to these fears—making them palpable via story—is a way of gaining a sense of control over them and a way of warning people about them.

The following story embodies—pardon the pun—the fear that many people have about artificial tanning and serves as a warning against it. A young woman was part of a bridal party and wanted to have a tan by the time of the ceremony but was nowhere near achieving this. Tanning salons limit customer exposure to thirty minutes per day, so she visited several salons each day to get the quickest tan possible. After several weeks of this, she began feeling very ill and also noticed that her body had a foul odor that wouldn't go away. She went to her doctor. She had actually managed to cook her body's internal organs; the smell was rotting flesh. She died two weeks later. The warning served up by this story seems obvious: Do not artificially tan to excess.

A similar warning-filled story has become quite popular. A guy met a very attractive woman at a club one night. He flirted with her, one thing led to another, and soon they were back at his apartment having sex. He thought to himself, "What a lucky night!" But the next morning he woke up alone and went to the bathroom. Scribbled in red lipstick on the mirror in large letters was: WELCOME TO THE WORLD OF AIDS. This story is known as "AIDS Mary" and has an "AIDS Harry" version. It delivers a warning about promiscuous sex.

Urban legends also frequently offer or imply a "moral to the story" in much the same way that the traditional American legend of George Washington ("I cannot tell a lie—I chopped down the cherry tree") supported the virtue of honesty. Urban legends thus typically tell a morality tale or express a cultural value. A cement-truck driver was on his way to deliver a load of concrete and happened to be traveling through his neighborhood. He happened to see a Cadillac convertible parked in his own driveway. After parking the truck, he crept up to the window and saw his wife talking with a strange man. Thinking that his wife was unfaithful, he backed the truck up to the Cadillac and filled it with concrete—the Cadillac sunk to the ground under the magnificent load. That evening he came home just as the car was being towed from his driveway to the junkyard. His wife was crying hysterically—it seems that she had been scrimping and saving for years to buy her husband a new

Cadillac on his birthday and it had just been delivered that morning by the dealer. Someone had filled it with concrete. The moral: Don't jump to conclusions. The cultural value expressed: Trust your loved ones, don't be so suspicious.

There are obviously key differences between rumor and urban legend—though again, these differences sometimes blur. For one thing, rumors tend to be shorter than urban legends. The story of the concrete Cadillac is quite a bit longer than, say, "I heard that our department is being downsized; what have you heard?" A narrative simply requires more space. A common view among folklorists is that rumors are "one-liners." This point highlights a related difference: rumors tend to be part of a story that is unfolding, whereas urban legends tend to consist of the whole story. For another thing, rumors may or may not be very entertaining, but urban legends are always so. A rumor that the department is downsizing is not funny (especially if you are a member of the department), is not so bad that it would be considered horrible, and would certainly not be considered "strange, but true."

The key to these differences is what the social interchange is really about. When people spread rumors, it tends to be about sensemaking and threat management; when they spread urban legends, it tends to be about good storytelling. And, as we've seen, when they spread gossip, it tends to be about building, changing, or maintaining their social network.

The relationship between rumor and urban legend is a bit more complicated than this, however, because they mutually feed off of each other. That is, a rumor that is repeated over a long period of time may eventually morph into a good story with many variations—it has become an urban legend. In 2005, six lorikeet birds were stolen by two people touring the Newport Aquarium. The pair smuggled them away from the exhibit by hiding them under trench coats. Fortunately, the birds were recovered soon afterward. When this event occurred, people almost certainly spread rumors about the episode, trying to make sense of it: Who are the thieves? Why would they take these birds? How did they slip past security? Will the birds be recovered? This, in combination with borrowed plot lines from the 2005 movie *March of the Penguins,* may have resulted in or added to a very good story about a kidnapped penguin. A story may become so good that the telling of it for dramatic effect and entertainment is what the social interchange is really all about—not the making of sense or the management of threat. Of course, many rumors simply don't hang around long enough for that to happen, or they don't acquire the needed story elements. A rumor that Goodyear profits are up, for example, seems unlikely to pick up a meaningful plot or a "moral to the story" that resonates with cultural values.

The reverse also occurs. A long-standing urban legend can acquire local details, such as specific times and locations, and people discuss the alleged episode in an effort to make sense of it or to manage possible risks—the urban legend then "touches down" for a while as a rumor. The story of the killer in the backseat, told around a campfire on a summer night, is an urban legend. But the unverified report, discussed by concerned parents over dinner, that a young Rochester woman narrowly escaped a convicted sex offender who was hiding in the backseat of her car parked at the Monroe County Fair—is a rumor. And so urban legends can—and do—periodically take on the characteristics of rumor.

And so there may be episodes of hearsay that are hard to categorize as urban legend or rumor—they may indeed bear some characteristics of both, or it may be an instance of an urban legend reappearing as a local rumor.

As with gossip, what is true about rumor is sometimes true about urban legend—both are types of informal communication, and urban legends can take the form of a local rumor. But pure rumor differs in important ways from pure urban legend; as we've seen, different situations tend to give rise to rumor and to urban legend. The cues that lead to belief in rumor may differ quite a bit from the cues people use in judging urban legend—and whether or not you believe urban legend to be true is not really important to the story. And while it is possible to manage a specific rumor, managing the entire set of variations that have morphed into urban legend would be a bit more daunting.

5

It's a Small World Around the Watercooler

The What, Why, and Where of Rumor Spread

> *The rumor forthwith flies abroad,*
> *dispersed throughout the small town.*
>
> —VIRGIL, *The Aeneid*

AT 3:45 ON THE MORNING OF February 8, 1972, Nancy Wyckoff—a student at Oregon State University—was found dead inside her dorm room; she had been fatally stabbed in the chest. Police had been summoned after nearby residents of the girl's dormitory heard Nancy's screams. A brutal crime indeed, but also perplexing: the killer had struck in midst of a campus already on high alert to the possibility of attack. How did he do it? In the week prior to the murder, two other females had been attacked, leading to the adoption of strict security measures by the campus administration. Doors to residences were locked at 7:00 p.m., visitation was limited to public areas, and student IDs were checked. A campus-wide 10:30 p.m. curfew was put into effect and after 9:00 p.m. all university buildings were locked. Entrances to women's residence halls were guarded around the clock. Then on the Wednesday prior to the murder, a male student claimed to have been choked to the point of unconsciousness. And on the Wednesday following the murder, another female student claimed that the same had happened to her. The police were skeptical of these claims and indeed these two reports turned out to be fabrications, but at the time were believed by the campus community and added to a palpable sense of threat. As a result, 70 percent of the student body left town on the weekend after the killing.

Psychologists John L. Shelton and Raymond S. Sanders documented the psychological effects of this ordeal on OSU students. Dormitory residents, especially those in close proximity to the events, experienced "fear, generalized anxiety, grief, depression, and confusion." Not surprisingly, many students had difficulty sleeping, but also had bouts of nausea, vomiting, headaches, and diarrhea. According to Shelton and Sanders's records, the hysteria peaked a couple of days after Nancy Wyckoff's death. Fatigued and depressed, students became frustrated and angry, had difficulty concentrating, and seemed unable to make decisions. Dorm rooms were supposed to be safe—especially with curfews, police guards, and lockdowns—but despite this, Wyckoff had been stabbed in her very own room. Understandably, residents felt quite vulnerable and, to use a more recent term, terrorized. They had not only to cope with the murder and attacks, but also with an invasive national press corps and repeated police interrogation. Some female students, in particular, became hysterical and their displays of distress contributed to a growing sense of panic on campus. Students began to arm themselves. Others expressed hostility toward security personnel, reporters, and the administration. Some male students organized small escort services for female students, thereby reinforcing their feelings of vulnerability. Others organized small groups to patrol each dormitory floor—a type of "neighborhood watch."

The counseling psychologists noted that students at this point became "more suggestible, and the spread of rumor was particularly evident following the alleged strangulation [of the male student]." Many students found themselves powerless to resist the impulse to continuously ruminate about the events and the possibility of future attacks. The situation resembled the aftermath of a natural catastrophe: "Many students, preoccupied with attempting to explain the behavior of the assailant, engaged in endless but unproductive speculation about his psychological state and motivation. This fostered the development of widespread hysteria." Interestingly, the crisis afforded an opportunity for some students to have some of their personal psychological needs met. For example, those who seemed to possess any "inside information" were instantly accorded higher status. And many students used the crisis as a means of fastidiously avoiding studying and homework.

This awful episode dramatically illustrates several answers to the question: What causes rumor spread? That is, what are the immediate psychological and situational factors that lead people to transmit rumors? This is the "what" question in rumor transmission, and it focuses our attention on causes behind rumor spreading. Notice by the way that the way we ask the question makes a difference in the answer. "What are the causes of a phenomenon?" emphasizes the inanimate forces at work in that phenomenon, much as you might focus on the chemical properties of cyanide on human organs in answering the question "What caused the man's death?" The medical examiner would ask the question in this way, whereas the detec-

tive would ask, why did he take the cyanide? What was he (or someone else) trying to accomplish? That sort of question would lead to
an examination of the motives, desires, and beliefs involved in the
episode. But we are getting ahead of ourselves; I'll begin with the
causes of rumor spread.

First of all, uncertainty leads to rumor spreading. People at
OSU were filled with uncertainty. Rumors were so prevalent
that a rumor control center was set up and staffed twenty-four
hours a day—specifically with the intent of combating uncertainty.
Uncertainty is the psychological state of doubt, of being filled with
questions about what events mean or what will happen in the
future. How did the killer do it amidst all that security? Who was
this person? A fellow student? Why would someone do such a terrible thing? How can I protect myself? When will these attacks
stop? The existentialist philosophers have said that uncertainty is a
basic condition of life, and we often encounter situations in which
it seems to be plentiful. Sociologists have called these situations
"undefined"—they are experienced as lacking a coherent pattern or
meaning. Uncertainty is an unpleasant state to be in. People in
search of missing loved ones, for example, report that the hardest
burden to bear is not the loss—but the lack of closure. Not knowing what happened to them. Waiting for news can actually be worse
than receiving it—and people seize upon rumors in an attempt to
end uncertainty.

For millions of asylum seekers in the world today, waiting and
uncertainty is a fact of daily life. Asylum seekers are refugees who
seek a residency status in another country. They flee their homeland
out of fear of persecution, because of their religion, race, national-
ity, or political opinion. Asylum seekers today often flee their
country of origin because of war or violent oppression. They are
sometimes kept in special camps, awaiting judgment about whether

they can stay, or must return to their homeland. In this political limbo, rumors often abound. Jawad, a refugee in a Denmark asylum camp, has documented examples of rumors rampant in asylum camps: "A rejected asylum seeker was deported to his home country." "An asylum seeker was transferred to a closed camp." "A financial reward was given to an asylum seeker after he agreed to return home." "The government is discussing the plight of asylum seekers." Jawad says the cumulative effect of these rumors is destructive and discouraging, but the rumors here are (futile) attempts to assuage chronic uncertainty. Waiting is emotionally wearing and makes people vulnerable to all manner of rumors.

Sometimes situations are filled with uncertainty because there isn't much information available. But often the problem is distrust in the official source of information. Before the fall of the Union of Soviet Socialist Republics (USSR), news was carefully monitored and controlled by the government; anything contrary to official Soviet policy was not published. Not surprisingly, the official news was distrusted. Political scientists Raymond A. Bauer and David B. Gleicher chronicled how rumors were extensively relied on by Soviet citizens in the 1930s and 1940s. Between 1950 and 1951, these researchers conducted more than three hundred oral interviews with Soviet refugees living in Europe or the United States. Although rumors were derogated by the government, they flourished. Sixty-six percent of the persons who listed word of mouth as a regular source of information also considered it to be their most important source of information. This measure of how "potent" or "salient" a source of information was, indicated that rumors were more potent than all other sources of information, including newspapers (48 percent), radio (24 percent), meetings (11 percent), and personal observation (36 percent). In other words, in an environment where official news could not be trusted, word-of-mouth information—in large part rumors—was the most powerful.

In addition to uncertainty, students at OSU were also filled with fear and anxiety—and this led to lots of rumor spreading. Whereas fear has a focus—"I'm afraid of snakes," for example—anxiety often does not—"I'm simply afraid." Anxiety is objectless—a vague, pervasive, and unpleasant feeling of distress, nervousness, and unease. Students, naturally, were afraid and worried for their safety. Learning that a brutal murder has taken place on your dormitory floor is certainly reason enough to feel real—and rational—fear. But in addition, students felt intense anxiety. The murder and attacks happened in what was supposed to be a safe haven—one's dorm room. Further, it took place amidst police, guards, student watch groups, and high vigilance. In that situation, one begins to speculate about the fellow across the hall—is he really a farm boy from Des Moines? Or is he a demonic psychopathic sadist? One begins to feel a sense of dread even in the hall restroom, among the stacks of books in the library, on the lonely quad at night. One is acutely aware of just how vulnerable we all are to malignant monsters.

Hearsay researchers Charles J. Walker and Carol A. Beckerle explored how anxiety led to rumor spreading in a clever experiment on the campus of St. Bonaventure University in upstate New York. Students came to Walker and Beckerle's lab and were told that the task of the study was to help a professor improve exam questions by answering those questions on a mock test. Then a confederate—posing as another participant in the study—informally exposed each participant to a couple of rumors. The rumors were explanations of what was (supposedly) really going on. For example, one rumor was that the true purpose of the study was to catch cheaters; the other rumor stated that the professor's true intent was to assess the quality of his classroom demonstrations. Each of the rumors was plausible and represented a couple of ways of making sense of this situation. Then each participant was placed randomly in one of two experimental conditions—high or low anxiety. In the high-anxiety condition, students watched on a TV screen what they believed was a live situation happening in another room. In this scene, the professor was harshly interrogating another participant in the study. The scene was, of course, not real and not even live—in fact it was videotaped to ensure that each high-anxiety participant saw the exact same stimulus. Understandably, watching this harsh treatment at the hands of a formidable professor—and expecting that one would undergo the same experience shortly— was quite anxiety provoking. (If you have ever witnessed a tough-talking judge berating a defendant in a courtroom just prior to your own appearance for speeding, you can get a feel for this condition.) In the low-anxiety condition, participants did not watch the scene; they merely read some test questions. Some time later, another confederate asked nonchalantly, "What is going on here today?" and if they received no reply, they asked this question again in another form. Participants in the high-anxiety condition shared one of the rumors much earlier (after an average of only two prompts) than participants in the low-anxiety condition (after an average of four prompts). Conclusion: anxiety led to rumor transmission.

Anxiety seems to work its effects by robbing people of a psychological sense of control. One basic human motivation is the desire to control our circumstances so that we survive and do well. A sense of control is that settled conviction that one is able to influence events, people, or objects around them. The sense of control might be achieved by simply flicking a light switch and observing the room flood with light. The desire for a sense of control seems to be inborn. In one study led by the research team of Michael Lewis at Rutgers University, infants lying in a crib faced a screen on which a picture could be flashed. The baby's arm was tied to a switch that would change the picture and the babies soon learned that if they pulled on the string, a new and interesting picture would appear. The babies seemed to enjoy this, and appropriately cooed and gurgled. But when control was taken away—that is, when the pictures stopped switching in response to the tug or when the pictures were flashed randomly—the babies complained: they cried or whined. It's easy to understand their discomfort; none of us likes to lose control over our environment. The computer screen freezes and won't respond to our tap-tapping. This loss of control strikes most people as very annoying. It seems that we are not all that different from these infants.

Think for a moment about how we might react to events that are potentially threatening to us. We might try to form and enact a plan that will help us avoid the threatening event or influence that happens to us. Students at OSU did this: they organized escort services and dormitory watch groups. They actively sought information so as to get a better picture of the problem and thereby learn how to avoid being attacked. The administration and security personnel also did this by putting into place a strict curfew and security checkpoints. We might say that these efforts—which included sharing rumors—were aimed at affecting one's environment. They were attempts to actively change or manage the situation. This type of control has been dubbed primary control.

But what of situations in which we are truly powerless to avoid negative outcomes? In such scenarios, we might try to feel better about the threatening events simply by seeking to understand them or by emotionally preparing for them. There is something comforting about understanding why something terrible is happening and about being able to "brace yourself" for the worst. Continuing to think that the world is understandable and predictable is important—it makes the planet seem a bit saner. Indeed, much of modern stress management tries to reduce stress by helping individuals to see how a potential negative event might be understandable or predictable. The OSU community pursued this strategy by trying to collectively comprehend the motive and psychological makeup of the killer. By discussing and endlessly ruminating on this, students were attempting to achieve what has been dubbed a secondary sense of control. Thinking that the killer was severely abused as a child, for example, would afford an (almost) comprehensible reason for these terrible events.

Rumors collected by Charles Walker and his associates in a number of other studies support this idea. In one investigation, Walker's team collected two hundred rumors circulating among 111 students at St. Bonaventure University. Using a team of trained students, he then analyzed the type of control that each rumor seemed to be offering. For example, if a rumor stated, "That course is taught by a very difficult instructor—avoid it if at all possible!" the team would categorize it as providing a primary type of control because students could use this information to avoid an unpleasant course. A rumor recipient would simply not register for the course and feel fortunate that they could do so. But the rumor "The Board of Trustees has voted to raise tuition by 10 percent" alerts students to an event that they can't do anything about. So why share it? Because hearing about it would afford a type of secondary control: simply knowing about the event would help people emotionally prepare for the worst. Students would be unable to avoid the tuition hike, but would feel better about it because they knew it was coming, could attribute the hike to rising costs or inflation, and because they could commiserate with one another about it. Walker's team expected to find many secondary control rumors, but was surprised to find that all of the rumors were about secondary control themes. That is, students appeared to be sharing rumors in order to feel better about uncontrollable events by simply trying to understand them or passively accept them. In a word, they were using the rumors to try to regain a *feeling* of control.

This attempt to regain control also seems to manifest itself in the popularity of dread rumors: in study after study, dread rumors outnumber wish rumors. For example, Prashant Bordia and his colleagues collected rumors at a large public hospital in Australia. The hospital was undergoing a restructuring. These employees had already been through quite a few changes, including new construction, new equipment, new organizational hierarchies, fewer beds, and relocation. Now, change is not always bad—indeed it could be good. But out of 510 rumors that could be classified one way or the other, 479 were dread rumors. Employees were most concerned about the possibility of losing their job or of negative impacts to their job as a result of the changes. Not surprisingly, hearing these dread rumors was associated with greater employee stress when compared with not hearing rumors or with hearing wish rumors. This seems natural enough: People are more likely to lose a sense of control and feel anxious when unable to alter the course of negative—as compared to positive—events that will affect them.

Of course, we feel more anxiety and less control about dreaded events that pertain to issues that are important to us; trivial events don't seem worth getting energized over. If you depend on public transit to get around, for example, a transit labor strike is important to you. In the spring and summer of 1986, riders of the Southeast Pennsylvania Transit Authority (SEPTA) faced such a strike. Talks had broken down, and many residents of the greater Philadelphia metropolis had to find alternate forms of transportation.

City officials were caught in a gridlock of negotiations with union leaders and progress was stalled. In the midst of this noisy situation, Jim Esposito—one of Ralph Rosnow's graduate students—distributed questionnaires at a large urban shopping mall, among transit patrons, and among Temple University undergraduates. He asked people questions such as "Describe a rumor that you have heard recently about the impending SEPTA strike" and "To about how many people did you mention this rumor?" Among other things, Jim asked about importance: "When you first heard this rumor, how important did you think its content was?" Not surprisingly, the more important the issue was to people, the more likely they were to spread rumors about the strike. "If SEPTA does strike, it will be a long one." "The fare increase would be at least twenty-five cents." "The Red Arrow line will strike at midnight tonight." Recall Allport and Postman's law of rumor: the likelihood of rumor spread is proportional to the uncertainty of the situation and the importance of the topic. Trying to figure out if SEPTA will strike or when the strike will end required energy and effort—but because it directly affected their lives, people did it.

Similarly, questions surrounding the murder of Nancy Wyckoff were immensely important to students at OSU—their very lives seemed in peril. This idea is implicit in many of the definitions of rumor. Rosnow and Allan Kimmel defined rumor as "an unverified proposition for belief that bears topical relevance for persons actively involved in its dissemination." That is to say, rumors are statements concerning issues that are important to participants, perhaps because the information is new (like news), perhaps because the information concerns a topic that affects them directly, or perhaps because the topic is one that interests them greatly. This explains why old rumors tend to die out—they are no longer novel or newsworthy. If I shared a rumor that former President Bill

Clinton had an extramarital affair with White House intern Monica Lewinsky, not many people would be interested—but at the time the stories first appeared, rumors about this episode were plentiful. It seemed important at the time.

One morning in 1993, I found a flyer in my mailbox in the psychology building at Temple University. A well-meaning employee had received the flyer via fax machine, had copied it out of concern, and then distributed it to all mailboxes in the mail room. Perhaps the first thing that caught my attention was the capitalized words urging automobile drivers: DO NOT BLINK YOUR HEAD-LIGHTS!!! My first thought was, "Blink my headlights? Why would I want to blink my headlights?" I mentally listed the situations in which I routinely blinked my headlights at oncoming traffic: when they had their high beams on, to signal them to go ahead at an intersection, and—if their lights were off at night—to remind them to turn on those headlights. I read further: it was the last of these situations that the flyer referred to. It claimed that after blinking at an oncoming car without its headlights on, the car had turned around and followed the unsuspecting "blinkers" to their destination and killed their drivers as part of a gruesome new gang initiation rite. According to the flyer, this terrible event had occurred several times in Illinois.

This sounded like many of the rumors I had begun to collect, so I called the Illinois State Police to check its veracity. A tired trooper answered the phone: "Is this about the headlights rumor? It's a hoax. It never happened. We've been getting calls about this for two weeks." And so, the flyer was false. Our research team thought this would be a great opportunity to collect data about the factors associated with rumor transmission. Prashant Bordia and I hastily created a set of interview questions, then canvassed the psychology building and interviewed everyone we could find—about thirty people. One of the questions we asked was, "How strongly do you believe the information on this flyer?" We expected a moderate to low level of belief—remember, these were highly intelligent, highly skeptical graduate psychology students and renowned professors. We were surprised that all but one person expressed very strong confidence that this tale was true. Indeed, almost all persons we interviewed had immediately called two or three members of their family or friends to warn them not to blink headlights. When we asked them why they believed it, a common response was "It sounds like something that could happen: gangs do bad things, gangs have initiation rites, gangs hurt innocent people, and this is a story about gangs hurting innocent people as part of an initiation rite." In other words, this was a plausible idea to the people we questioned. It must have been a plausible idea to many Americans, because the flyer spread by fax machine to just about every major corporation and organization in the United States.

The headlights hoax provides an example of how belief in a rumor leads to the spreading of that rumor. One way of putting this is that people don't always simply hear a rumor and spread it in the same way as, say, a contagious virus might spread. Rather, rumors are discussed and evaluated. They pass through a plausibility filter. Of course, what is plausible to one group may be fantastic to another, so it may seem like people are operating without a filter. A closer look, however, will show that stronger confidence in the rumor leads to greater rumor spreading. Reporters and interested people sometimes ask me if educated persons are less likely to believe rumors, perhaps because they assume that educated people are less gullible than the average human. I don't know the answer to that, but the headlights hoax's success among highly intelligent people demonstrates that at times, even the highly educated elite can "fall" for a false rumor—as long as it seems plausible to that particular rumor public at that particular time. The plausibility filter probably operates because of social forces at work in long-term relationships. There is a general rule of conversation that when we pass along information, that information should be true—even when spreading a good story, told for effect. This may be because we are concerned about our reputation. If we have a long-term relationship with someone, we want to be sure that the information we pass on to that person will not unnecessarily alarm them or raise their hopes. And so we pass along only those items that we have some confidence in.

With regard to rumor spreading, up to this point I've focused on what Aristotle called "efficient" or immediate causes. The efficient cause of a sculpture, for example, would be the force and motion of the chisel applied to marble. But as human beings we can fruitfully approach the same question with what Aristotle called final causality and ask: What is the person or group trying to do by spreading the rumor? The final cause of the sculpture might be that the artist is attempting to create the likeness of *David,* or suggest the masterful power of man, or maybe just keep unemployment at bay. Interested in final causes, we might put our question: *Why* do people spread rumors? This sort of question focuses us on the reasons, motives, desires, goals, and beliefs of those involved in rumor transmission. Or to put it yet another way, the intent behind rumor spreading.

One reason people spread rumors is simply to understand a situation so that they might act effectively. We can gain a lot of understanding through informal discussions with others—even using unverified statements in circulation. We like to find the facts, figure out what might happen in the future, and discern appropriate reactions to situations.

Imagine you are a parent of a child at Plymouth High School near South Bend, Indiana. One day in October 2007 you hear from a friend that a student is going to bring a gun to school. It seems that this student—a female—had been harassed by three boys in class. The young lady then threatened to bring a gun to school and shoot the boys if they did not stop. Given this information, what is the appropriate action for you to take at this point? You could (a) do nothing—she doesn't really intend to bring a gun to school, or (b) keep your child out of school for a couple of days—school shootings are unlikely, but they do happen. To answer this question, you need more information, such as: Does the female student in question have a history of mental illness? Does she indeed own a gun? Is she emotionally stable? Did she really mean what she said, or was it a flirtatious remark? In addition, it would be helpful to know what other parents are doing. If other parents are keeping their children at home, then perhaps one should do likewise. At Plymouth High School, both types of rumors undoubtedly circulated. "I heard that she does own a gun, but that she's never fired it" would be an example of a rumor about the situation in question. "I heard that Mabel is keeping her Johnny home from school tomorrow" would be an example of a rumor about what other parents are doing. In both cases, people are using rumor with the intent of understanding so as to act effectively in the face of uncertainty.

People share rumors like this also to help others act effectively. Several years ago, a friend of mine received this e-mail forward in her in-box:

> I got this message about a virus that can produce lot of damage to your computer. If you follow the instructions which are very easy, you would be able to "clean" your computer. Apparently the virus spreads through the address book. I got it then maybe I passed it to you too, sorry. The name of the virus is jdbgmgr.exe

and is transmitted automatically through the Messenger and address book of Outlook. The virus is neither detected by Norton nor by McAfee. It remains in lethargy ("sleeping") for 14 days and even more, before it destroys the whole system. It can be eliminated during this period. The steps for the elimination of the virus are the following:

1. Go to Start and click Find.
2. In Files and Folders write: jdbgmgr.exe.
3. Be sure that it searches in C.
4. Click Search Now.
5. If the virus appears (with icon of a small bear) and the name jdbgmgr.exe don't open it !!! in any case !!!
6. Click the right button of the mouse and destroy it.
7. Empty the recycle bin.

If you find the virus in your computer please send this mail to all the people in your address book. Thanks.

My friend checked her computer and sure enough found the icon. She immediately alerted all persons on her address list, hoping that it was not too late for us to avoid damage to our computers. Perhaps you've also received this popular e-mail forward, known as the "teddy bear icon virus" hoax. If you followed the instructions, you would have found the teddy bear icon next to a file named jdbgmgr.exe, as the e-mail claimed. However, not to worry; jdbgmgr.exe stands for Java DeBug Manager—it is a Microsoft program used by Java programmers and will not harm your files. And, unless you are a Java programmer, deleting the program will not harm or impair your computer in any way. The warning was a hoax. My friend, however, was concerned that she had infected everyone in her address book with a harmful virus, and so she forwarded this message to all of us. She was motivated by a desire to help us avoid what would certainly be a great loss. Psychologists call this a pro-social motive and argue about whether it is driven by true concern for others or for oneself—these two motivations are often hard to disentangle. Other psychologists argue that acts such as these are driven by a fundamental commitment to moral principles—to do unto others as you would have them do unto you. Whatever the ultimate aim, my friend's act of spreading this rumor was certainly intended to keep us from harm.

The teddy bear icon example also illustrates that sharing rumors is a social interchange, not just an intellectual puzzle. People often spread rumors in order to enhance or maintain their relationship with others. In other words, rumor sharing makes other people like or respect us more. How might this occur? We've seen how this can happen by helping others to act effectively, avoid harm, or not miss an opportunity. Sharing a rumor with another person can also increase the teller's social standing in the eyes of the hearer, at least temporarily. The teller is "in the know" and regarded as something of an authority for a time. This happened to students at Oregon State University; those with any of the latest developments or rumors were instantly accorded greater status.

Many times, sharing a rumor is just something that people do together, to identify one another as part of the same "crowd" or as people with a similar perspective. The truth or falsity of the statement is perhaps of secondary importance. Among Republicans: "Those spendthrift Democrats!" Among Democrats: "Those robber-baron Republicans!" Think of the types of unverified statements that are acceptable—and not to be questioned—in your own particular circle of friends. Recall the headlights hoax above. At the end of each interview we told people that the story was untrue. It was usually an awkward moment—the first of many I was to have over the years. People didn't really appreciate being enlightened. They would have preferred me to join them in commiserating about the sense of powerlessness and anxiety they felt: "It's awful what gangs do these days!" "A person can't drive safely anymore." "What is the world coming to?" Instead, the statement "I called the Illinois State Police and they said it is a hoax" was socially inappropriate. It did nothing to enhance my relationship with each person—in fact I sensed some annoyance. It was my first taste of being a "killjoy."

A friend once forwarded me a false rumor about a U.S. presidential candidate; I contacted her and told her the rumor was false and encouraged her to send a retraction to all the people she sent the original to. I never heard from her again. I had failed to recognize that the telling and hearing of this rumor was primarily a social act, not to be disrupted by the facts. People are not always primarily interested in the truth when they speak together, but rather to find ways to affiliate and bond with one another.

One study that Prashant Bordia and I performed with students from the Rochester Institute of Technology (RIT) explored how this social awkwardness affected rumor transmission. Students read scenarios in which they were asked to imagine that a friend had told them that the (nearby) University of Rochester's (UR) ranking in the *U.S. News & World Report* had dropped four places—a serious decline indeed. (This was a fictitious rumor, by the way, and participants were informed of this directly after the study.) They were asked how good or bad this was for the UR and overall, they agreed that is was very bad news—higher education has become a competitive business, and colleges and universities regularly depend on such ratings to build their reputation among students. In another condition, they were told to imagine the friend had told them that the UR ranking rose by four places—a significant increase. These statements qualified as rumors because students "heard" them from "a friend of yours at RIT"—certainly an unverified bit of information. Such hearsay about the reputations of colleges is indeed prevalent and may factor heavily in applicants' decisions to apply or attend. For example, "I heard that University XYZ is a party school"; "is glorified high school"; "will let anyone in"; "is very good"; or "is very warm and friendly." The participants in this study—all of which attended RIT—were then asked to imagine that they happened to be at a party with other students from the UR. At that point they were asked, "How likely would you be to share this information [with the UR students]?" RIT students were much more likely to share the positive rumor with the UR students than the negative one. Sharing a negative rumor would have been socially inappropriate. People actively strive to promote and preserve good impressions of themselves in the eyes of others—telling them something bad about their group is usually not the way to do that. Much better to share the positive rumor.

We also strive to promote and preserve a good impression of ourselves in our own eyes. Mike Kamins and his associates performed a similar study at the University of Arkansas. Students were asked to imagine sharing either a rumor that the rival school had been rated less favorably than their own, or rated more favorably. They were then asked to imagine talking with members of their own school and queried about how likely they were to share what they had heard. They were more likely to spread the negative rumor about the rival school than the positive one. In addition, students in the negative rumor condition thought they would "feel better" after telling the rumor, as compared to students in the positive rumor condition. (This is not a very flattering conclusion about human nature.) Kamins's team also had students imagine sharing positive or negative rumors about their own school; they were more likely to share positive rumors about their own school. Remember that the recipient of the rumor was another student at the same school. The researchers therefore theorized that telling negative rumors about the rival school, and positive rumors about one's own school, functioned to make the tellers feel better. Putting a rival group down with a member of your own "club" can push your own group up by comparison. And because you are part of your group, your own sense of self gets a boost as well. Rumors can thus be told to boost one's self-esteem.

Psychological self-enhancement is perhaps the intent behind racist rumors. For some persons, it helps to put others down so that their own group—and by extension, their own self—looks better. Allport and Postman documented such rumors in the United States during times when African-Americans were enslaved or discriminated against by white Americans. These rumors supported derogatory ideas about African-Americans as criminal, dangerous, sexually promiscuous, and violent. One common rumor was that African-American servants were caught using the "lady of the house's" combs. Another was that African-American males were caught raping blond virgins and robbing white men. Similarly, people sometimes use negative rumors about other groups as a way of avoiding looking at the things in themselves for which they feel most ashamed. Looking for opportunities to be angry at others is one—not very effective—way to deflect deep-seated bad feelings about ourselves. This usually takes the form of blaming socially acceptable targets—often minorities or other groups to which one does not belong. The problems one faces in life can therefore be explained as the fault of others. If we are in the practice of boosting our self-esteem in this way, we become eager purveyors of negative rumors about groups to which we don't belong. This may explain why derogatory rumors about other groups are well known among people in our own group, but derogatory rumors about our own group are rarely discussed. They are not very self-enhancing.

Spreading a derogatory rumor to boost self-esteem is psychologically self-enhancing. In similar ways, spreading it to boost one's profits is financially self-enhancing and to boost one's power is politically self-enhancing. For example, spreading rumors about a business competitor's products, ingredients, or political ideology may draw customers away from the competitor. Of course, for these planted rumors to work, they must be plausible and important to the hearer. Sources of rumors like this often allege that the competitors' products contain carcinogens, then offer their own product as a pure substitute. It doesn't take a Ph.D. in psychology to conclude that a likely motive for this type of rumor spreading is pecuniary gain. A false rumor of this sort is that sodium laureth sulfate—a common ingredient found in shampoo—causes cancer. While searching the World Wide Web for "sodium laureth sulfate" as recently as November 2007, I found numerous Web sites operated by small multilevel-marketing businesses proclaiming this substance to be cancerous, then hawking their own alternative "natural ingredient" products.

In his 1990 work, *Rumors: Uses, Interpretations, and Images,* Jean-Noel Kapferer presciently wrote: "Rumors are ideal weapons in primaries—struggles between people within a single party." False rumors about Senator John McCain—including that he had fathered an illegitimate black child—that were spread by "push polls" during the South Carolina Republican primary election in 2000 are widely believed to have been instrumental in McCain's defeat that year. Push polls are propaganda devices purporting to be legitimate telephone polling efforts. A "pollster" will first call and ascertain who the household member is likely to vote for; if they indicate the propaganda target, they will be asked a question that insinuates the rumor. Push pollsters in South Carolina asked respondents who indicated that they were in favor of McCain, "How likely are you to change your vote if it became known that McCain fathered an illegitimate black child?" On the other side of the aisle, rumors about rumor mongering circulated during the feisty 2007–2008 Democratic primary season. In November 2007, conservative columnist Robert Novak claimed that the Hillary Clinton campaign told Democratic Party insiders that they possessed scandalous information about Barack Obama but that they were not going to publish it. Novak stood by his statements despite receiving criticism from both the Obama and Clinton campaigns. By far the most popular target of rumors during the raucous primary season was the senator from Illinois. False claims that Obama is (or was) a Muslim, that he swore his oath of office on a Koran, that he refuses to pledge allegiance to the flag, and that he was raised in a radical terrorist school have enjoyed wide circulation.

So, we've seen the what and the why of rumor spread, but what about the where? This question emphasizes the pattern of rumor spread through space and over time. By "space" I don't necessarily mean country, city, or precinct; but rather social space—the web of relationships and social networks in which we are embedded. The question of where rumors spread focuses us on the paths a rumor takes within social networks, the speed of a rumor as it travels across social networks, and the extent of a rumor's dissemination through social networks. It also raises the questions: Where does a particular rumor "settle down to live," and where does it "shake the dust from its feet?"

Sociologist Theodore Caplow was an officer in the army during World War II (assigned to the Amphibian Engineer Corps in the

Pacific Theater). The army was concerned—as was the entire military—about rumors, especially about war operations. "Loose lips sink ships!" was an oft-seen slogan in posters urging war personnel to hold their tongues. Caplow's duty as part of his S-2 unit, the intelligence gathering arm of his regiment, was to prepare an intelligence report; this included a section on rumors. He did this on a monthly basis over a two-year period using contacts from every company in the regiment. These contacts enthusiastically reported rumors to him and within a few hours of being heard, Caplow would regularly set these rumors down in writing. He also recorded the circumstances in which these rumors originated, and estimates of how widely they had diffused, how valid they were, and the pattern of flow surrounding them. Caplow noted that the informal channels of communication—the social networks—were particularly important for understanding the process of rumor spread. Officers, for example, would rarely communicate with enlisted men, and vice versa. Military rumors therefore tended to diffuse within these established groups rather than travel from one group to another. Rumors did cross from one group to another, usually through a well-recognized cross-group connection, but this was less common than the within-group chatter. Rumors thus tended to flow along established social networks.

Similarly, close networks in the African-American community help to explain the raft of hearsay besetting Cory A. Booker, the mayor of Newark, New Jersey. Negative rumors about Mayor Booker abounded in 2007: "One of his top aides moonlights as a cocaine dealer." "Mayor Booker is not black." "He lives in a fancy house in the suburbs." These rumors were false, but they filled a gap in knowledge about Cory Booker—analysts say that he is not well known among city residents, creating uncertainty about him and his administration. Perhaps these rumors are instigated by angry "old guard" black leaders who have not been included in the power structure—as had been the case with former mayors—or those who are trying to regain power. This would be a political self-enhancement motive. Booker particularly angered some by signifying willingness to lay off and outsource up to 20 percent of the city's municipal employees—many of whom are African-American—to meet a severe budget shortfall. So, the rumors may therefore be motivated by financial self-enhancement. We've seen these types of causes and motivations before. But I want to emphasize that the rumors played well in established African-American social networks: barbershops, basketball courts, and after church on Sundays. Without these networks, even highly motivated rumor spreaders in an information vacuum would have had few places to spread their hearsay.

Network structure affects rumor propagation. At a basic level, the existing social pattern of relationships encourages flow here and impedes it there. The course of a river's flow is determined by the lay of the land; in a similar fashion, the path a rumor runs is shaped in part by the social topography.

Caplow also noted how quickly military rumors can disseminate: "In one case, the rumor of an impending operation appeared in a detachment isolated on a tiny island without radio communication approximately one day after it was introduced to the main body of the regiment." Rumor's ability to travel quickly has been noted for some time. The ancient Roman poet Horace said, "Nothing is swifter than a rumor." And in our own laboratories, Prashant Bordia and I collected hundreds of questionnaires from students asking them to rate the term "rumor" along several dimensions, one of which was "timeliness." Invariably, students rated rumors as very timely. How is it that rumors can travel with such speed?

The "small world" arrangement of most social networks explains how rumors can move so rapidly. Undoubtedly you have heard or used the expression, "Gee, it's a small world after all!" when discovering that two people that you know also know each other. I frequently have this experience and it's always a bit surprising—why should Nelson, from one part of my life, happen to know Natasha, from another part? (This phenomenon should serve as a cautionary tale that nothing can be done "in a corner.") The world is thus "smaller" or more connected than I thought it would be. How does this happen? Some people, as you might imagine, have contact with many others—in social network terminology these people are called "hubs." Most people, however, are less well connected. And some have few interactions indeed—we call these lonely souls "isolates." The resulting social network is known as a small world and is very common indeed. It turns out that in this type of network, the average number of "steps" between any two people is surprisingly small. Within my faculty community of about one thousand professors, for example, I do not know most by their first name. But I undoubtedly know someone who does know them on a first-name basis—or at least I know someone who knows someone else who knows their first name. These connections form in ways that one would expect—I know the dean of our college who knows the dean of Natasha's college who knows Natasha, for example—and in ways one may not expect—I play racquetball with someone in Natasha's department. My large campus community is therefore a small world after all; it is more closely connected than I thought given its size. Your social network is probably a small world too.

If there are fewer "steps" between people than we ordinarily suppose, then it is easy to see how a rumor might travel so quickly—it simply doesn't have very far to go. Social psychologist

Stanley Milgram performed the classic study in this area in the late 1960s. Milgram wanted to know just how well connected we are. He gave a letter to 160 people in Omaha, Nebraska. The letter was addressed to a stockbroker in Boston, but instead of using the postal service, people were requested to pass it along to a friend or acquaintance, who was asked to also pass it along to a friend or acquaintance, and so forth until the letter was finally delivered to the stockbroker. Imagine being in this study: you might begin by mailing it to your old classmate who lives in New York City, they might send it to a family member in Boston, and that family member might mail it to their Boston stockbroker. From that point it seems likely that it would reach the target fairly quickly. At each resending of the letter the relay would also mail a postcard to Milgram's lab to keep track of the letter's path. Forty-two out the original 160 letters reached the Boston stockbroker. The median number of degrees of separation (intermediate resendings) was 5.5— this is a small number indeed. The widespread notion that there exists only six degrees of separation between any two people on the planet may or may not be true, but the number is almost certainly smaller than we would suppose given the earth's enormous population. Rumor transmission studies that trace the flow of rumors in organizations show transmission along small world pathways: the rumor spreads quickly by reaching hubs (people who are well connected), who then disperse it widely. Most people then tell a small number of people in their circle, and some do not pass it on at all. Before you know it, the rumor has traveled from Omaha to Boston.

"Going viral" is an expression in online circles. It describes a situation in which an electronic message spreads quickly and widely, much as an infectious biological virus would propagate via human contact. Such was the case in the town of Bend, Oregon, population 75,290, in July 2007. One concerned Bend mother wrote an e-mail asserting that a dead mouse had been found in a sack of popcorn kernels at a local movie theater. She stated that she had heard this from a theater employee. Notice that she wrote the e-mail out of an apparent pro-social motive—she didn't want people to get sick. In addition, the e-mail was plausible because in the previous year, rodent droppings had been found on the theater floor by county health department officials. But more recent visits by the health department found no such problems. The e-mail was very "contagious." The woman sent it to only her friends and family with encouragement to forward it to as many other residents of Bend as possible. Given the small world nature of most social networks, it is not surprising that the rumor then quickly spread throughout the town. Many people received multiple copies from different sources, indicating that the e-mail was thoroughly saturating this network. The rumor had an immediate effect on theater attendance, of course. People stayed away from the theater until they heard more information. One interesting aspect of going viral is that when a message is forwarded, it is tacitly being endorsed by the forwarder. And when it has been forwarded by so many people, it may gain a certain degree of credibility, and in this way increase the likelihood that it will be forwarded yet again. "Nothing succeeds like success," and nothing gets passed on like passed-on rumors.

Not only did this rumor spread quickly, it spread *widely.* How does this happen? The answer lies in the mathematics of exponents. Consider the path of a particularly interesting or important rumor, such as the headlights hoax. Imagine that Harry tells just five friends or family members not to blink their headlights. The number who heard this rumor "downstream" of Harry is five. Now imagine that each of those people in turn tells five other persons. The number who has now heard the rumor grows to thirty (5 times $5 = 25$, plus the original 5). Now imagine a third wave of rumor transmission; the number jumps a whopping 125 people

(25 times 5). After just ten waves of transmission the total number of downstream recipients has exponentially ballooned to more than 12 million people. If the rumor continues to spread like this, it will soon reach every person on the face of the planet.

This math explains how rumors can reach a vast number of people and how it can happen so rapidly. With the advent of the Internet and the ease of electronic communication, the numbers in the example are probably conservative—if you are like me, you often receive e-mail forwards addressed to far more than five people. And, according to a recent Harris poll, 79 percent of Americans are now regularly connected to the Internet. Actually, the more interesting question is, if rumors spread like this, why doesn't everyone receive them? Despite diffusing extensively and being faxed to nearly every major company in the United States in 1993, some people haven't heard the headlights hoax—why not?

Just after World War II, the eminent social psychologist Leon Festinger and his colleagues wanted to study how communities organized and communicated in real-world settings. They focused on a low-rent living community that had been built during the war to accommodate shipyard workers. In 1947, the community consisted of one hundred single or semiattached houses in a four-block area. From time to time, unsuccessful attempts had been made by some residents to start community activities such as holiday parties for children, Saturday night dances, boxing lessons for teenage boys, a softball league, art classes for kids, a gardening group, and sewing classes. For various reasons all of these efforts had failed. If you are fortunate to be part of a community where these types of activities happen, you will know that they are very beneficial, but they don't automatically happen. As a result, residents in this former shipyard worker project didn't feel much of a sense of community.

Enter social psychologist Leon Festinger and his team of research associates. Festinger wanted to know how a sense of community developed and, more practically, wanted to intervene to create a sense of community by fostering widespread involvement in community activities. (These were the days of bold projects in social psychology.) Initially posing as an interested volunteer, Festinger's research associate attended an exploratory meeting of the "tenants' committee," a volunteer neighborhood activity committee, to which only five persons had come. Through the research associate, Festinger hoped to guide the development of neighborhood activities. Festinger's associate was indeed the driving force in what happened next. At the tenants' meeting, she suggested that a large general meeting be held two weeks hence. She offered to obtain the help of consultants who would come to the meeting to advise tenants on community activities in which they were interested. (These consultants had expertise but were also part of the research team.) Further, she spearheaded the canvassing of the neighborhood so as to ensure a high level of attendance at the general meeting.

Her efforts paid off: Two weeks later, forty-three community members attended the general meeting. During a panel discussion at the meeting, the community activity experts—three professors on Festinger's research team—focused on three types of activities in which community members had expressed interest: a nursery school, a recreation program for school children, and adult education groups. The experts then led small group discussions of each of these groups, and encouraged practical steps to be taken in realizing these activities. In effect, subcommittees had been formed and new volunteer leaders began assuming responsibility. In the subsequent weeks, these subcommittees met, planned, began to fund-raise, and continued to recruit participants. Within a month, the goal of realizing a widely supported set of community activities appeared to be a reality.

The picture was not all rosy, however. In the midst of these community-building activities, an opposition group emerged and grew, instigated primarily by a member of the tenants' committee. The resistance came in the form of pessimism, criticism, and then opposition to the activities themselves. For example, another member of the original tenants' committee often expressed pessimism that community activities could succeed with these "low-type" tenants, based on her past experience. If you have ever been in the presence of someone like this, you know how discouraging it can be. Her defeatist attitude was somewhat infectious. Resistance also came in the form of criticism of the general meeting. Why were so many professors so interested in this community? (Their research interest in this community was not initially conveyed and so there was real uncertainty.) Critics began to express suspicion about the true purpose of the activities, and they wondered why a nursery worker would be provided for free. Resistance came in the form of the abrupt cancellation of subcommittee meetings by the committee member who outright opposed the activities, especially the nursery school.

At this point, an officer of the tenants' committee created a rumor to explain the uncertainties surrounding the activities and capitalized upon a growing national fear of Communism at the time. The rumor alleged that the volunteer leading the nursery school initiative, as well as the experts who spoke at the general meeting, were all "avowed Communists." The rumor emerged, was actively promulgated by its originator, passively accepted by other women who transmitted it, and led to the cancellation of all community activities for several weeks. No one wanted to have anything to do with a Communist plot. (The rumor was eventually dispelled, the nature of the researchers' interest was fully disclosed, and community activity development happily resumed— without the involvement of the rumor's author.)

Capitalizing on this unexpected turn of events, Festinger interviewed sixty-six residents several months later about how this rumor had spread through their community. He was interested to know how friendship patterns and motivation to tell the rumor affected the flow of this informal hearsay. Festinger divided his interviewees into three groups: those who had close friends in the community, those who only had acquaintances in the community, and those who had no friends in the community. Those who had close friends were far more likely to have heard the rumor than those with only acquaintances and those with no friends. Festinger concluded that the Communist rumor tended to circulate within friendship groups rather than between them, and that friendship intimacy afforded an easy avenue of communication. Only occasionally was it transmitted outside these boundaries. The rumor tended to travel along already established friendship groupings.

But social networks are not rumor destiny; motivation also plays a role in who one shares a rumor with. At each "rumor relay station," transmitters make a decision about who would like to hear this rumor—and who wouldn't. Dead mouse in the Bend movie theater? E-mail that message to Uncle Paul whose kids go to the movies every week in Bend, but not to Uncle Pat in Boston. Blinking headlights part of a gang-initiation ritual? Fax it to my sister Paula before she starts on her commute home so she doesn't blink. No need to send it to Aunt Patty, as she no longer drives a car. Like the letters sent by Milgram's subjects, each of these rumors has a particular "address" or segment of the population that would find it interesting, important, or effective. Rumor relays keep this in mind when passing hearsay along. Festinger found evidence for this in his study: 67 percent of the people who were involved in the new community activities told the rumor to someone else after hearing it; none of those who did not participate did so. To those involved in the community activities, the rumor would be of high interest and relevant. Similarly, 62 percent of people with nursery school–age children heard the rumor, while only 28 percent of those without such children heard it. Again, parents of nursery school–age children would be interested in a rumor that the planned school was part of a "Communist plot." Festinger concluded ". . . that the circulation of a rumor through a social structure does not depend merely upon the existence of adequate channels of communication; some motivation to tell the rumor must also be present."

Nowhere is the interaction of social network structure and motivations more clearly observed than in the content of rumors that circulate through groups that oppose each other. I previously discussed a false rumor that circulated about both President George W. Bush and Senator John Kerry in the 2004 presidential election. This derogatory rumor highlighted the alleged hypocrisy of the candidate when he stated that his favorite Bible passage was John 16:3, not John 3:16. Presumably, the rumor that bashed President Bush flourished in Democratic Party soil—if you were a Democrat you were more likely to have heard the Bush-bashing version, and probably more motivated to resend it. Conversely, the one bashing Senator Kerry traveled well on Republican Party terrain—if you were a Republican, you were more likely to have heard the Kerry-bashing version, and also more motivated to send it. The outcome is a set of very different and conflicting shared realities.

Bernard Brooks, David Ross—both mathematicians at the Rochester Institute of Technology—and I have simulated the propagation of this kind of negative out-group rumor on various types of social networks. People in our simulations were represented as dots, and relationships as lines that connected those dots. Someone who had many relationships, for example, would be symbolized as a star: a dot from which many lines emanate. Social networks are commonly depicted using such sociograms. In our simulations, the sociogram was first divided in half: some dots were colored red to represent one group and others blue to represent a rival group. As in real life, people from one group in our simulations tended to be densely connected; birds of feather do flock together. Thus, red dots were decidedly more connected with each other than with blue dots, and vice versa.

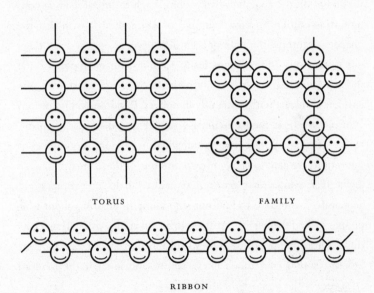

TORUS   FAMILY

RIBBON

Three of the social networks used in our simulations are depicted above. Sixteen-person torus, ribbon, and family networks are diagrammed here. Each face represents an individual and connections are indicated by lines. In the torus network, each individual has four "neighbors"—north, south, east, and west—in a two-dimensionally uniform distribution that resembles a lattice.

The ribbon configuration shows how an individual may be connected to four neighbors aligned as on a street—two across the road and one on either side. If you live on a residential street of single-family homes, you most likely know your neighbors to the left and right and in the two houses opposite you; those down the street are merely familiar strangers. The family configuration depicted shows how the majority of one's social interactions may be with one's "family" or local cluster of contacts. If you are part of a family, each of you knows and interacts with one another, especially if you eat dinner together every night. Each of the preceding configurations differs in how "clumpy" or segmented it is in that the chances of interacting with one set of people, as opposed to others not in that set, differs dramatically. Families, for example, are the most segmented, in that family members interact most with one another and least with nonfamily members. Random configurations (not pictured), as the name implies, are arranged so that the probability of connections between individuals is random. Random configurations are akin to being thrown into one of those uncomfortable icebreaker games at parties designed to help newcomers get acquainted: you have to find out something interesting about four people picked from a hat. At these dreadful affairs you end up chatting with several people, but they probably don't know one another. Doesn't sound very much like a family, and indeed, the random structure is the least segmented of the four.

In our model of rumor transmission, we first calculated the likelihood of one person passing the rumor to another person with whom they are connected. We based this likelihood on the ideas presented in this chapter. For example, red to red transmission of a rumor that is negative about blues was specified to be more likely than red to blue transmission of such a rumor, and also blue to blue. This followed from the research showing that people are more likely to share a negative out-group rumor with someone from their own group than from a member of the rival group. It would be bad manners to share a negative rumor about blue people with a blue person. And, it may boost my self-esteem to share the blue-is-bad rumor with my red friends. In addition, the more one believes the rumor, the more likely one is to pass it on. As we've seen, belief leads to rumor spreading. Further, the more novel a rumor is, the more likely one is to pass it on—old rumors die out. Finally, the process was also interactive: hearing the rumor repeatedly leads to greater belief in it. (We'll see this in the next chapter.) Thus, for any two connected dots where one of them has heard a rumor, we had an equation that calculated the likelihood that the rumor would be transmitted from one dot to another.

To begin the simulation, one of the red dots was seeded with a negative rumor about the blue people, or vice versa, and the initial belief in that rumor was set at 50 percent. We then observed the pattern of propagation and belief over time. It was like playing SimCity®. Our simulations showed a clear set of results: In-group belief in the out-group negative rumor outpaced out-group belief in these rumors. That is, the negative rumor about reds was heard and believed more quickly and more strongly—and diffused more extensively—among blues. That is not so surprising. What was intriguing was that this tendency was affected by how segmented the network was. Specifically, it was accentuated in the family structure. During the simulation of rumor spread in the highly segmented "family" configuration, the rumor remained almost entirely within the in-group—it simply didn't have much opportunity to be transmitted to the out-group. That's because most of the connections in the family structure are with in-group members. In the least segmented group, the random structure, in-group and out-group belief trends were very similar—in-group and out-group members had the most opportunity to share the rumor because of their increased contact.

Our computer simulation mirrors what we know about how different rumors arise in different groups, how they tend to circulate within these groups due to segmented social structure, and are then believed more strongly over time. The outcome is often a starkly different set of shared realities between the competing factions. During the sensational trial of former football star O. J. Simpson, the prosecution presented evidence linking Simpson to the scene of the murder of his ex-wife, Nicole Brown, and her friend Ronald Goldman. The evidence included a bloodied glove allegedly used by Simpson, and DNA test results. Among African-Americans, a majority of whom thought that Simpson was innocent (or at least not proven guilty beyond a reasonable doubt), rumors abounded that the Los Angeles Police Department had planted the evidence. Among whites, most of whom believed Simpson guilty, these rumors were not believed. In other words, rumors of a corrupt, evidence-planting LAPD circulated widely in African-American circles and were strongly believed; among white networks, this was not the case. The segmented nature of these networks probably contributed to the polarization in beliefs about these rumors.

Even when motivation is not an important issue—as when the content of the rumor doesn't flatter or offend any group—segmentation in networks might lead to adopting different rumors in different clusters. This could happen simply because other persons in our social clique exert a stronger influence on us than persons in a different social clique. If I'm part of a densely connected pocket of people who make sense of an ambiguous situation by believing a particular rumor, I'm inclined to adopt that rumor as a sensible explanation as well. Festinger saw this in his investigation of the Communist community worker rumor, and commented that once a particular rumor explanation has been adopted, the social pressure to conform to that explanation can be very powerful indeed. Segmentation therefore seems to produce rumor diversity. To continue with our landscape metaphor, different types of animals and trees tend to grow in areas that are cut off from one another by mountains, rivers, and oceans. Segmenting the land seems to give rise to greater variety in plant and animal life. Among humans, Africa is the original home to persons of color, Europe to the pale skin, and the Far East to a more olive complexion. In the same way, do different versions of rumor tend to flourish more among segmented than nonsegmented social networks?

To investigate this idea, my research team and I conducted an experiment where students were presented with ambiguous situations and various rumors that tried to explain these situations, discussed them with other students, and tried to decide which rumor made the most sense. We varied the extent to which their social network was segmented and then we measured the diversity of the rumors in each group. Here's how it went.

Groups of sixteen students came to my laboratory (and the labs of my fellow investigators Martin Bourgeois and Prashant Bordia) to participate in a study of "social sensemaking on the Internet." They were seated in front of a bank of computers. During the study they all read several ambiguous scenarios. After reading one scenario, they read four alternative statements—rumors—that made sense of the scenario, and they had to choose which rumor made the most sense to them. They also indicated how confident they were in that choice. Then they could discuss the scenario and the rumors via the computer terminal with four other individuals in the room. Discussion proceeded over four rounds of communication, and after each of these rounds they again chose the rumor that made the most sense to them.

For example, participants read a fictitious scenario in which "a professor was found dead from a gunshot wound." Alternative A stated that the professor was killed by an angry student, B that he committed suicide, C that he accidentally shot himself, and D that he was killed in a robbery attempt gone awry. After reading these alternatives, participants indicated privately which of four rumors made the most sense to them and how much confidence they had in that alternative; then they sent and received a message from each of the four people they were connected with. These messages indicated which alternative made the most sense to them and often communicated why it made the most sense. A participant might write: "I think the professor was killed by an angry student because the situation stated that he often belittled students in class." Or, "Alternative B [suicide] seems more likely because professors are often a depressed bunch." After each round of messages had been received, they again registered their choice of rumor and confidence in that choice. Despite the artificiality of the situation, it captured the "feel" and basic elements of rumor discussion: an unclear situation, some rumor hypotheses, and attempts to sort it out with other people you are connected with.

Unbeknownst to the students, we varied the configuration of the network they were in. That is, during the discussion of each scenario, the group was configured into torus, "family," "ribbon," or random spatial arrangements as presented above. We anticipated that the more segmented a network was, the more diverse the final set of chosen rumors would be. This indeed happened. The clumpiest configuration—family—retained diversity best over rounds, but all other configurations lost diversity. That is, the family configuration protected against the emergence of rumor "majorities"— situations where most of the persons in the group choose one rumor—while none of the other configurations did so. As a consequence, majorities tended to emerge more when the network was not configured as family. The greater segmentation that categorizes the family configuration served to shield participants most from exposure to global majorities—and the social pressures that go along with this exposure. In other words, the family configuration limits the exposure that the "family" cluster has with the rest of the network. Pockets of rumor "minorities" could therefore continue to exist. And of course, the presence of rumor minorities signifies greater rumor diversity.

These results reveal how different "shared realities" arising from rumors may tend to emerge among segmented types of social structures and may remain less susceptible to alteration. That is, the more segmented a society, the more diverse its set of rumors and the more varied its perceptions of reality become. This is like the cultural differences that arose between the French and the English simply because they are on either side of the English Channel. Variety is the spice of life and we wouldn't want everyone to think the same way. In situations of competition however, it might fan the flames of conflict. *Vive la différence!* might give way to the Hundred Years' War (which lasted 116 years!).

6

Believe It, or Not

WHY WE BELIEVE SOME RUMORS AND NOT OTHERS

> *Do not believe in anything simply*
> *because you have heard it. Do not*
> *believe in anything simply because it*
> *is spoken and rumored by many. . . .*
> *But after observation and analysis,*
> *when you find that anything agrees*
> *with reason and is conducive to the*
> *good and benefit of one and all, then*
> *accept it and live up to it.*
>
> —HINDU PRINCE SIDDHĀRTHA
> GAUTAMA, FOUNDER OF BUDDHISM
> (C. 563–C. 483 B.C.)

THE BROOKLYN BOTTLING COMPANY was on the brink of bankruptcy in 1987. The grandfather of BBC's current owner—Eric Miller—had established the family-owned enterprise fifty years earlier. Now this small New York–based soda manufacturer was struggling, dying the slow death of mom-and-pop soda makers squeezed out by carbonated giants Coca-Cola and Pepsi. It was on the verge of being consumed by these competitors; a case of little minnows in the same sea as big fish.

Fortunately, Miller then found his niche: gourmet and specialty sodas aimed at ethnic customers that the big companies had ignored. Miller marketed the 20-ounce bottle of Tropical Fantasy

Fruit Punch for forty-nine cents in predominately poor areas of New York City. At the time, the giant soda makers were selling the usual 16-ounce bottles of Coke and Pepsi for about eighty cents. Miller began offering more soda for less money. A fruity taste in a soda pop was unusual and he faced few competitors. In addition, Miller bottled soda manufactured in Latin America, such as the apple-flavored drink Manzana, made by the Colombian company Postobón. The taste was familiar to Caribbean Latino immigrants. On top of that, Miller offered bodega owners—small grocery stores in Spanish-speaking neighborhoods—free cases of his soda for stocking it on their shelves. The strategy was a huge success. By 1990, Brooklyn Bottling sales soared to $12 million, 50 percent more than the previous year. Brooklyn Bottling was beating the beverage behemoths.

Then someone brewed a false rumor and spread it via a flyer:

ATTENTION!!! ATTENTION!!! ATTENTION!!!

.50 CENT SODAS

BLACK AND MINORITY GROUPS

DID YOU SEE (T.V. SHOW) 20/20 ???

PLEASE BE ADVISE, "TOP POP" & "TROPICAL-FANTASY" .50 SODAS

ARE BEING MANUFACTURED BY THE KLU KLUX KLAN.

SODAS CONTAIN STIMULANTS TO STERILIZE THE BLACK MAN,

AND WHO KNOW WHAT ELSE!!!!

THEY ARE ONLY PUT IN STORES IN HARLEM AND MINORITY

AREAS. YOU WON'T FIND THEM DOWN TOWN . . .

LOOK AROUND . . .

YOU HAVE BEEN WARNED

PLEASE SAVE OUR CHILDREN

Whoever distilled this rumor was a bright *brewmeister* as we shall see. It made sense of something peculiar that was true—Tropical

Fantasy *was* marketed in inner-city neighborhoods and minority areas. The rumor therefore capitalized on an unintended uncertainty arising from Miller's marketing stratagem. Why were these sodas so cheap? And why were they only marketed in poor neighborhoods? We've seen how rumors make the most of such unanswered questions. The flyer also had the appearance of authenticity in that it referred to a credible source: a report from the well-known television news documentary program *20/20*. This report, of course, was nonexistent.

The flyer fed upon plausible fears in the African-American community. The Ku Klux Klan had a long history of attempts to dominate, demean, and destroy persons of color. Fears of sterilization of black men typically sound laughable to white ears today, but a brief review of history renders the fear rational. African-American bioethicist Annette Dula—an affiliate at the prestigious University of Pittsburgh Center for Bioethics and Health Law—writes extensively on the racial aspects of bioethics. Dula describes how early proponents of birth control and sterilization adopted the goals of the eugenics movement, which advocated the improvement of the human race through various forms of hereditary intervention, most notably by discouraging or even restricting the reproduction of people with "bad" genes and encouraging the reproduction of those with "good" genes. It's easy to see how the eugenics movement is compatible with racist ideology that views some races as hereditarily better than others.

Dula documented the efforts of the eugenics movement to reduce the birth rate among African-Americans in the twentieth century. Eugenicists urged white women to have larger families and promoted birth control among African-American women out of fear that the white race would commit "race suicide." African-Americans were explicitly described as inferior stock by early eugenicists. Birth control methods—whether adopted voluntarily or involuntarily—were seen as the means by which the propagation of black people could be curbed. Guy Irving Burch of the American Eugenics Society stated: "We must prevent the American people from being replaced by alien or Negro stock, whether it be by immigration or by overly high birth rates among others in this country." Margaret Sanger, the influential founder of the American Birth Control League, which later became the Planned Parenthood Federation of America, put it this way: "More children from the fit and less from the unfit."

As a result of these ideas, several states attempted to pass compulsory sterilization laws for mothers of illegitimate children in the 1950s, and government began to subsidize family planning clinics in the 1960s. It turns out that the number of these clinics was proportional to the number of black and Latino Americans in a region. These efforts and ideology did much to instill suspicion in the African-American community that the majority was attempting to maintain their dominant power status over the minority by diminishing their numbers. Given this context, it didn't seem unlikely that a soft drink sold in poor neighborhoods would sterilize black males. A quotation from a Harlem roofer at the time gives us a flavor of just how this framework made the Tropical Fantasy rumor plausible: "It sounds kind of far-fetched, but this goes to the heart of race and the system. . . . The 49-cent sodas can't be chanced."

By May 1991, sales of Brooklyn Bottling Company had fizzled by 70 percent because of the rumor. The flyer was actively being passed around African-American networks. Miller acted aggressively to counteract it. He first had the New York City Department of Health certify the soda as safe. Employees scoured neighborhoods and spread "truth kits" that refuted the rumor. Mayor David

Dinkins, himself an African-American, drank the Tropical Fantasy drink in public. These efforts appear to have paid off—by June of the following year sales had rebounded to former levels. Brooklyn Bottling, now more successful than ever, survived the sterilization rumor.

Why do people believe rumors, especially ones that seem so unbelievable? I've been asked this many times by individuals who simply can't comprehend how people can put confidence in what seems like an outrageous rumor. Since the claim at hand isn't plausible in the least to these questioners, they conclude that the group of believers is gullible, unintelligent, intellectually indolent, or perhaps just possesses lower standards of belief. Feeling genuine pity for such persons, they regard them as targets that are easily taken advantage of. Alternatively, they scorn them with an air of sarcasm. With P. T. Barnum they say, "There's a sucker born every minute." Actually, Barnum didn't say that—and the story of the quotation is instructive here.

The aphorism "There's a sucker born every minute" is often attributed to the legendary circus kingpin P. T. Barnum, but Barnum's biographer was unable to verify this. A more probable source is David Hannum, a Syracuse banker who in 1869 unwittingly purchased a phony stone colossus known as the Cardiff Giant. This strange story begins with a surreptitious cigar manufacturer named George Hull, who sculpted the giant from a ten-foot-long block of gypsum, buried it in Cardiff, New York, "discovered" it, and put it on display (charging admission, of course). Crowds of spectators journeyed from all over the state of New York to see the "petrified American goliath." Hull's hoax was hugely successful. He soon sold most of his interest in it to a group of businessmen headed by Hannum, who exhibited it for even higher admission fees. The

Cardiff Giant was a national sensation and caught P. T. Barnum's entrepreneurial attentions; he wanted to display it himself. Unable to persuade Hannum to sell, Barnum created a replica, claimed it to be the original, and called Hannum's exhibit a hoax. (This last part, ironically, was the truth.) Referring to the duped patrons of Barnum's more successful exhibit, Hannum—not Barnum—is then alleged to have said, "There's a sucker born every minute." He then sued Barnum for defaming the original. Hannum lost when George Hull confessed all in court; finding that the giant was a phony, the judge ruled that Barnum could not be sued for calling it a forgery. Adding a strange twist to this tale of double deception, Hannum's quote was then misattributed to Barnum. A central irony of this fascinating, and true, nineteenth-century story is that it was Hannum—who ruefully called Barnum's customers "suckers"—who was in fact himself suckered into paying a great sum of money for a counterfeit colossus of rock.

Why did "suckers" believe this hokum? Two main theories about the giant held that he was either a petrified man or a three-hundred-year-old statue carved by Jesuit fathers. To the mind of a nineteenth-century citizen, the idea of a giant petrified man was plausible. It's not that difficult for modern sensibilities either. The tallest man living today is Leonid Stadnyk of the Ukraine who measured 8 feet, 5½ inches in 2007. The tallest man ever—that we have records for—was Robert Pershing Wadlow of Alton, Illinois. On June 27, 1940, this real-life goliath scaled at 8 feet, 11.1 inches. The Cardiff Giant was not much taller at 10 feet, 4½ inches. In addition, in an age of archeological discovery, finding a fossilized member of an ancient race of giants was easy to envision. Also, the idea meshed well with Biblical texts that seemed to indicate the existence of giants in early antiquity and doubtless the literalist-modernist controversies brewing at the time amplified interest in the affair. Remember also that Hull's intent was to deceive. He had taken pains to present a figure that appeared to be petrified, even going so far as to wear down the sculptors' chisel marks with acid to simulate petrifaction and pound tiny holes across the sculpture to mimic pores. Finally, an early medical expert who examined the giant did not see through Hull's deceit. All in all, the petrified man and Jesuit statue ideas didn't seem implausible at first.

The Encarta Dictionary defines "belief" as "acceptance by the mind that something is true or real, often underpinned by an emotional or spiritual sense of certainty." Belief that something is indeed so is a settled confidence in the matter, a conviction in its veracity, an assurance of its reality. Belief can be weak, moderate, or strong; to measure belief in a rumor I ask, "How strongly do you believe this statement?" or, "How confident are you that this statement is true?" People have no problem appreciating this point. Believing is a fundamental element of the human experience. Belief is first of all an "acceptance by the mind." Though it may seem automatic, it is actually a decision that a person renders about a state of affairs. We are entertained when we see a magician hack a beautiful assistant in half with a sharp blade because we fail to believe it—if we did, we would instead be horrified. We reject what is apparently right in front of us. Instead, we choose to accept that he has somehow made it appear that the saw has passed through her torso—but in reality it is not so. We are vindicated in our belief when the assistant is ultimately revealed unharmed.

This acceptance applies even to events that seem "self-evident." As I write this, I believe I'm seated in my car in the parking lot of Wegman's grocery store (my wife is inside shopping). It's raining hard. My ears hear the raindrops pounding against the roof of the vehicle. I have no reason to think that a truer state of affairs exists. But like Neo in *The Matrix,* I could be deceived with regard to this reality—a prisoner of evil machines who have constructed a false interactive world that is force-fed to my neurons while I lay helpless and naked in a pod, one of billions of human beings that the merciless machines rely on for energy. It *could* be. But I choose not to receive that explanation; I believe that I recline here and it is raining hard. My point is that even so-called "self-evident" facts require from me some level of acceptance of the reality. This is a natural element of how we apprehend the world.

When hiking down a steep mountain trail, I sometimes arrive at a place where I must jump to the next flat stone below in order to proceed. The hop can be a several-foot drop, especially if I'm descending a sharp embankment. Each time I face a decision: Do I accept that there's a safe stone platform just below, or am I in reality at the edge of a deadly and dangerous cliff? To pass on my merry way, I must acknowledge that there is solid and safe rock residing there. What leads me to make this leap? Well, if I see the stone, I jump. Seeing is believing, right? Not really—I still have to trust my eyes before I believe them. Alternatively, I may be enveloped in a soupy fog and fail to see the flat rock below—what then? Fortunately, others in my hiking party have told me that it's there—in which case I believe my buddies and accept their picture of the path. The latter situation would be a case of placing confidence in the group's consensus in the midst of a situation full of uncertainty and anxiety—not dissimilar to what we do in a rumor discussion.

Still, in a soupy fog situation this would be a tough step to take—after all, it might be my last move. In such an uncertain scenario, how do I get to the psychological "place" where I can put one foot in front of the other? The definition of belief provides a hint about this dilemma: belief is ". . . often underpinned by an emotional or spiritual sense of certainty." I can hop down because I *feel* a sense of sureness that the rock is there. Analogously, I can believe a rumor because I feel that it is true. In other words, the rumor is plausible to me. Put another way, the content of the rumor must first resonate within me else I fail to accept it.

Each time I lecture undergraduates about the connection between media violence and aggressive actions, I'm reminded of how implausibility is an impediment to belief. I present the settled conviction of social science: There is as much evidence linking the viewing of violent television with aggression as there is connecting smoking with lung cancer. (Watching a violent TV show won't necessarily cause a person to punch their neighbor, but overall it will make this response more likely after provocation.) My students—and perhaps my readers—often have a hard time emotionally with this because many like and are immersed in violent media, yet they don't see themselves as acting in an aggressive manner. The statement lacks resonance with them; it fails to elicit that "emotional or spiritual" sense of certainty. In a word, it doesn't seem plausible. And so, while my students answer the item correctly on an exam for a good grade, they don't actually accept it. Some outright discard it arbitrarily as "a load of crap"—perhaps as politically correct propaganda pushed on them by grown-ups who want to spoil their fun. But most permanently send it to "belief limbo": "Well, I don't know about that—it could be so, but I don't think so. . . ."

I once pitched a presentation to government officials from an intelligence-gathering agency. I thought that this organization might be willing to fund some of my research. Rumors, after all, reveal that which is plausible to a community and tell us how they feel threatened. Part of intelligence gathering is about understanding community sentiment. Rumors also sometimes contain valuable war time information not officially available. The intelligence officials were less interested in these types of projects, however, and instead asked me, "Can you come up with a way to spread a rumor that Osama bin Laden is a born-again Christian?" Such a rumor, according to these officials, would undercut Al Qaeda's support among Muslims. It would be a classic propaganda rumor. I responded that such a rumor would never be believed because it would be extremely implausible to the Muslim mind. It lacks the resonance—the emotional certainty, the plausibility—that we've been discussing. Whatever else bin Laden is perceived to be in the Islamic world, he is certainly a Muslim and opposed to the spread of Christianity. (I received no funding from this agency.)

Perhaps the main reason that people believe rumors, then, is because they accord with the hearer's feelings, thoughts, attitudes, stereotypes, prejudices, opinions, or behaviors. Concordant rumors therefore feel plausible—the hearer is in the psychological place where he wants to accept the hearsay. The resonance metaphor is helpful here: just as a musical note sung brightly by the tenor Pavarotti can make an entire chord of piano strings vibrate, a rumor can strike a chord of cognitions. Because of their experiences with the Ku Klux Klan and with the eugenicist ideology of birth-control movement leaders, rumors of black sterilization resonate with African-Americans. In contrast, rumors that Osama bin Laden has converted to Christianity do not reverberate with Arab Muslims.

A rumor may resonate with hearers' anxiety. Tropical cyclone Sidr hit the poverty-stricken South Asian nation of Bangladesh in November 2007. (Hurricanes are called tropical cyclones in this part of the world.) Although over 3000 people died, the toll from Sidr could have been much worse. A previous storm in 1991 had killed 140,000 people; in 1970 an astounding 300,000 to 500,000 lives were lost. This time, an early warning system successfully mobilized Bangladeshis to preventive action. Twenty-seven hours before the tempest hit land, the Bangladesh Meteorological Department issued evacuation orders. Then 42,000 volunteers, organized by the Cyclone Preparedness Center, spread the word across the country to head for shelters or sturdy housing. Volunteers used megaphones, mosque speakers, or simply called out loudly in remote villages. The effort successfully minimized the loss of life that could have occurred.

After such a calamity, it's natural for people to feel widespread anxiety. Jarred from their normal routines, the possibility of another disaster is salient. We would therefore expect rumors of additional calamities to be common in these circumstances. They are. Early rumor researcher Jamuna Prasad recorded rumors that circulated in the aftermath of a terrible earthquake in the Indian province of Bihar in 1934. These rumors frequently predicted imminent destruction. After this catastrophe, for example, a rumor circulated that the city of Patma would be obliterated by severe earthquakes. Leon Festinger thought that these rumors provided a way for people to justify their lingering anxiety. Festinger speculated that survivors felt worried, even though the threat had passed. The rumor accorded with these feelings of anxiety, and was therefore judged to be plausible and was believed—often strongly enough to be acted upon.

Sadly, such rumors can lead to panics and further death. After the Bangladeshi disaster, thousands again fled their homes for the safety of shelters when they heard a false rumor of an impending tsunami. Rumors that "the seawater is rising again!" were spread by unidentified young men on motorbikes, proliferated through cell phone networks, and resulted in what news reports described as mass hysteria and panic. In the coastal subdistricts of Sadar and Patharghata, two people died of heart attacks and five from stampedes as crowds clamored (unnecessarily) for the safety of concrete buildings. People may have believed these rumors—enough to run for shelter quickly—in part because they saw others rushing for shelter, but also because they resonated with residual anxiety in the aftermath of the tropical cyclone.

"There's a war on, you know!" was the regular reply to complaints uttered by civilians during World War II. The slogan gave meaning to the inconvenience inflicted by wartime rationing. If you didn't live during this era, it's difficult to grasp just how invasive, annoying, and irritating the rationing program was. In the spring of 1942, the U.S. Office of Price Administration (OPA) issued war ration books and tokens to every American family. These tokens put limits on purchases of rationed products. The roster of rationed goods was extensive and included bicycles, canned fish, canned milk, cars, cheese, coffee, fats, fuel oil, gasoline, kerosene, meat, processed foods, rubber footwear, shoes, stoves, sugar, tires, and even typewriters. The war effort was all-consuming. Typewriter factories were making armaments, automobile manufacturers were making airplanes, and farms were harvesting food for armed forces. In addition, the global conflict disrupted international trade. Rubber was the first nonfood item to be rationed because Japanese forces had occupied the Dutch East Indies, home to 90 percent of the world's rubber plantations. The rubber scarcity led to campaigns to collect and recycle unused tires. Gasoline shortages led to compulsory rationing—voluntary efforts had proved ineffective—and austere restrictions on driving. Gas "stickers" were issued by local OPA boards and limited the gallons of gasoline one could get. Drivers using their vehicles for "nonessential" and "nonmilitary" purposes were issued black "A" stickers and were permitted to purchase no more than four gallons of gasoline per week. Four gallons did not go a long way, especially in an era of fuel-inefficient cars. By the winter of 1942, half of all U.S. automobiles were A-stickered. In addition, the maximum "Victory" speed limit was 35 miles per hour, and car pools were encouraged. Rationing was rough.

At that time, rumors of government waste and special privilege arose. One such story of bureaucratic squandering stated "Scrap rubber collected is wasted by being allowed to deteriorate because there are not adequate facilities for storage and reclaiming." A rumor of big-business profiteering proclaimed "There is plenty of coffee in the U.S. The big companies have cornered the market and are holding out for higher prices." Social psychologists Floyd H. Allport (Gordon's brother) and Milton Lepkin at Syracuse University deemed these rumors "lurid and dramatic" and they wondered why some people would believe them. In May 1943 they selected a set of twelve such stories reported to the Syracuse Rumor Clinic (a rumor control center), put them in a questionnaire, and sent the survey to parents of students at eight Syracuse, New York, public schools. All of the rumors were bogus and baseless; each had been researched by the rumor clinic. The survey asked respondents whether or not they had heard—and how strongly they believed— each statement. Despite the fact that open belief in this sort of hearsay was considered unpatriotic, persons in the sample had already heard about three of them on average—a significant proportion. Moreover, some of the statements were considered plausible. For example, when presented with the statement "A certain prominent government official has three cars and a large underground storage tank filled with gasoline for his own use," 44.5 percent of the sample at least "wondered whether it could be true." Others were more universally disbelieved; 86.5 percent did not believe "gasoline storage tanks of the producing companies are so full of gasoline that oceangoing tankers are dumping their cargoes at sea." For Allport and Lepkin, however, the critical question was, what predicted greater belief in these rumors?

To test this idea, they polled participants on how strongly they felt that the rationing program was "unfair" or "unnecessary." Allport and Lepkin suspected that a negative attitude toward the rationing program would predispose people to believe rumors about how the program was wasteful, unwarranted, and inequitable. They reasoned that people would tend to believe a rumor that agreed with their preexisting attitude. Did the Syracuse survey support this idea? Indeed it did. The best predictor of belief in rumors of waste and special privilege was a negative attitude toward the rationing program. Those who perceived the program to be unfair or unnecessary were 14 percent more likely to believe the rumors than those who found it fair and necessary. (A 14 percent increase is not destiny, but it is substantial.) The researchers are worth quoting:

> [W]hen an individual is hostile toward something, or toward somebody, he is the more ready to believe unfounded statements to the discredit of that object or person. He seizes upon something he can use as a "justifiable reason" for his hostility; and at the same time he has an opportunity, through belief in the damaging rumor, to attack the object he dislikes and vent his feelings upon it. The belief in rumors derogatory to racial or religious groups might, perhaps, be found to be based upon a similar motive.

In other words, a hostile attitude may predispose someone to reason that a false rumor is possible, plausible, and perhaps even likely. Believing the rumor then allows one to spread the rumor and in so doing vent one's feelings of hostility. In the last chapter I showed how transmitting these types of rumors is sometimes motivated by self-enhancement; here we see that belief in rumor may also be so motivated.

Rumors—particularly wedge-driving rumors—may resonate

with aggression and hatred in the hearer. The work of rumor researchers is replete with examples of racist rumors that echoed attitudes of white supremacy, and sentiment that was anti-African-American, anti-Catholic, and anti-Jewish. Robert H. Knapp was in charge of rumor control for the Massachusetts Committee on Public Safety during World War II. With the aid of *Reader's Digest* magazine, he collected 1,089 rumors in the month of September 1942. Knapp noted the high percentage of wedge-driving rumors in the United States (65.9 percent) and classified them with regard to their target. Surprisingly, these rumors were almost entirely about groups in the U.S. population or Allied nations. For example, an anti-British rumor claimed, "The British are sabotaging their own ships in American ports so that they will not have to put out to sea." Allport and Postman documented similar types of rumors at around the same time, such as, "The Jews get the cushiest jobs in the army."

Similar wedge-driving rumors exist today. I regularly give students in my social psychology class index cards and ask them—without identifying themselves—to write down rumors they have heard about groups of people. I then collect the cards and read them out loud. The rumors listed are reflections of well-learned stereotypes that bear a lot of resemblance to Knapp's and Allport and Postman's rumors: Women are bad drivers, Jewish people are shrewd businessmen, white people are domineering, African-Americans are oversexed and criminal, Irish are drinkers, Italians are Mafioso, Arabs are terrorists. Despite declines in overt racism over the past six decades, wedge-driving rumors have survived.

Imagine that a murder has occurred in your neighborhood. Naturally, you are somewhat alarmed and this incident becomes an important item of interest to you. A couple of rumors are making the rounds.

One derives from Detective Webb, whom you know. (He is with the investigation.) The other comes from Harriet, an elderly spinster you know but who has no connection to the case. In which report—the rumor from Webb or the hearsay from Harriet—would you place more confidence? In a study with my student Scott Rabideau, participants presented with these rumors overwhelmingly placed more confidence in the word of Detective Webb. Undoubtedly they believed his rumor more strongly since they saw him as a much more credible source than Harriet—this makes sense given that he was described as close to the criminal investigation. The source of the rumor is the teller of the tale or the person whom the teller attributes the rumor to. Source credibility has long been known to lead to greater acceptance of any message. All other things being equal, one is more likely to have confidence in the opinions, statements, attitudes—and rumors—emanating from a credible source. Social psychologists have identified two important ingredients in source credibility: One is the person's expertise—their perceived proficiency in the matter at hand. Expertise may stem from credentials (she's a nurse—she should know if coughing stops a heart attack), experience (he wrote a book on rumor—he should know if source credibility leads to belief), or special knowledge. Hearsay from Detective Webb is more credible by virtue of his being "in the know"—having special knowledge—in this matter.

The other factor is the teller's trustworthiness—the sense that the source is motivated to help the listener, has the hearer's best interests in mind, and has no ulterior agenda. Sociologist Elaine G. Porter probed the diffusion of negative informal information about the use of birth control in the Dominican Republic in 1977. Porter assembled data from 722 women who had attended clinics in Santiago. She was especially interested in why 21 percent of the first-time users of contraceptives had discontinued use by four months after their initial training. She wondered whether negative stories about the side effects of birth control had contributed to discontinuance. These included accounts of contraceptive failure and serious medical side effects such as stomach pains, vaginal infections, illness, and even cancer. Another negative tale alleged that contraceptive pills accumulate in the abdomen. Porter found that negative word of mouth was widely disseminated and contributed significantly to women's decisions to stop taking birth control, but only when the teller was considered a trusted source. Women believed these negative stories more when they came from a source in which they had placed their trust—either about birth control matters or about any matter—or someone they viewed as expert by virtue of having used birth control. If the source of a rumor is not trusted, the rumor will naturally be less likely to be believed.

Credibility is such an important factor in promoting belief that successful hoaxes often appear to come from an authoritative source. The false Tropical Fantasy Fruit Punch rumor flyer urged readers to contact the highly credible television news documentary series *20/20*. Remember too the false rumor—also spread via flyer—that the head of Procter & Gamble appeared on the *Phil Donahue Show* and bragged that the company contributed 10 percent of its profits to the Church of Satan. The flyer claimed that readers could write to the show and receive a transcript of the alleged program as proof.

Reputation plays a vital role in source credibility, and, therefore, in belief in rumor. In Theodore Caplow's study of World War II military rumors, a source's credibility was considered by servicemen participating in the discussion of rumors. Reputations were gained or lost over time in this process. People remembered if

Private Paulson or Corporal Carter had previously passed them bogus falsities or bona fide facts. "Hey, I heard this from Wally—so take it for what it's worth!" This is why it is surprising to us when credible sources such as newspapers get it wrong—we typically trust in journalistic institutions because ordinarily they're not in error. The proverb "Don't believe everything you read in the newspaper" does affirm that you should believe most of what you read in the newspaper. If newspapers were routinely wrong, we would stop subscribing to them. Likewise, if the individual who relays a rumor is in general incorrect, we would cease to listen to him.

On a dreadful July day in 1993, Deputy White House Counsel Vincent W. Foster Jr. was discovered dead from a gunshot wound in Fort Marcy Park near Washington, D.C. Foster was a key staff member in the Clinton administration and a close personal acquaintance of Hillary Rodham Clinton. In her autobiography, the former First Lady described Foster as one of the finest lawyers she had ever known. He was instrumental in overcoming resistance to Mrs. Clinton's hiring at the respected Rose Law Firm in which she later became partner. Foster's foray into national political service was marred by an aversion to public scrutiny. Consequently, he suffered from clinical depression and anxiety. Just prior to his passing, this was aggravated by several scathing editorials in *The Wall Street Journal*. A shredded draft of a resignation letter turned up in his briefcase; among other complaints, the letter lamented that "I was not meant for the job or the spotlight of public life in Washington. Here ruining people is considered sport." Foster's death was declared a suicide by three separate investigatory bodies. Despite this, conspiracy theories and rumors arose almost immediately and continue to circulate.

One Wall Street investor whom I interviewed as part of my dissertation studies had listened to the news story of Foster's suicide. He had also heard the remarkable rumor that Foster's death was murder, not suicide. The theory was that the Clintons had played a part in Foster's death as part of a cover-up of incriminating evidence connected to the Whitewater controversy, which involved alleged improper actions by the Clintons with regard to their real estate holdings in the Whitewater Development Corporation. (No credible support has ever surfaced regarding these rumors.) At first this investor scoffed at the story, attributing it to politically motivated pundits. But after receiving the rumor several times that morning, he suspended his skepticism and adopted a more neutral "let's wait and see" stance. Repeated hearing of the rumor raised his level of belief.

The idea that simply hearing a rumor repeatedly might raise one's level of belief in it is slightly unsettling. And yet this appears to be the case. In a recent study at the Rochester Institute of Technology, repeatedly reading a rumor increased belief in it. Participants read a student narrative and were asked to imagine themselves as the main actor in the story line. For example, during Day 1, participants read:

> You wake up this morning feeling refreshed after a good night's sleep and ready to start the week. On your way into school you get a call from your friend Justin and he tells you that he heard that there was a coyote loose on campus last week because of the high deer population. Putting the information out of your mind, you walk to your first class. . . . While leaving class you overhear a few students talking about how they heard that a professor was giving a student good grades because he found out the professor plagiarized and was bribing him to keep quiet. You make your way out of the room and head over to the

dining hall to get something to eat before your next class. While in line you hear a student worker say that he heard that the rent for on-campus housing will be raised substantially next year because there are planned renovations. You notice what time it is and decide to get your food to go so you won't be late for class.

As you can see, this portion of the narrative exposed the reader to rumors about coyotes loose on campus, a plagiarizing professor, and rental increases due to renovations. Participants were eventually exposed to six separate rumors, and each was repeated from one to six times. For example, by the end of the narrative "week" some students had heard the coyote rumor on the first day from their friend Justin, the second day while waiting in line for coffee, the third day while conversing with Pete, the fourth day while talking with someone on the bus, and so forth. On the seventh day, participants were asked how strongly they believed each statement, plus a statement that they had never seen.

A graph of the relationship between the number of times participants heard a rumor and belief in that rumor turned out to be a nice "diminishing returns" sort of curve—that is, belief rose steeply from zero to one hearing, less steeply from one to two hearings, less steeply still from two to three hearings, and so forth. On average, confidence in a rumor rose from about 40 percent when it hadn't been introduced in the narrative at all, to 60 percent when it had been heard six times. Repeated hearing of hearsay led to greater belief.

Repeated hearing may increase belief for a couple of reasons. One might simply be what has been called "social proof": if the rumor survives, it is more likely to be true. This rationale depends upon the assumption that people generally try to refrain from passing along bogus information; therefore, if a rumor continues to circulate it is more likely to have some foundation in reality. Though it has been exposed to many people, it hasn't yet been "knocked down," and so there must be something to it. I'll have more to say about this idea in the next chapter, which is about rumor accuracy, but for now it's sufficient to say that in situations where people are capable *and* motivated to "knock down" false rumors, active circulation over time does tend to produce more veridical rumors. That is, in these types of social environments, a surviving rumor is more likely to be true than one that dies.

But the second reason that repeatedly hearing a rumor increases belief is more intriguing—and should give us pause. Repeated hearing leads listeners to feel familiar with the statement and that familiarity increases belief. This idea is based on what is known as the illusory-truth effect: familiarity with a statement leads to greater belief in that statement. Participants in studies by Ian M. Begg and associates at McMaster University were exposed to statements and were told that some of the statements were true and some were false. For example, students first heard "Eighteen newborn opossums can be placed in a teaspoon" as a statement from a source that always told the truth, and "Three hundred thousand pencils can be made from the average cedar tree" as a statement from a source that always lied. In other words, students were introduced to claims that were identified at the outset as either true or false. They heard or read these statements and in this way became familiar with them. Later they were presented with the statements again and asked to rate their truth value. Because of source credibility, we would expect that they would rate the true statements as truer than false statements, and this indeed happened. But at the same time, students were asked to rate the truth value of new statements—statements they were unfamiliar with—and they rated the false statements as truer on average than the new statements. This is surprising because all statements had been tested beforehand and were equally plausible. So in other words, familiar statements—even though they had been identified as false—were remembered as truer than statements that were unfamiliar to students. The illusory-truth effect is counterintuitive; there is no logical reason that a statement with which we are more familiar should be invested with greater confidence. It may be that we use a simple heuristic in judging the truth of a statement—"That sounds like something I've heard before—it must be true!"

The implication of all this is that if "everyone is saying it," then our belief in the hearsay rises. All other factors being the same, familiarity breeds confidence—not contempt.

After the surprise attack by the Japanese at Pearl Harbor on December 7, 1941, the United States was in a state of high alert and emotional tension. Rumors that the damage sustained by the U.S. military was far more devastating than official news reports had conveyed were widespread. One word on the street was that the "entire Pacific fleet had been sunk at Pearl Harbor on December 7." Another that "one thousand planes had been destroyed on the ground." According to these alleged assessments, the United States was now completely vulnerable to attack. Belief in these rumors was pervasive. In February 1942, Allport and Postman asked a group of two hundred undergraduate students: "Do you believe that our losses at Pearl Harbor were greater, much greater, the same, less, or much less than have been officially stated?" Of the sample, 69 percent thought that the losses were "greater or much greater" than the official reports. These demoralizing stories were so upsetting that President Roosevelt felt the need to repudiate them in his weekly "fireside chat" radio address that he happened to deliver just three days after the survey. After the broadcast, Allport and Postman scrambled to compose another sample of two hundred students in order to ask them to what extent they believed Pearl Harbor rumors now. Did Roosevelt's refutation reduce belief in these rumors? Yes: 46 percent of those who had heard Roosevelt's address now stated that Pearl Harbor losses were "greater or much greater" than official statements indicated. Roosevelt's refutation significantly diminished belief in Pearl Harbor rumors.

Refutations of the rumors of waste and special privilege also reduced belief. Floyd Allport and Milton Lepkin's study was performed in Syracuse, New York, with false rumors collected by the Syracuse Rumor Clinic. The clinic was charged with gathering and investigating rumors—and managing them as well. The clinic also published a regular newspaper column that recounted the rumors and then refuted them. Some persons in the sample "regularly" or "occasionally" read these columns; others never read them. Allport and Lepkin found that the proportion of column readers who at least wondered whether the rumors could be true was significantly smaller than the proportion of nonreaders who were similarly wondering or believing. In other words, people who read the published refutations were less likely to believe the rumors. Of course, it may be that the group of people who read the columns differed in an important way from the group that didn't. However, the researchers took special care to investigate this explanation and found the readers and nonreaders were comparable along a number of dimensions, including education and occupational status. Moreover, Allport and Lepkin compared column readers who had read the refutations with column readers who had not, and still found that reading the refutation substantially reduced the tendency to believe. Allport and Lepkin therefore concluded that reading the clinic refutations lessened belief in the rumors of waste and special privilege.

More recently, Prashant Bordia and I conducted a series of studies to test whether or not denial of a rumor reduced belief. In these studies, students typically read a scenario in which they imagined hearing a rumor that was of some importance to them, rated how strongly they believed the tale, then read a denial of the rumor, and finally rated belief in the rumor a second time. In every case belief decreased, even when the source of the denial was not rated as very trustworthy or honest. I'll explore these studies—and others—in the last chapter, which is about managing rumor, but I wanted to note here that denial reduces belief. Of course, put the other way, the absence of a denial leads to belief. In the case of the Brooklyn Bottling Company, apparently no one believes the damaging rumor any longer. Why not? It seems likely that Eric Miller's efforts to refute the fallacy that Tropical Fantasy Fruit Punch sterilizes black men were fruitful. Had he not taken steps to stop the rumor, Tropical Fantasy might indeed be a forgotten brand. Had a refutation effort been absent, it seems likely that belief in the rumor would have continued to amplify in the African-American community. The absence of a refutation, then, is another factor leading to rumor belief.

Belief in rumor tells us about some of the mechanisms that are used in assigning confidence in an idea and it reveals the underlying attitudes and sentiments of a rumor public. Belief is also an important topic because it seems likely that the more one believes a rumor the more likely one is to act upon it. That raises an interesting question: Can rumors still be acted upon despite not believing in them?

Clearly the answer to this question is yes. It doesn't seem to take much belief to lead to rumor-based behaviors. I was first introduced to this idea while pilot testing my stock market game Broker. Developing any material or apparatus for use by participants often requires several rounds of pretesting. On this occasion, a lone student was operating Broker and I asked her to speak her thoughts out loud as she worked her way through the game. This technique is designed to ensure that the materials and procedure are doing what they are supposed to be doing. She was closely following the Goodyear stock price change and was then repeatedly confronted with unpublished rumors from "brother-in-law Harry." She was clearly annoyed at Harry. Despite Harry's minimal character development, she voiced palpable anger at him. Consistent with a systematic set of questions asked of all subjects about sources of information, Harry was not viewed as a credible source, and his rumors were not believed. Despite this, participants relied on Harry's rumors to the same extent that they relied on news from the front page of *The Wall Street Journal*. In other words, a minimal belief in Harry's rumors seemed to be all that was necessary to affect trading behavior in the same way as front-page news.

This is not a new idea. Jamuna Prasad noticed that many of the rumors circulating after the 1934 earthquake in India were only weakly believed but were transmitted and acted upon anyway. Prasad called this "watered down" belief, a posture in which disbelief is suspended. Watered-down belief is a reluctance to say that something is false. Similarly, Ralph Rosnow, John Yost, and Jim Esposito collected rumors among faculty members at Temple University in the early 1980s. At the time, the faculty union and university administration were conducting a series of intense labor negotiations, and an aura of uncertainty and anxiety pervaded the campus. Among other items, professors were asked what rumors they had heard, how strongly they believed these rumors, and whether or not they had passed them on. As we discussed in Chapter 5, belief in the rumor led to passing it on, but Ralph's team found that the relationship was not necessarily uniform. In other words, it only took a little belief in a rumor for it to be spread.

Only the strongly disbelieved rumors were not spread at all. To make the rounds then, a rumor need not be entirely plausible, only moderately so. This helps explain the comment by the Harlem roofer about the Tropical Fantasy rumor: "It sounds kind of far-fetched. . . ." That is, to him the rumor was only moderately believable—he realized it was a bit far-fetched. But he acted upon it anyway.

The remaining part of the Harlem roofer's comment contains a hint about why only lukewarm belief is necessary before spreading or acting on a rumor: ". . . The 49-cent sodas can't be chanced." In other words, the risk of sterilization from a soft drink—improbable as it is—is not worth whatever savings one accrues through purchasing this pop. In Chapter 2, I discussed how dread rumors capitalize on the "better safe than sorry" rationale, but the other side of the story is that this thinking seems to "kick in" at moderate—and even low—levels of probability. Of course, this risk assessment strategy is the lifeblood of the insurance industry. It is unlikely that John Insured will die soon yet he carries a hefty life-insurance policy. Why? The money he sends away each month to Northwestern Mutual could be used for furniture, fun, or family finances. But the consequences of his death would be devastating to his family—financial insecurity and even poverty—so he continues to mail the money away. Insurance salespersons know this and seek to make the possibility of an early demise more salient—and thus more probable—to potential customers. Similarly, the consequences of not spreading or acting upon a rumor may be dire—such as sterility—and so even though it is improbable people act upon it. Even though it is only believed a little bit, it influences.

What about logic and reason? What if the rumor simply makes no sense or doesn't comport with the available data? After all, in an earlier chapter I stated that rumor is a form of explanation. If the explanation is unreasonable, will people still believe it? Facts are often compelling—but not always. How can this be so? First consider that the definition of "unreasonable" can vary quite a bit depending upon a person's preexisting axioms and attitudes. For example, if I'm confronted with a rumor that Miss Scarlet bludgeoned Mr. Boddy with the lead pipe in the ballroom, I'll check these assertions against the facts as I know them: Where was Scarlet at the time of the murder? Is she strong enough to swing a lead pipe with the force necessary to kill a man? Does she profit from Boddy's death? But the facts as I know them are rarely stand-alone entities; they are embedded in what I already hold to be true—my conception of reality. To continue with the example, if I come from a culture in which it is inconceivable that a woman would beat a man to death with a lead pipe, then this action is subjectively less likely to me. I say "less likely"—not impossible. People's views do sometimes accommodate reality that contradicts what they currently hold to be true.

Second, since our reasoning efforts are often motivated, this indirectly—and often unintentionally—affects our judgments. Practically speaking, we are predisposed to reason our way through some matters and not others, to stop seeking evidence for some hypotheses and not others, and to accept as plausible some theories and not others. If the servants hate Miss Scarlet because she habitually demeans and belittles them, they are more likely to entertain the possibility that Scarlet did it. Her alibi will be thoroughly investigated and any slight discrepancies will be noted and emphasized. Conversely, the possibility that Colonel Mustard—a favorite of the servants—did it will be only briefly considered and his alibi will be quickly accepted. The rumor of Scarlet's role will arise and linger; Mustard's will quickly abate. The servants do not directly convict Scarlet and acquit Mustard of the crime—that would shock their own sensibilities; rather it is done indirectly by means of motivated reasoning. This explains how the cues to belief we've explored in this chapter exert more influence when the facts are in question than when they are not, but even when the facts are well established, strongly motivated people will meander from them. The video revealing Mustard's deadly deed will be called into question; after all, "Hollywood can create anything."

In this chapter, I've tried to show how tenuous our judgments— including our judgments of the truth of a matter—might be. Does this leave us in a postmodern miasma? One might conclude that we are unable to grasp reality and are doomed to wander about in a soupy rumor fog; some would say that there is—or may as well be—no objective separate reality. There is *only* rumor. These are rather depressing thoughts. Before abandoning all hope let's explore a related question: How well does this system work overall? That is, do people in fact typically end up believing true rumors—or false ones?

7

Facts Are Stubborn Things

TAKING STOCK OF THE WORD ON THE STREET

> *Rumor travels faster, but it don't stay put as long as truth.*
>
> —WILL ROGERS, U.S. COWBOY,
> COMEDIAN & COMMENTATOR
> (1879–1935)

IN AN APRIL 4, 1999, *New York Times* column on career and workplace issues, a reader wrote the following plea:

Help! I overheard on the way to a staff meeting that résumés are being accepted for my job as managing editor of a quarterly magazine for a nonprofit group. I know my performance isn't the problem. After all, when I started two years ago, I organized my department from scratch and have reformatted the magazine; reader interest has increased, and we receive nothing but raves with each issue. Instead, the catalysts seem to be office politics—a new director of communications has arrived—and the fact that I had to be away for a week because of a family emergency. I'm still invited to meetings and otherwise treated as if nothing is wrong, but I have decided to look for other work. How should I be handling this?

Management consultant and Washington, D.C., writer Michelle Cottle's insightful counsel to this edgy editor was as follows: "Rumor Might Have It, But Have It Dead Wrong." Heading for new horizons after overhearing one rumor seems a bit extreme, continued Cottle. Her advice was check out the facts, the rumor might be completely false. One scenario is that the statement might simply have been a malicious wish broadcast a bit too loudly by a dissatisfied subordinate. Another possibility is that the organization is actually preparing the editor for a promotion and is for that reason in search of a replacement. Cottle wisely advised the reader not to create uncertainty by attempting to confirm the rumor with coworkers. Instead she recommended that the manager approach her boss on the matter either subtly ("How's my performance—can you give me some feedback?") or directly ("I heard a rumor that I am being replaced—is this true?"). Knowing one way or the other is better than being mired in the emotional morass of employment uncertainty.

Rumors we encounter can indeed be false—or true. There are many times when it has not been or cannot be verified, yet one must act. For the rumor consumer, what then is one to do?

One way of answering that question is to determine what psychologists who study judgment and decision making in conditions of uncertainty call the "base rate" of each possible outcome. If a bin of one hundred well-mixed Ping-Pong balls contains seventy blue balls and thirty red ones, how likely is it that a blindfolded participant reaching into the bin will select a red ball? The correct answer is of course 30 percent. This is the base rate for the outcome "red ball chosen." Similarly, we might ask what the base rate is for the outcome "rumor is true." If the percentage of rumors overall tends to be true in particular situations, we may do well to act upon them in those circumstances; if they tend to be false under other conditions, we should in those cases ignore them. It may seem unusual to ask this question about rumor—but really it is the same dilemma we encounter with any bit of information about which we are uncertain. In the unfortunate event that you are diagnosed with cancer, you and your physician will settle on a course of treatment by considering and comparing the base rates of success for chemotherapy versus radiation for persons in the past that had your particular type of cancer. Given the same negative side effects, it is wiser to choose the treatment having a higher success base rate. Likewise, in this chapter we seek to broadly estimate true rumor base rates under various conditions.

What is the base rate for true rumors overall? That is, how likely is it that upon hearing a rumor, it will subsequently prove to be true? Only a handful of academic studies have asked this question, and the results have varied widely. Researchers in these investigations typically enter a situation, collect rumors (or elements of one or more rumors), then simply determine what percentage of them are veridical. This has been dubbed the "accuracy percentage."

In some settings the accuracy percentage is very high. I introduced Theodore Caplow's study of World War II military rumors in Chapter 5. Caplow collected rumors as part of his monthly regimental intelligence report over a two-year period. He recorded that these rumors were not only virtually 100 percent accurate, but also comprehensive. "[E]very major operation, change of station, and important administrative change was accurately reported by rumor before any official announcement had been made," he wrote.

Rumors in his study seem to have functioned as an advance warning communication system. Management professor Keith Davis, a pioneer in the study of the grapevine, conducted a number of investigations in organizational settings and found that for noncontroversial company information, the organizational grapevine was between 80 and 99 percent accurate. Evan E. Rudolph surveyed 124 employees at a telephone company and traced the flow of twelve different "information episodes" over a three-week period in the early 1970s; the overall accuracy percentage was 94 percent. Organizational grapevines seem to produce a crop of mostly accurate rumors. Of course, the small percentage of a rumor that is in error could be disproportionately important. Davis documented the case of a rumor that a general manager's daughter married a welder. Ninety percent of the rumor details were correct—for example the day, time, and location of the ceremony. But one important point was incorrect: the welder's bride was not the manager's daughter—the mix-up was due to the daughter and the bride coincidentally having the same name.

In other situations, rumor accuracy is no better than chance or is abysmally low. Harvard academics John Pound and Richard Zeckhauser collected forty-two takeover rumors published in the Heard on the Street column of *The Wall Street Journal* from 1983 through 1985. Just 43 percent of these rumors proved true within one year after the rumors were published. Rumors amid crisis or calamity are typically inaccurate. In June 1950 the late cross-cultural psychologist Durganand Sinha recorded rumors after a massive rainfall-induced landslide in Darjeeling, India. Sinha attempted to verify these rumors and found most to be false or exaggerated; the accuracy percentage was minute. During the winter term of 1975, communication researchers Sanford B. Weinberg and Ritch K. Eich established a rumor control center for scuttlebutt arising from a strike by graduate student employees at the Ann

Arbor campus of the University of Michigan. Stories of stalled campus buses, disrupted dormitory food service deliveries, and aggressive picketers were common. Weinberg and Eich checked out rumors that were called into a phone line advertised in the student-run newspaper. Only 16.2 percent of these hotline rumors were found to be true (77.4 percent were false and the remainder were inconclusive).

Video game freelance journalist Kyle Orland observed an interesting pattern of accuracy in a recent nonacademic review. Orland investigated eighty-eight video game rumors published in the Quartermann column of *Electronic Game Player Magazine* during 2003 and rated each rumor on a scale of 1 to 5, where 1 signified "completely false" and 5, "completely true." Orland's average accuracy rating was a dismal 3.1, or an overall accuracy percentage of about 50 percent. What is more fascinating, however, is that accuracy tended to bifurcate. The majority of the rumors were either completely true or completely false, and very few were half-true. Prashant Bordia and I found this same result in a pair of workplace rumor studies we conducted in the late 1990s. In one of these investigations, 146 participants from the United States and Australia recalled a true rumor and a false rumor they had heard in their place of employment, and then rated the accuracy of each. The results were striking: very few rumors were "in the middle" with regard to accuracy; the vast majority were either all or mostly true or all or mostly false. It seems that rumors do not like to stake out a middle ground. Moreover, "all or mostly" true rumors became more accurate over the life of the hearsay—they became more true with time. In contrast, "all or mostly" false rumors either became less accurate or stayed just as false over the life of the tale. The true got truer; the false either got more false or simply remained as false.

We dubbed this pattern the "Matthew Accuracy Effect" after the similar Matthew Science Effect coined by Columbia University sociologist Robert K. Merton in 1968. Merton observed that—in terms of accolades—well-known scientists tend to receive an increasing share of scientific honors over time while lesser-known researchers receive a disproportionately smaller part of the public praise pie. It may seem unfair, but opportunities and fame are not distributed in accordance with one's accomplishments. Rather, as scientists become better known, they receive lopsided—as compared with their lesser-known colleagues—increases in funding and opportunities to collaborate with other scientists. Nothing succeeds like success. Further, more people refer to and remember their work, even when they are not the primary author of a project; they therefore become much more famous than their less successful colleagues. The phenomenon of "the rich get richer and the poor get poorer" has been noticed in many of life's arenas other than fame, funding, and wealth. Matthew effects derive their name from a passage in the Gospel of Matthew where Jesus states, "For everyone who has will be given more, and he will have an abundance. Whoever does not have, even what he has will be taken from him." The idea here is that those who act responsibly with the resources entrusted to them will be given even more assets to oversee; things entrusted to those who act unwisely will be taken from them. Employers give more autonomy and authority—and higher salaries—to workers who have proven trustworthy; employees shown to be capricious are supervised closely and soon let go. Something akin to this principle seems to be working itself out with regard to rumor accuracy.

How does this happen? What is the machinery that leads to greater rumor accuracy in some instances and thoroughgoing falsehood in others?

If you are a teacher, instructor, preacher, or professor, here is a bit of good advice for your presentations: Get organized. Students will forgive much, but not a disorganized lecture. Deriving a meaningful nugget from a scattered speech is strenuous work on the part of the pupil. Listeners are unlikely to learn anything but perhaps the main point of your presentation, especially if their attention is distracted. Secondary themes and nuanced meanings will simply not be noticed. This state of affairs is much like what was experienced by participants in a study by social psychologist Robert S. Baron and his associates. Baron's team was interested in understanding why people who listen to a story of someone's misdeeds rate that person more negatively than people telling the story do. This is known as the teller-listener extremity effect—the listener's rating of the person is more extreme than the teller's. Baron's study makes a convincing case that the culprit behind this effect has to do with the limits of human attention while attending to a disjointed message. The tales that people tell one another are often so hard to follow that listeners are only able to process the main story line; the finer points and subplots are simply missed. Let's take a closer look at Baron's investigation, instructively titled "Why Listeners Hear Less Than They Are Told."

Participants first viewed a video of a college-aged man describing how he had unintentionally gotten drunk at a party, sped away intoxicated, ran a stop sign, caused a serious automobile accident, left the scene, sped away from police who pursued him, and assaulted an officer of the law. This is indeed a serious set of misdeeds, but the video also contained information that mitigated the man's guilt: he had little experience with alcohol, didn't know the drinks were spiked with 180-proof booze, his friend was even more intoxicated than he was, he had been pressured to drive the car, drinking and driving were out of character for him, and he expressed regret for his actions. Judges and juries take such mitigating information into account all the time when parceling out punishment for offenders. Thus, the video conveyed the main story line about the man's misdeeds—which were pretty bad—plus the mitigating factors involved in the incident. After viewing this video, subjects evaluated how good, self-centered, hurtful, sensitive, responsible, aggressive, and sorry the speaker was. Then they tape-recorded a detailed verbal account of the video message from memory; these subjects were called "tellers" because they told the story. The tape-recorded account—which amounted to a second-hand report—was then listened to by another person; these participants were called "listeners." Listeners then evaluated the man based on these secondhand stories.

As had happened in other studies of the teller-listener extremity effect, listeners consistently evaluated the person more negatively than tellers. Baron's research team explained this in the following way: the listeners had less to work with than the tellers. Whereas tellers had viewed an organized and polished presentation, the listeners often listened to a disorganized and disjointed one. When a message is unclear, listeners are forced to pay greater attention to it and end up being aware of not much more than the main idea. In this case, the main story line was rather negative— hence their ratings were more severe. They really only "heard" part of the story. In contrast, messages that were more coherent and organized were more easily attended to and so the mitigating factors of the case were more salient to listeners and taken into account more fully when rating the drunken driver. In short, the secondhand accounts were more haphazard than the original video, so listeners tended to encode the main story—which was negative— and miss the mitigating factors.

Baron supported this explanation in several clever ways. First, he asked listeners to rate the clarity of the secondhand report and found that the clearer the report was perceived to be, the less harshly the listener rated the target. Muddled reports led to more negative ratings for our drunk driver. Second, Baron presented participants with either an organized video presentation or a disorganized one in a follow-up study. The disorganized presentation imparted the same information, but in a chronologically jumbled way. For example, the speaker would sometimes insert, "Oh, I forgot to tell you . . ." and then tell a part of the story that should have been related earlier. In addition, the disorganized presentation was full of those distracting habits of speech with which we are all so familiar, namely the nonwords "ah" and "um." Baron found that the disorganized accounts produced more disapproving ratings than organized ones, even though they contained the same information. Third, Baron made it harder for some subjects to pay attention by playing a moderately loud incoherent babble of people talking in the background as listeners listened to the teller. This background noise was indeed distracting and led to more negative ratings by listeners. In sum, the less clear the message or the less attention listeners were able to pay to the presentation, the more harshly they rated the target of the story.

Very high levels of anxiety are also known to interfere with attention, as well as a number of other cognitive processes; worried people find it difficult to concentrate, remember, and think clearly. Conversely, performance on many types of tasks seems to be optimal at moderate levels of anxiety. It is likely that rumor distortion that arises from attention and other cognitive deficits while listening to disjointed accounts is made worse under conditions of extreme anxiety. Rumors circulating in the aftermath of disasters owe their inaccuracy in part to this emotional state. The prevalence of exaggerations, errors, and fabrications in such situations is likely due to difficulties in attending, remembering, and thinking that accompany terror, fear, and angst. This may be one reason why highly excited or fearful groups become more suggestible and less critical of ideas. This too tends to reduce accuracy.

All this leads to some practical advice if you are ever defending yourself with a speech that contains a description of both your culpable acts and the extenuating circumstances surrounding those acts: be sure your communiqué is clear, coherent, concise, free of "ahs" and "ums," and delivered in a quiet setting so that listeners— who are hopefully not in a fearful state—can attend fully to the entire story. This is especially the case if listeners are not permitted to ask questions of you, as in a jury trial. The application to rumor accuracy is also clear enough: ordinary people are not orators and the rumors we relay are often disjointed and jumbled. Our listeners are only able to pay so much attention and might only be able to manage the main part of the story, resulting in a more extreme— and simplified—version of reality than the one originally imparted. This version would be necessarily less accurate than the original. Again, this is especially the case if listeners are highly anxious and do not have opportunity to discuss the rumor.

Listeners are not only limited by how much attention they can pay to complex messages, but also by how much of the message they can store in memory. If you have played the telephone game, then you are already familiar with how limits to memory may lead to inaccurate rumors. One person whispers a message along to another person, who then passes it to a third, and so on down the line. I described this whisper-down-the-lane serial transmission procedure previously in this book—it was the centerpiece of Allport and Postman's work. Allport and Postman typically conducted these studies in classroom or lecture settings in the following fashion. First, six or seven volunteers left the room. An illustration or photograph was then projected upon a screen in full view of the audience. The scenes were quite detailed.

One black-and-white drawing depicted what appears to be the

site of a skirmish during World War II. The setting is a French village in which four combatants are positioned in front of the ruins of a small shop. Three of them are clearly clothed in military garb—the fourth may or may not be a civilian. One soldier is lying prone and peering through his binoculars, one is aiming his rifle, and a third reclines on his back and appears to be injured. The fourth—the only dark-skinned combatant in the scene and possibly a civilian—is about to loft a grenade. A nearby street sign signifies that Paris is 21½ kilometers away and Cherbourg is 50 kilometers distant. The ruined shop still bears a sign above its doorway, PAIN ET VIN (bread and wine), next to which are stacked eleven artillery shells. In the background stands a battle-scarred church with a steeple atop of which is a cross. On the face of the steeple, the hands of a clock tell us the time: ten minutes till two. A truck with a red cross marked on its outer canvas and—paradoxically—a box marked TNT beneath the canvas is also seen in the background, along with a couple of soldiers taking cover or on the run. Several tree stumps are discernible, and we can see only the frame of another small structure that has apparently been gutted. Above, bombers are dropping their load near the church and an air battle appears to be in progress.

At this point, one of the volunteers was brought back into the room and seated in a spot where he could not see the projected drawing; let's call this person Alpha. A person in the audience was then assigned the task of describing the drawing in detail to Alpha (or a detailed description was read aloud by the experimenter). This wasn't so difficult because that audience member could look at the drawing while describing it. No discussions or questions were permitted between the tellers and the listeners in this study. Next, a second volunteer was reintroduced into the room—let's call her Bravo. Bravo, like Alpha, was situated so that the drawing remained out of her sight. And so, without the benefit of actually seeing the scene, Alpha did his best to describe to Bravo as much as he could accurately recall from the description he had heard. After this first report, Charlie, a third volunteer, was seated next to Bravo. Bravo described to Charlie as much of what Alpha described to her as she could accurately remember. And so on, continuing with Delta, Echo, Foxtrot, and Golf. The last volunteer finally recited the terminal report—often amidst audience laughter because it bore little resemblance to the original description of the drawing.

To get a sense of what Allport and Postman demonstrated, cover the paragraph above describing the drawing and try to recall as many of its nearly twenty details as possible. How did you do? It is immediately difficult to remember more than a handful of details after being exposed to them only once and without the aid of rehearsal, discussion, or other memory aids. There are simply limits to what ordinary Homo sapiens can remember without assistance. Consequently, the first type of change wrought in rumors transmitted in this fashion is that many details are lost, or as Allport and Postman put it—"leveled"—from the description. (Think of leveling or razing a building to the ground during demolition.) An initial set of twenty details, for example, would typically get leveled to a mere group of five by the time the terminal report was produced. The other side of the leveling coin, of course, is that the remaining details survive—they continue to be transmitted— and are sometimes even emphasized or exaggerated. Allport and Postman called this "sharpening." The following four terminal reports from our example illustrate these processes:

- A church is on fire, there is a cross. I don't remember the next part.
- There is a church steeple. There are four Negroes working. The church has a clock. It is ten minutes past two.
- In Italy. Knocked-down church. Bombers dropping bombs.

- French battleground. Looks as though there had been fighting; woman standing in front.

Each of these reports has been leveled to only a handful of details and in that sense is less accurate than the original description. Some details have also been sharpened—the church is not only damaged, it is now "on fire," and "one Negro" has multiplied into "four Negroes."

Leveling and sharpening didn't occur randomly but rather as a function of what the transmitters found easiest to remember. For example, Allport and Postman noticed that hard-to-remember proper names and places were quickly lost. In contrast, vivid actions ("Bombers dropping bombs"), peculiar phrases ("ten minutes past two"), contextual labels ("this is a battle scene"), orienting phrases ("in Italy"), and movement ("a large black man is throwing a hand grenade") were more likely to make it to the terminal report. Notice also that some outright errors have crept in—"four Negroes," "ten minutes past two," "in Italy," "woman standing in front," "church is on fire." The limitations of human memory are the culprits causing these inaccuracies; if our memory functioned as well as a tape recorder, leveling, sharpening, and other errors would not accrue.

Allport and Postman's research, Baron's experiments, and a long line of important rumor transmission investigations have employed the serial transmission method. This method is unnaturally taxing on attention and memory capabilities, and so these studies maximize the kinds of inaccuracies that result from inattention and memory loss. After all, the serial transmission procedure was originally designed as a way to investigate memory processes and therefore tell us much about how distortion develops from deficiencies in the unaided human capacity to pay attention and remember. How applicable are these results to real rumor phenomena?

They are applicable to one facet of real rumor episodes—and are therefore instructive—but generally not to the situations as a whole. Serial transmission is not the norm. There are times when rumor is serially transmitted with no discussion, such as when a rumor is broadcast via the radio, when you read a forwarded e-rumor once then share it with someone else, or when some urgent situation curtails discussion. Also, there are circumstances when the rumor is so uninteresting that people are not motivated to ask questions, ask the teller to repeat the message, or beg for clarification. These situations are almost certainly in the minority, however; real-life rumor transmission involves two-way communication, restatements, clarifications, hypothesizing, questions, and a whole repertoire of sensemaking activities, as we have seen. But despite this lack of realism, serial transmission studies do explain a lot about how limits to our cognitive capabilities drive inaccuracy.

With every face-to-face social interaction, attention and memory deficiencies degrade the rumor message. The extent to which this happens, however, depends on other factors known to improve accuracy. I'll explore these factors more closely, but it is well to briefly highlight here how a couple of them—discussion and accuracy motivation—have mitigated distortion in serial transmission studies. Person-to-person discussion reduces the distortion brought about by serial transmission of rumors. When participants in the serial chain are allowed to repeat messages, ask for clarification, respond to questions, and phrase the message in alternate ways, accuracy improves quite a bit. It's not hard to see why— discussion involves repetition, rehearsal, meaningful encoding, active listening, message checking, and interaction; all of these features aid memory and boost attention. This way of transmitting a rumor is—again—more realistic. Rumor transmission is more often a discussion than a one-way transfer of information. In addition, when serial transmitters pass along messages that are important to them—when they are really trying their best to pass along accurate versions of what they heard—the terminal reports also become less distorted. It's also not difficult to understand why accuracy motivation mitigates the distortion inherent in serial transmission—people are simply trying harder. In real life, people can be motivated by accuracy concerns—or by other goals, as we shall see next.

Problems in human attention and memory are only half of the story of how cognitive deficits lead to rumor inaccuracy. Details don't just get lost from memory, they get reorganized and replaced so as to be more meaningful. The task of remembering something is much more like reconstructing and reorganizing dismantled puzzle parts than replaying a videotape. Cognitive "missing pieces" then give room for motivated reconstructions, a process Allport and Postman called "assimilation." Assimilation is the guiding of the leveling, sharpening, errors, and additions that are introduced into rumor transmission. That is, inaccuracies that result from memory and attention deficiencies also give opportunity for the alterations that are consistent with the teller's preexisting knowledge, expectations, stereotypes, interests, defenses, and prejudices. Rumor is therefore like a Rorschach test in which the personality—or some other aspect of the participant—gets projected onto the tale in its retelling.

Assimilation can be a relatively cool intellectual process. Details might be changed to fit the general theme of the story, as when details that didn't fit well into the battle scene described above were altered. For example, the combatant lofting the grenade could have been a civilian but was always described as a soldier—a fighting soldier fits more neatly within a battle scene than a fighting civilian. The Red Cross truck was remembered as an ambulance even though in reality the drawing depicted its load as explosives. Assimilation can also reflect personal interests, training, or perspectives. For example, Allport and Postman noticed that military audiences referred to the actors depicted in the battle drawing simply as "men" whereas civilian listeners labeled them "soldiers." Military audiences also typically sharpened the time of day and location more than civilians. Occupational training and interest biased their perceptions. Female audiences characteristically sharpened clothing and bargains more than male audiences did in a drawing depicting shops on a street—because of women's greater interest and experience in these matters, according to Allport and Postman.

Similarly, leveling and sharpening might be guided by a desire to construct a story that is more understandable to the hearers. This can be accomplished by leveling out the parts of the story that are inconsistent with well-learned stereotypes. Research by social psychologists Anthony Lyons and Yoshihisa Kashima demonstrated this. Australian students read a story involving "Gary"—a fictitious Australian Rules football player. Australian Rules football—otherwise known as "footy"—is a highly physical contact sport resembling soccer and American football. The story told how Gary had been given some time off from playing professional football and decided to drive up the coast for a couple of days with a friend. At each stage of the narrative, an equivalent number of clauses that were consistent with the macho football player stereotype and inconsistent with that stereotype were presented.

For example, after reading the story setting, all participants read a stereotype-consistent sentence, "On the way, Gary and his mate drank several beers in the car," then a stereotype-inconsistent clause, "After a while, Gary decided to buy himself a bunch of flowers at a roadside flower stand." Participants continued to read the narrative in which, unfortunately for Gary, a policeman with a Breathalyzer test happened to be at the flower stand, tested Gary, and found him over the legal alcohol limit. "Gary became angry and began to shout at the policeman" [stereotype-consistent]. "Gary began to feel very scared about the situation" [stereotype-inconsistent]. "Gary decided to escape arrest" [stereotype-consistent]. "He jumped back into his car and took off down the road." "As they drove on, Gary found himself crying, which blurred his vision" [stereotype-inconsistent]. Because of this, the car careened off the road. "He quickly jumped out of the car. He began kicking the door in anger" [stereotype-consistent]. "After a time, Gary fell to the ground in tears" [stereotype-inconsistent]. As you can see, Gary the footballer seems to have both a tough and a tender side to his personality!

After reading the story twice, participants drew the floor plan of their house for five minutes in order to prevent them from rehearsing the story mentally (this was a serial transmission study). Then they wrote down as much of the narrative as they could remember. These written reproductions were then given to a new set of subjects. These second-generation participants also read the reproduced story twice, were distracted, then wrote down as much of the story as they could remember. This cycle was repeated a total of four times. Thus, the saga of Gary the Australian footballer—which started off with an equivalent number of stereotype-consistent and stereotype-inconsistent sentences—was serially transmitted in writing four times.

Lyons and Kashima anticipated leveling—and this indeed happened. But they predicted that stereotype-inconsistent sentences would be leveled more than stereotype-consistent clauses. This also occurred. Over four retellings, stories contained more stereotypical material than sentences that did not fit with the stereotype. This happened because people are motivated to tell stories that are coherent and understandable to the listener. The parts that don't "fit" are more easily dropped as they are passed. A stereotype-consistent story is more easily understandable than stereotype-inconsistent material. Allport and Postman would say that the rumor had assimilated to the footballer stereotype because of a strong motivation to tell a coherent story to another person.

The coherence motivation affects rumor accuracy. Because we lose information, the terminal rumor is almost certainly less accurate than the initial one. When the facts are mixed—as they often are in unvarnished reality—the operation of a strong coherence motivation in the presence of well-learned stereotypes will tend to reduce accuracy.

The motivation to present a story that is more coherent to a listener hints at a broader set of relationship-enhancement reasons that affect rumor accuracy. Hearsay is embedded in a social context—and has social consequences. Part of the desire to reshape rumor to be more coherent to an intended audience is so that we form a common understanding—and thus a closer relationship—with our audience. Among Australian college students, a machismo Gary the footballer story is more understandable—and probably more entertaining—because of the widespread stereotype of these athletes. What if the audience members were a cohort of mothers of young children? A story emphasizing Gary's tender side might "sell" pretty well to this sensitive sample and we might witness a sharpening of stereotype-inconsistent clauses. At the point of the "sale"—the rumor transmission—the teller will try to make the story more understandable and *acceptable* to her hearer.

I tend to tell you a story that you will like so that our relationship will be strengthened and we can be reassured of our mutual understanding, interests, and liking. Chip Heath's study of the transmission of disgusting urban legends supports this idea. More disgusting urban legends—which are more entertaining among college students—were more likely to be transmitted than less disgusting tales. RIT college students were more likely to share a positive—as compared to a negative—rumor about the University of Rochester's change in college rankings with students from that esteemed school because they wanted to create a pleasant interaction with their listeners. My own reluctance to tell people that the rumor they just shared with me is false stems from my desire to maintain a cordial connection with that person.

In the (predominately Democratic) academic culture in which I am embedded, animosity toward President George W. Bush and his administration has been at a fever pitch for some time. It's generally considered a faux pas to say something positive about the man. Negative Bush rumors are always welcome and rarely questioned; derogatory digs, sidebars, and even PowerPoint slides are often inserted into nonpolitical academic presentations and electronic discussions; and small talk almost always includes a mutual demonization of our current commander in chief. To share a positive rumor about George W. Bush—"I heard that W was nominated to receive the Nobel Peace Prize"—would be a conversation stopper and if the sentiment persisted would severely strain the relationship. MoveOn.org constituents do not hold a monopoly on this conformist dynamic—Republican klatches during the Clinton years were equally preferential toward defamatory rumors of our forty-second president. Claims of Clinton's involvement in the death of staffer Vince Foster, the Whitewater Development Corporation, and unproven episodes of sexual misconduct were the kind of stories that one would like to have ready at a right-wing cocktail party. These hatefests are unfortunately an important element of social bonding in many communities. They signify a common point of view, validate one's own positions and opinions, and help to readily explain the evils of the world. A contrary attitude—even expressed in the form of a tentative rumor—threatens those happy states, and acceptance into the local social club is therefore not open to those who can see both sides of the story. There is a reason for the old adage to avoid discussing religion and politics at work or social gatherings—many people find it unpleasant to hear coworkers, friends, and family members express divergent views about topics one cares deeply about. This powerful social dynamic almost certainly produces inaccurate rumors that are selectively leveled, sharpened, altered, and added to so as to be more socially acceptable to a particular audience. Be cautious, then, of rumors that are pleasing to the social milieu in which they circulate.

For the same reasons that we should beware of rumors that are pleasing, flattering, and reinforcing to others, we would do well to suspect hearsay that has this same effect upon ourselves. Self-interest, self-enhancement, and self-justification motivations tend to produce inaccurate rumors by favoring some rumors or rumor elements rather than others. (Full disclosure: I served as an expert legal witness for the Procter & Gamble Corporation on the topic of rumors in the court case described below.)

The Amway Corporation is a thriving multilevel-marketing company. Amway, whose parent company is now called Alticor, manufactures a variety of personal and health consumer products. In 2006, *Forbes* magazine named Alticor the twenty-seventh largest independently owned business in the world, with $7.29 billion in annual revenues. Amway distributors are so named because of their role in distributing Amway products as "independent business owners" (IBOs are not Amway employees). In multilevel-marketing organizations, incentives motivate IBOs not only to sell products and services, but also to recruit other distributors. If I am a distributor and convince you to become one also, I become your "sponsor" and you are "downstream" to me; I then receive a portion of your sales revenue—and that of any new IBOs that you sponsor—from that point on. Because of the laws of exponentiation, a large "distributor organization" can quickly materialize into a vast multilevel hierarchy (there are currently more than 3 million Amway IBOs worldwide in eighty countries). Such a framework of close economic ties facilitates rapid and widespread communication, aided by a technology developed especially for this purpose called the "AmVox" machine. AmVox is an electronic telephone answering and forwarding device available to Amway distributors. A message read into an AmVox machine at the top of a large hierarchy and sent downstream can reach an enormous number of Amway distributors within a very short period of time.

Recall the false rumor that the head of Procter & Gamble appeared on the *Phil Donahue Show* and supposedly revealed that the company was giving 10 percent of its profits to the Church of Satan. Alleged "proof" of this claim could be found in the P&G logo at the time—a crescent man-in-the-moon and stars symbol, which is actually a popular drawing from the early days of the company prior to the American Civil War. Of course, no Satanic symbols are now—or ever were—part of any P&G logo. Flyers on which this totally fallacious tale were printed urged Christians everywhere to boycott P&G, and conveniently displayed a list of forty-three P&G products to avoid.

In April 1995, a down-line distributor in a large IBO network read this flyer into the AmVox system. A transcript of that message follows:

I wanna run something by you real quick that I think you will find pretty interesting. Just talking to a guy the other night about this very subject and it just so happens that a guy brings information in and lays it on my desk this morning, so here it goes. It says the president of Procter & Gamble appeared on the Phil Donahue Show on March 1, '95. He announced that due to the openness of our society, he was coming out of the closet about his association with the church of satan. He stated that a large portion of the profits from [P&G] products go to support his satanic church. When asked by Donahue if stating this on television would hurt his business, his reply was, "There are not enough Christians in the United States to make a difference." And below it has a list of the [P&G] products which I'll read: [the message then lists forty-three P&G products]. It says if you are not sure about a product, look for the symbol of the ram's horn that will appear on each product beginning in April. The ram's horn will form the 666 which is known as satan's number.

The AmVox message continued:

I'll tell you it really makes you count your blessings to have available to all of us a business that allows us to buy all the products we want from our own shelf and I guess my real question is, if people aren't being loyal to themselves and buying from their own business, then whose business are they supporting and who are they buying from. Love you. Talk to you later. Bye.

The message quickly found its way "upstream" to a very high-level distributor, who then disbursed it down line via the AmVox system and appended this approving introductory comment: "This is a great message. Listen to it."

Notice how the elements of the message now include a stamp of approval from a source perceived as credible (a high-level, trusted, and authoritative IBO), and an admonition that distributors should not purchase competitors' products. The clear implication of these additions was that if a distributor purchased P&G products, they were supporting a Satanic business. And because it was spread by people who had something to gain by it, it appears that self-interest was at least one of the motives involved. In 2007, a federal jury in Salt Lake City must have arrived at a similar conclusion: they awarded $19.25 million to P&G in a civil lawsuit brought against four high-level Amway distributors. (This verdict may still be appealed.) To be fair to the distributors involved in spreading this Satanic story, they claimed that their error was simply a thoughtless oversight and that their motive was not self-interest. And to his credit, at the urging of Amway several days later, the highest-level distributor issued a strong retraction, again via the AmVox machine. For the rumor consumer, perhaps the lesson to be learned from this tale is to beware of rumors that contain an element that benefits me and/or my group. The content might be driven by seductive self-interest—psychological or pecuniary—rather than objective considerations.

The case presents an opportunity to think about how self-interest may affect rumor content and transmission, but also may hinder the spread of retractions—thus enhancing the chance that an inaccurate rumor will survive. Unfortunately, forwarding the retraction of a false rumor that one has already disbursed is less likely than passing along the original message, again because of self-interest. Normal rules of conversation dictate that we convey valid information, and forwarding a message often implies my additional stamp of approval. Sending a subsequent retraction amounts to admitting that I forwarded a falsehood; this is usually embarrassing. If you have ever forwarded or passed a rumor, but later learned it was false, it is unlikely that you sent a retraction to every person to whom you first distributed the story. (But if you did, I commend you.) For e-mail rumors, the chances of this happening might be increased if you specifically request that it be immediately re-forwarded to all of the original rumor recipients, in perpetuity. For example, the original message could be re-sent with the following introductory note designed to chase the rumor as it propagates:

I JUST LEARNED THE MESSAGE BELOW IS FALSE. SORRY FOR THE ERROR—I SHOULD HAVE CHECKED THE FACTS FIRST. PLEASE FORWARD THIS CORRECTION IMMEDIATELY TO EVERYONE YOU SENT THE ORIGINAL MESSAGE TO UNTIL IT IS STAMPED OUT. THANKS.

Even with these specific directions, however, rumor retraction messages might die a quick death; it is simply not very flattering to publicize our errors.

The reluctance to retract a rumor is likely to have operated in July 2007 in the city of Montgomery, Alabama. Hundreds of e-mails spread the false report that a child had been raped in a shopping mall restroom. However, when police questioned the child's mother they ascertained that the little girl had concocted the tale to save face over accidentally urinating on her own clothes while in the lavatory. The child had naturally been embarrassed over the accident. Police then requested that anyone who spread the rumor should also spread a retraction. It seems unlikely that even a significant minority would do this, however—it requires effort and it is uncomfortable to admit to being fooled. In my own experience, I cannot recall receiving even one retraction for any of the hundreds of false rumors that have been sent my way. In one memorable example of the reluctance to send a retraction during the U.S. presidential election of 2004, an acquaintance sent me the false rumor that Senator John Kerry had stated that his favorite Bible passage was John 16:3 when he obviously meant to say John 3:16—a much more popular verse. The rumor explained the mistake as a manifestation of the candidate's alleged hypocrisy. I mentioned in an earlier chapter how the exact same rumor was circulating about George W. Bush at the time. The point here, however, is what happened when I explained to the sender that this was a false rumor. I urged him to send a retraction to all of his original contacts. His reply was that he was aware that the rumor was false, but that "one false rumor deserves another." In other words, self-interest—evidenced both in the decision to propagate a false rumor and a reluctance to retract it—trumped accuracy in this case. Like an unchecked virus, the false rumor continued to spread.

The motivational picture I've painted till now is pretty gloomy so far as accuracy is concerned, but take heart: the desire to ferret out facts is also alive and well. The intention to understand the facts of a matter appears to be as deeply ingrained a motive as the desire to please others and feel good about ourselves. Cultural prohibitions against deceiving are ubiquitous. And, as mentioned above, one basic rule of communication is to repeat only true information. In addition, the goal of acting effectively in many situations requires a knowledge of the actual facts. Accuracy motivation does at times prevail even when it is not flattering for sensemakers or when it makes them unpopular among their fellows.

I want to take a brief philosophical detour and assert that the goal of ferreting out the facts is at least theoretically possible: there is some true information to discover. Scientists take this as axiomatic and so shall I. Even persons strongly motivated to perceive matters in a biased manner recognize the difference between facts supported by evidence and fancy based on desire. As John Adams stated, "Facts are stubborn things; and whatever may be our wishes, our inclinations, or the dictates of our passion, they cannot alter the state of facts and evidence." Though the rumor may have assimilated to self-interest, cohered to a cultural stereotype, or been leveled through transmission, an actual state of affairs exists that might possibly be recovered. In Hans Christian Andersen's timeless fable *The Emperor's New Clothes,* the naked king pretends to be dressed in regal garb because he wants to feel that he is intelligent and competent (a self-enhancement motive), the court and the townspeople pretend likewise because they want to ingratiate themselves to him (a relationship-enhancement motive), but everyone knows the truth spouted by the little boy: "The emperor has nothing at all on!" This old tale still resonates with us precisely because humans are ordinarily capable of differentiating between what they want to perceive and what they actually perceive. It might be fanciful thinking on my part, but I take it as axiomatic that facts exist and that in many cases they can be discovered.

Ironically, the motivation to be accurate may also draw steam from the desire to enhance relationships or view oneself positively, at least under conditions of transparency. In long-term relationships and in situations where the rumor can be verified or falsified, one's reputation for spreading facts or fallacies depends upon one's record of accurate statements. People take into account how reliable a person has been in the past. As the Chinese proverb states, "Fool me once, shame on you. Fool me twice, shame on me." People may greatly desire to spread a rumor that pleases their listeners, but they are constrained by considerations about the truth of their tale—they do not want to appear gullible, foolish, or flippant. In a study of murder rumors with my student Scott Rabideau, participants never neglected to consider how credible the rumor was, even when motivated to tell a good story. Similarly, research on positive thinking has long shown that only those positive thoughts that are credible in our own eyes are effective in raising our mood. Unsubstantiated positive thoughts are regarded for what they are: wishful thinking. The desire to be regarded by others—and by oneself—as a credible source of information can therefore also be a force pushing people in the direction of accuracy.

Not surprisingly, if people are motivated toward accuracy then they are more likely to produce accurate rumors. In situations where getting the facts of the matter at hand is of paramount concern—and given that the group is capable of ferreting out these facts—accurate rumors are likely to emerge. Theodore Caplow's study of military rumors exemplified this. The topics of these rumors—troop movements, military campaigns, status of the war—were of great import to soldiers; these rumors were extremely accurate. Organizational rumors about matters that impact job security or job quality typically spawn anxiety and are very important to employees; workers are therefore often highly motivated to learn the truth of the topic at hand. This is undoubtedly one reason why organizational rumors are often highly accurate. Prashant Bordia, Rob Winterkorn, and I investigated rumors in a company undergoing a radical downsizing—by the end of our study, about half of the work group being investigated had been laid off. A week prior to the formal announcement of who would be terminated, a rumor circulated naming the unfortunate individuals to be let go. This rumor was 100 percent correct—every person on that list was laid off. This story dovetails with Keith Davis's findings that the organizational grapevine is extremely accurate, at least for noncontroversial company matters. And it agrees with another study Bordia and I performed in which we asked employed students to recall a workplace rumor that had since been proven true or false—the overwhelming majority of subjects recalled true rumors, suggesting that there were more of them to remember. At least for rumors where the outcome is eventually known, accurate organizational hearsay appears to be the rule rather than the exception—in part because employees want valid information more than they want preferred information.

In July 2007, a widely aired television report that Chinese dumplings sold in Beijing were being filled with shredded cardboard instead of meat turned out to be entirely fabricated. How this report was discredited demonstrates the power of a motivated group to uncover the facts. Zi Beijia, the part-time reporter who created the hoax, was apparently under pressure to produce a news story. After unsuccessfully investigating many stands selling *baozi*—steamed and filled buns—Zi allegedly cooked up the phony investigative piece using his home DVD recorder. He staged the manufacture of dumplings filled with meat and cardboard. The news report sparked a loud public outcry, and the mayor ordered an immediate investigation. Even though more than one hundred *baozi* stands were sampled, no cardboard contents could be found. Professor Chen Min, at the nearby China Agricultural University, then simulated the manufacture of the cardboard-filled dumplings based on Zi's report and found that cardboard filling—even in small amounts—was easily observable and rendered a dumpling difficult to chew. It therefore didn't seem plausible that *baozi* makers had indeed been supplementing their filling with cardboard. Investigators therefore focused on the reporter; Zi broke down under interrogation and is now spending some time in jail.

For the rumor consumer, then, situations in which people are

primarily motivated to find the facts of the matter at hand—
because the facts are important to them, because they want to view
themselves as seekers of truth, or because they want to preserve
their reputation for accuracy—favor the production of accurate
rumors.

Of course, motivation is not a *sufficient* ingredient for accurate
rumors. Performance in any area depends upon motivation plus
ability. Given a desire to ferret out the facts, the ability to ferret
them out determines whether or not a sturdy story or a fallacious
fable emerges. Chief among these abilities is the capacity to check
the rumor. Caplow's study of military rumors is again a good example of this: not only were these soldiers motivated to find facts,
Caplow relates that they were able to approach their superior officers regarding these rumors. Obviously, the ability to check the
veracity of a rumor by at least some members of the group within
which the rumor is circulating will favor rumor accuracy.

Checking begins with making sure you heard the rumor correctly, as when you ask the teller to repeat what she said, call for
clarification, or ask questions. I previously called this "discussion"
and showed how it counters the losses inherent in serial transmission. We might refer to this as "message checking." Message checking may also take the form of questioning others besides the teller,
or cross-checking. Given an accuracy motivation, this kind of activity can reverse the effects of individual memory loss. What I forget,
you may remember as we "compare notes." Groups that collectively
check one another's recollection of a message will use the following rule of thumb: The more people who remember a particular
detail, the more likely it is that the detail existed in the message's
original version. The interaction may also serve to jog memories.
This collective memory reconstruction process—as long as it is

accompanied by accuracy motivation—can be quite powerful in reducing message distortion and reproducing accurate information. The classic film *Twelve Angry Men* exemplified this idea. In this dramatic story of the deliberation phase of a murder trial, jurors jog each other's memories of the facts of the case. Witness statements about the time of the murder, whether the defendant "hit" or "slapped" the victim, the appearance of a key witness for the prosecution, and whether or not another witness had small indentations on her nose were all accurately recalled through juror cross-checking. (I highly recommend this film, as it dramatizes many of the principles conveyed in this chapter, including cognitive limits, dependence on stereotypes, capacity to check, motivation, conformity, discussion, and percolation.)

Veracity checking—ascertaining the truth of the message—may be as simple as searching the World Wide Web. In today's connected world, checking has become a much easier task, at the very least in the case of rumors circulating on the Internet. Such rumors can easily be checked by searching Web sites dedicated to this purpose, such as Snopes.com, TruthOrFiction.com, or UrbanLegends.About.com. The U.S. Department of Energy also maintains the Computer Incident Advisory Capability (CIAC) Web site hoaxbusters.ciac.org that contains a list of Web sites devoted to checking on all manner of Internet hearsay, hoaxes, and scams. The operators of these sites spend their days investigating the truthfulness of hearsay spreading on the Internet—so that we don't have to. (I encourage readers to routinely turn to these sites.)

Veracity checking may simply involve making a phone call to a person who knows the real story. In 1996, I conducted a series of interviews with corporate communications officers in the Rochester area. I was interested in how they handled rumors they had encountered. In two of these instances, completely false rumors died when someone called a company official in the know. In one situation, a reporter heard of a dangerous crack in a nuclear generator and promptly called the plant—the story was then squelched. In another event, rumors among employees that the company would be taken over were quickly stopped after speaking with company officials whom they trusted. Journalists regularly perform this type of checking. In 2007, a false rumor that Pete Wilson, a former governor of California, had died arose when a San Francisco radio announcer by the same name passed away, but was kiboshed when reporters and friends checked it out. Governor Wilson, along with Mark Twain, had reason to say "Rumors of my death have been greatly exaggerated!"

Unfortunately, rumors often go unchecked. In another duplicate-name mixup, I once interviewed a corporate manager who had by chance overheard a false story circulating that he was about to leave the company for greener pastures. The manager was justifiably concerned about this hearsay because he was up for promotion. He immediately went to his boss, fearing that this falsehood would negatively impact his chances. He was right; it turned out that his superior had indeed heard the rumor and was about to grant the promotion to someone else because of it. In the story at the beginning of this chapter, the employee had neglected to check; in this instance, the boss had neglected to check. These examples raise a puzzling general question: Why don't people check?

Checking does require some effort, however small, and this in and of itself may stop some persons—particularly if they have little energy to spare. And checking may seem harder than it really is, especially if we've never done it before. Some situations genuinely hinder checking, as when one's sources of information are unfamiliar (e.g., you've just begun a new job; you are stranded in a strange city; a natural disaster has disrupted normal channels of communication), one has very few relationships outside one's social clique (e.g., you are in an isolated section of the world; you only communicate with people in your clan or group), there is an urgent need to act (e.g., "There is a suicide bomber on the bridge! Run!"; "The dam is bursting! Get out now!"), or when a topic is classified. It may even appear to be impossible if we do not trust official sources of information. Perhaps the boss in the preceding paragraph figured that the manager I interviewed couldn't respond honestly to a question about his intention to leave; what would then be the point of checking?

More often, checking is simply not perceived as the responsibility of the rumor participant. Though the conversational norm is to pass along true information, people do not ordinarily perceive themselves as checkers of that information, especially if they couch it in tentative terms—something like, "I'm not sure of this but I heard that . . ." Unless they are a journalist, expert trial witness, or, say, author of a nonfiction book, they may be unaware that they could be held accountable for what they say and therefore ought to check their facts. Checking may also involve potential social costs that are not readily apparent to others. At the very least, it signifies that one has a source of information that one might not wish to reveal, or that one has participated in an informal sensemaking discussion session. Saying "I heard that . . ." sends the unintended message that you were listening—and this might not be altogether appreciated or approved of.

People also don't check because it might result in learning something that embarrasses your source or is not very flattering to you. After hearing a rumor that a fellow employee was fired improperly, one may not really want to know the whole story—it might strain your relationship with him or with your employer. Similarly, the managing editor at the beginning of the chapter who would rather send out her résumé than check with her boss may not have wanted to risk hearing for certain that she was slated for replacement. As silly as it sounds, leaving the job often seems a safer option—in an emotional sense—than waiting to find out if one is fired. Perhaps you can relate more easily to this if you have ever dealt with the risk of rejection by first rejecting others. You can't get fired if you quit first; you can't get hurt if you leave the relationship first. This is the insidious manner by which we allow rumors to succeed in dividing us: they remind us of our deepest fears and insecurities so much that we'd rather not risk them being true. Instead of facing our fears squarely—often by simply checking the rumor—we choose to avoid the matter altogether.

The ability to check the veracity of a rumor may hinge upon certain characteristics of the group and assets of its members. For example, some people in the group may be in a position to know for certain if the rumor is true or false. Obviously, having such an insider enables a rumor public to meaningfully check veracity, as Caplow's soldiers did. Tightly connected organizational grapevines are likely to include higher-level sources who leak information; this may be another reason why organizational rumors tend to be accurate. Even when no insider is available, accuracy can emerge when members are quite knowledgeable about the subject surrounding the rumors and thus better able to sift facts from the hearsay, as in Prashant Bordia's investigation of the false rumor that the early Internet service provider—Prodigy—was tapping users' hard drives. During the extensive e-mail discussion of this rumor, several experts weighed in. They typically prefaced their remarks by displaying their technical credentials and then demonstrating how tapping users' hard drives was technologically improbable or impossible. In other words, the group had a few experts who—

while not Prodigy insiders—were well-informed about critical issues bearing upon the validity of the story.

Group norms about acceptable standards for evidence also affect the group's capacity to check. Groups with higher standards tend to produce more accurate rumors—journalists are a good example of this. Major news media generally published accurate stories in the aftermath of September 11, 2001, while nonmedia Web sites and blogs fared much worse. There were only four documented cases of news stories reporting a false event, and these were quickly corrected. Further, these erroneous stories had been based upon errors in official statements or on outright hoax attempts by citizens. In contrast, the eminent sociologist Gary Alan Fine studied how a false rumor spread and persisted among sixth-grade boys. This well-known—and fallacious—fable purported that Pop Rocks candy, when ingested with carbonated soda, exploded in a boy's stomach. Of course, we shouldn't be too critical of these youngsters—the standard of acceptance for most people most of the time seems to be set very low and hinges mostly on how plausible the rumor seems at the time. Further, under conditions of high anxiety or extreme threat, the norm of acceptability may effectively disappear—every rumor is then passed no matter how improbable. In panic situations, one is therefore likely to find a plethora of rumor hypotheses in circulation.

Finally, the degree to which a group demands conformity may dramatically affect checking behavior. More conformity generally leads to less checking, and to less-effective checking. We've explored conformity as a facet of situations where some rumors are welcomed and some are not, but it's also important in the context of the group's capacity to check. Groups in which a diversity of opinion is tolerated are more likely to successfully check rumor veracity than groups that punish such alternate explanations—if only because a greater number of alternative explanations are available for review. Journalist James Surowiecki makes a similar point in his excellent text *The Wisdom of Crowds*. Surowiecki convincingly marshals a host of social psychological literature to support the idea that groups in which many different opinions exist and conformity is not demanded typically arrive at more effective solutions than any one individual within that group. Under these conditions, groups can be wiser than even the wisest individual in the group. The classic example of this phenomenon is the jelly-bean jar puzzle. A sufficiently large group presented with the task of estimating how many jelly beans are in a jar will produce a wide variety of estimates, but the average of these will almost certainly be within a few jelly beans of the actual tally. This happens because overestimates and underestimates tend to cancel one another out. In the context of rumor, people are presented with an ambiguous state of affairs and are asked to estimate what the facts are. Assuming accuracy motivation, the collective estimate of the facts will tend to be accurate as long as a diverse set of rumors is available and conformity is not demanded. These types of conditions typify active and diverse rumor discussions.

The U.S. presidential election of 2004 was another close race with the results being decided by a relative handful of voters in Ohio and Florida. Given the Florida experience in 2000—the razor-thin count, alleged voting anomalies, the saga of hanging chads, and the ensuing legal battle—it is not surprising that theories of voter fraud arose almost immediately. These theories were quickly adopted by disheartened Democrats whose dashed hopes had been heightened by early voter exit polls showing a lead by Kerry. One story originated from a Salt Lake City statistician who noticed a "surprising pattern" in the Florida results that showed gains for President Bush in Democratic districts that had employed electronic voting devices. The statistician disseminated her sophisticated analysis into the blogosphere and it spread with breathtaking speed. Hits to her blog rose exponentially and her posted analysis was even referenced by members of Congress calling for an investigation of voting machines in Florida several days later. But because her report propagated so rapidly, counterarguments to her analysis also arose quickly. Several Ivy League political scientists soon pointed out that these districts had a long record of voting Republican in presidential elections. Further, no concrete support for any theory of fraud materialized. And it turned out that the exit polls giving Kerry the early lead were simply in error. Investigations by researchers from the California Institute of Technology and Massachusetts Institute of Technology, and by Senator Kerry's legal team came to similar conclusions: No patterns of voter fraud or tampering had occurred. Out of an active discussion in a crowd of diverse independent-minded thinkers—who on the surface, at least, were seeking the facts—meaningful checking occurred and an accurate portrait emerged.

I am often asked how the rise of the Internet has affected rumor accuracy. On the one hand, it has paved the way for unbelievably rapid and far-reaching dissemination, often motivated by self-interest and social approval. The world is a much smaller place than it used to be. Fallacies and false rumors can therefore disperse with amazing alacrity and this has undoubtedly contributed to the spread of baseless rumor. On the other hand, they can also disperse more quickly to dissenters and those who would rebut them. If an active and diverse discussion then ensues, accuracy is more likely to emerge. Out of the vigorous and varied debate described in the previous paragraph, people were able to ferret out the facts. The Internet has amplified the ability of people to conduct active and diverse discussion, check the facts, and think collectively. It has made even more true today a statement attributed to Abraham Lincoln: "You can fool some of the people all of the time, and all of the people some of the time, but you can not fool all of the people all of the time."

This conclusion may seem strange because of the plethora of fallacious rumors circulating on the Web. If the Internet results in better collective intelligence, why do so many dumb online rumors persist? Again, the answer is simply that fallacies persist when discussion is not active and not diverse. The structure of the World Wide Web itself often limits diversity. University of Michigan computer scientist Lada Adamic analyzed hyperlink connections of liberal and conservative Weblogs. Liberal blogs overwhelmingly connect to liberal blogs; conservative blogs almost always link to conservative blogs. Only about 10 percent of the links cross ideological lines. In other words, although the Internet affords the opportunity for opinion diversity, it does not typically happen. The Internet rumor discussion might end up being active, but only occur among like-minded people—such scenarios increase conformity rather than reduce it. Alternatively, an active discussion may not occur and this also will effectively reduce rumor diversity. In these situations, a rumor is simply presented to a discussion group, accepted without comment, and people move on to the next topic. It passes unchallenged. In either scenario, accuracy is not likely to emerge.

For the rumor consumer then, one question is: Has this rumor been checked or independently verified? And to what extent is the group able to check, given its motivational inclinations, sources of insider information, expertise on issues pertinent to the hearsay, group standards for evidence, diversity of opinions, and discussion activity? By estimating the group's capacity to check a particular rumor, one can get a rough sense of the accuracy base rate.

We've seen that a diverse set of factors leads rumors along different accuracy trajectories—either toward or away from veracity— over time. Just how much time it takes for a rumor to become more or less accurate depends on rumor activity. That is, rumors will tend to become accurate in groups that are accuracy motivated and capable of checking, and do so more quickly if the rumor is being actively discussed. Conversely, rumors will tend to become more fallacious in groups that are not accuracy motivated nor capable of checking, and also do so more quickly if the rumor is being actively discussed. Rumor activity will hasten each process.

Prashant Bordia and I have called this the "percolation model of rumor accuracy," after the old-style coffeemakers. Also called *caffetterias*, these nostalgic stainless steel affairs operate by continuously recirculating hot water through coffee grounds until reaching the proper temperature. Water in a bottom chamber is heated until it begins to boil, whereupon it is forced upward through a vertical tube, visibly bubbles about in a small dense glass compartment, seeps through an upper chamber consisting of a perforated metal basket full of coarsely ground coffee, and drops back down into the bottom chamber. Increasingly hot water continues to cycle through the top and bottom chambers, percolating again and again through the coffee grounds by means of gravity. In the percolation model, the quality of the coffee grounds is analogous to conditions favorable or unfavorable to rumor accuracy. Good coffee beans represent conditions promoting accuracy; bad grounds represent conditions that facilitate fallacy. Applying heat inputs energy to the process and causes water to recirculate. Analogously, importance and anxiety energize people to engage in rumor circulation. More heat brings about more rapid water recirculation; more importance and anxiety bring about more intense rumor recirculation. Each process then operates more quickly. Little heat may never even result in getting the water to boil—a rumor will not even arise. Whatever the energy level, as long as water circulates, good grounds will at some point produce good coffee (conditions favorable to accuracy will produce accurate rumors), while bad grounds will create bad coffee (conditions favorable to fallacy will result in falsehoods). This idea is compatible with the Matthew Accuracy Effect in which rumor accuracy bifurcates—true rumors get truer and false ones become more false. A rumor's true character—in the sense of accuracy—will emerge.

Understanding rumor accuracy processes helps us become better rumor consumers because we are now better able to estimate how likely it is that a particular group in a particular situation with particular motivations will either ferret out the facts or fashion a fallacy. Rumor consumers should take into account cognitive difficulties in transmission, motivational predilections, ability of a group to check veracity, time, and rumor activity. On the basis of these assessments, the consumer can then make a more informed estimate of the likelihood of a rumor being true.

In the next chapter I turn to a more practical side of rumor wisdom—how to prevent and manage hearsay, especially hearsay that is harmful.

8

Managing the Rumor Mill

> *Can't you understand what's happening here? Don't you see what's happening? Potter isn't selling. Potter's buying!*
>
> —GEORGE BAILEY,
> *It's a Wonderful Life* (1946)

RUMORS CAN RESULT IN A RUN ON A BANK. Rumors that a financial institution is insolvent may produce a pack of patrons who literally run to the bank in an attempt to pull out their money before it is lost. Because a lending institution has only a fraction of its deposits available at any one time, this panic can cause the bank to become insolvent. Long lines form outside the beleaguered depository as people withdraw all of their assets—just to be safe. In August 2007, for example, some patrons of Countrywide Bank feared that this lender would declare bankruptcy because of subprime mortgage failures affecting its mammoth mother company,

Countrywide Financial Corporation. One Orange County, California, customer drove his Porsche to a Countrywide office in the city of Laguna Niguel, waited half an hour in line, then cashed out his entire $500,000 account; he promptly wired it to another bank. "It's got my wife totally freaked out," he said. "I just don't want to deal with it. I don't care about losing ninety days' interest, I don't care if it's FDIC-insured—I just want it out."

A bank run is the situational centerpiece of a memorable scene from the Frank Capra classic, *It's a Wonderful Life*. In this scene, Bailey Building & Loan manager George Bailey has just married and is leaving town in a taxi for his honeymoon. As they ride through Bedford Falls, hoards of people are seen swarming the bank. The cabdriver remarks, "Don't look now, but there's something funny going on over there at the bank, George. I've never really seen one, but that's got all the earmarks of a run." A passerby then shouts to the cabbie, "Hey, Ernie, if you got any money in the bank, you better hurry." Realizing the danger, George rushes to his office and confronts a crowd of anxious customers in the grip of panic.

It is the era of the Great Depression. Many folks are out of work and struggling to make ends meet. They have all heard the widespread rumor that the money in their accounts—the money they've entrusted to the B&L—is gone. To make matters worse, the avaricious, opportunistic, and wealthy Mr. Potter has capitalized on this fear by offering everyone fifty cents cash for every dollar they have in the Bailey Building & Loan. To understand this ploy, imagine not being able to get at the $10,000 you have in your bank account; after hearing a rumor of bankruptcy you think that you have surely lost it all. In a moment of panic, you sign over your entire account to Potter in exchange for $5,000 cash. You fear that your $10,000 account is a worthless gamble and are glad to trade it for a sure thing. In your agitated state of mind, Potter's offer seems like salvation, but in reality he knows that your money is safe. He has kept his head. When the panic is over, he will cash in your account and take your $10,000, thereby doubling his investment—while you lost half your savings. Potter knows that a mass exodus of patrons will kill the B&L, cripple the assets of the townspeople, and further their economic dependence on him. Bailey Building & Loan of course operates on a shoestring and at that moment has no cash whatsoever available until the bank reopens in a week. It's a tough moment for the tiny institution.

George first tries to calm them: "Now, just remember that this thing isn't as black as it appears. . . ." They aren't satisfied, and he explains again why the money is not always immediately available in the savings and loan business:

> You're thinking of this place all wrong. As if I had the money back in a safe. The money's not here. Your money's in Joe's house . . . right next to yours. And in the Kennedy house, and Mrs. Macklin's house, and a hundred others. Why, you're lending them the money to build, and then, they're going to pay it back to you as best they can. Now what are you going to do? Foreclose on them?

Still in the grip of fear, people begin to leave for Potter, thinking that getting half their money is better than losing all of it. George vaults over the counter, reframes the situation as a battle in the larger war with Potter, and attempts to impart hope:

> Now wait . . . now listen . . . now listen to me. I beg of you not to do this thing. If Potter gets hold of this Building and Loan there'll never be another decent house built in this town. He's already got charge of the bank. He's got the bus line. He's got

the department stores. And now he's after us. Why? Well, it's very simple. Because we're cutting in on his business, that's why. And because he wants to keep you living in his slums and paying the kind of rent he decides. Joe, you lived in one of those Potter houses, didn't you? Well, have you forgotten? Have you forgotten what he charged you for that broken-down shack? Here, Ed. You know, you remember last year when things weren't going so well, and you couldn't make your payments? You didn't lose your house, did you? Do you think Potter would have let you keep it? Can't you understand what's happening here? Don't you see what's happening? Potter isn't selling. Potter's buying! And why? Because we're panicky and he's not. That's why. He's picking up some bargains. Now, we can get through this thing all right. We've got to stick together, though. We've got to have faith in each other.

In response to this impassioned plea, a woman cries out, "But my husband hasn't worked in over a year, and I need money." And another, "How am I going to live until the bank opens?" Men chime in: "I got doctor bills to pay." "I need cash." "Can't feed my kids on faith." At that moment it looks as though the crowd will desert the struggling savings and loan outfit.

Suddenly, George's new bride, Mary, holds up a roll of bills—their wedding gift money. "How much do you need?" she shouts. George then uses this cash to enable people to make small withdrawals to tide them over until the bank reopens. With this act he gains their trust by putting his own assets at risk. That trust and dependence upon one another ultimately allowed many people to own their own Bedford Falls homes and to prosper, safe from Potter's usury. Frank Capra's masterpiece later provides a glimpse of the sleazy, depressed, and decrepit slum—renamed

"Pottersville"—that would have arisen without the kind of action displayed by Bailey in the midst of the bank panic. The vulnerable townsfolk from Bedford Falls and the fragile Bailey Building & Loan Association were saved that day from falling into Potter's trap. This happened because George Bailey helped people make good sense in a situation filled with potential threat; he had wisely managed a dangerous fear rumor.

In the previous chapter we considered our role as rumor consumer; here we contemplate the role of rumor manager. Rumors are of concern to anyone who desires to lead, manage, inform, influence, persuade, or guide other people through whom a story might circulate. Rumor management is therefore of interest to many role players, including administrators, advertisers, coaches, debaters, managers, marketers, parents, politicians, public relations officers, religious leaders, speakers, supervisors, teachers, and team leaders. These functions might be formally designated, or might emerge spontaneously in a crowd, team, or group. Rumor management is of particular interest if you happen to be the target of a negative rumor—how can one effectively defend one's self, group, organization, company, clan, or state against malicious hearsay? Defending against dirt is an activity that just about everyone wishes they could do (or could have done) better, including middle-schoolers, ministers, multinational corporate communications officers, political candidates, and State Department spokespersons.

The term "rumor manager" isn't intended to convey that rumors are always bad or that they can always be controlled. Rumors aren't necessarily destructive, but when they're harmful we desire to reduce their negative impact. Put positively, we want to help people make proper sense of their situation when there are gaps of understanding and potential threats. Proper and ethical rumor management then is the goal: to help—or when necessary, prod—people to make sense of their worlds and to cope with threat or potential threat in ways that are truthful, helpful, positive, pro-social, and productive. Rumors cannot always be managed; despite our best efforts, the motives, circumstances, and connections involved in a particular rumor situation may overwhelm our attempts. Nor would it be ethical to exert strong control in most instances. People have the right to make sense together free from outside interference. In fact, rumor may be the best way that a particular group has of ferreting out the facts—as in the reliance on rumors by ordinary citizens in the former Soviet Union. To attempt to manipulate the process fails to recognize people's autonomy as sensemakers. Rather than dictatorial control, the brand of rumor management I advocate seeks to influence—it recognizes that people will form their own conclusions and aims to persuade them as that process unfolds. It's not a way of spinning or hiding the facts—that would ultimately be futile. Rather, it's how we help people make good sense in a situation.

Sixty-seven percent of employees in the United Kingdom and France hear information about an important matter first through rumor, according to an April 4, 2005, report issued by the global employee research and consulting firm ISR. The study was based on responses from 40,818 European workers, 63 percent of whom agreed with the statement "We usually hear about important matter through rumour first." According to the study's authors, this indicates that employers are poor communicators. Leaving employees uninformed fuels the rumor mill. Conversely, good communication lessens the need for rumors. Further, good communication is associated with company performance. The investigation tracked stock prices for fifty-seven multinational companies over two years.

In the companies in which an above-average number of employees felt that the company was keeping them properly informed, stock prices rose an average of $7.80. In companies in which a below-average number of employees were satisfied with communication, stock prices fell an average of $8.10. ISR executive director Yves Duhaldeborde suggested a causal connection between communication and performance:

> Good leaders are good communicators. . . . Employees care about their manager's ability to communicate and want to know as much as possible about their organizations. They want to understand its core values and feel involved in key decisions. Managers need to change their approach. . . . Clear, unambiguous communication helps ensure employees are willing to work harder, understanding and supporting their company's goals and vision. Without it employees are likely to just tread water and this will be reflected in financial performance.

The study points to the ubiquity of rumor in organizational settings and suggests that the rumor mill is alive and well because communication is poor in those environments. Conversely, when communication is good, rumor activity is dampened. The study also suggests that an active rumor mill is an indicator of a poorly performing company.

Uncertainty reduction is undoubtedly the mediator here—better communication saps uncertainty and thus there is little need for rumor sensemaking. We might say that better formal communication displaces a group's informal efforts to understand a situation. Uncertainty reduction takes the form of dispersing timely and useful information about issues of concern to people (e.g., layoffs, disasters, terrorism), especially when unusual events occur or when change is in the offing. Timely communiqués—memos, meetings, announcements, press releases, discussions, newsletters—can all serve to reduce uncertainty. In a hierarchical communication network, a particularly vital group of people to keep well informed are formal communication "hubs"—persons officially connected to many other persons, such as supervisors—who can then disperse rich sets of information rapidly. Use of such information liaisons to reduce uncertainty has the added benefit of allowing discussion and clarification. In organizational settings, employees typically prefer such face-to-face two-way communication with their supervisors.

Uncertainty will often be reduced simply by confirming the rumor. During times of change, it might not be possible to dispel all ambiguity—for example: "10 percent of all workers will be laid off, but we don't yet know which 10 percent"; "We do not know who was behind the attacks on the World Trade Center today"; "I do not know when people will be airlifted out of New Orleans." In such cases, uncertainty reduction can take the form of stating the values and procedures by which the upcoming change decisions will be made, explaining why a full set of information cannot be given, and setting a timeline for when information will be available. In other words, even when the full story cannot be related, a rumor manager can attempt to limit uncertainty as quickly and as fully as possible.

Uncertainty is something a rumor manager should attempt to foresee in advance. One corporate executive I interviewed tried to anticipate rumors by consulting someone he referred to as a "radar man"—a trusted associate who would consider if a company communiqué might contribute to or curtail uncertainty. Memos and announcements intended to clarify may instead raise further questions. Uncertainty is also something that leaders should try to regularly gauge. This may be a challenge. Even when doubt is rampant, people may be disinclined to ask questions of official sources and this reluctance, of course, leads to an entrenchment of ambiguity. The corporate manager in the above example attempted to keep tabs on uncertainties by recruiting someone he dubbed a "sonar man"—an employee who would quickly report rumors he had heard among coworkers. The sonar man enabled this manager to address uncertainty related to the rumor early on. This approach is a bit risky, however—the sonar man might be perceived as a "snitch," especially if the parties involved aren't getting along. It is preferable to cultivate a norm of transparency; that is, a sense that most (or even all) information is accessible—one need only ask. Environments in which a norm of transparency is palpable will not require sonar and radar men—people will ask questions of their own accord as a matter of course.

To this end, developing a norm of transparency and reducing uncertainty may be as simple as periodically posing the question "Has anybody heard any rumors lately?"—and then being sure to respond honestly, quickly, and convincingly. If the facts aren't known, a rumor manager should admit this but soon attempt to gather and disburse the facts. The willingness to survey people for rumors and the rapidity and reliability with which responses are attended to conveys the idea that information is freely available and open for all to see. In my lectures on rumor management, I typically ask students about rumors they've heard. This almost always unleashes questions concerning the college, the program, university rules, or faculty attitudes. A false rumor I uncovered each year for many years was the perception that a former president of our university was going to slash the art program. Having checked this rumor out each year I am able to dispel it completely—art is alive and well at RIT. This had a reassuring effect upon art students, and I hope it has dampened this perennial falsehood.

The cultivation of a transparency norm may also be facilitated by a rumor control center hotline or rumor response Web page. Rumor control centers are often established during times of crisis for the purpose of collecting hearsay and reducing uncertainty. They typically operate by recording rumors called in by phone, investigating their veracity, and disbursing the information via newspaper, a Web site, or simply responding to people who call. Rumor control centers during World War II were instrumental in reducing belief in rumors of waste and special privilege. Other rumor control centers have been set up to dispel uncertainty during times of crisis, such as the Nancy Wyckoff murder at Oregon State University and a graduate student employee strike at the University of Michigan at Ann Arbor. The city of Baltimore launched a rumor control center after the assassination of Martin Luther King Jr. in order to curb unrest over civil rights issues at that time. In periods of peril, such as the aftermath of September 11, 2001, calls to the rumor control center rose dramatically.

Rumor response Web sites operate in a similar manner. The Katy Independent School District of Katy, Texas, operates one such site in order "to provide the Katy community with accurate, factual information." The site collects rumors by e-mail, phone calls, or word of mouth, then posts a response to its Fact or Fiction? archives. Katy rumors have included tales that the district would disallow student participation in the See You at the Pole student-initiated prayer meeting, the athletic stadium hot dog stand cost $600,000, and the high school is the "biggest and most expensive high school in Texas." Similarly, Rumor Central, an online service maintained by Charlotte County in Florida, provides a "one-stop spot for current information on the hot topics of the day," according to county officials. Rumors include stories that the county is wasting money on using recycled water to keep private golf courses green, is arbitrarily charging residents $115 for permits on existing septic tanks, and is wasting time and money on the eradication of iguanas. Both rumor control centers and Web sites demonstrate a transparency norm that reduces uncertainty as long as the questions put to them are indeed responded to rapidly, in a convincing manner, and based upon the facts. Shifty, evasive, and dishonest responses will soon discredit any rumor control hotline or Web site.

Sometimes organizations and individuals have employed a "no comment" response to rumors, thinking that responding to a tale will draw attention to it and lead some people to believe it. However, research by Prashant Bordia and I showed that a "no comment" response—by itself with no explanation of why the no comment stance has been adopted—tends to heighten uncertainty and is therefore generally counterproductive if the goal is to squelch the scuttlebutt. People expect a statement of some sort; the "no comment" response leads them to wonder why no one remarked about this rumor and to entertain the possibility that the rumor is indeed true. A rumor that Starbucks would offer free Wi-Fi service made the rounds in 2007 and early 2008. The rumor was grounded in the observation that the competition was heating up—megagiant McDonald's had recently announced that its twelve hundred locations in the United Kingdom would offer free wireless service and nine thousand franchises in the United States would follow suit. Other coffee competitors were also offering wireless service. Starbucks's response to these rumors? "No comment." Its communication policy is not to respond to rumors or speculation—and so these conjectures continued unabated. Similarly, Volvo chose a "no comment" strategy when asked about rumors that it would try to buy a rival German truck manufacturer. After offering the "no comment" response, the rumor continued to circulate and drove up the stock price of the rival truck maker. The general rule of thumb, then, is that a "no comment" response increases uncertainty.

There are times when direct and publicized approaches to

dispelling uncertainty are not desirable, feasible, appropriate, or legal. This may be especially true for rumors that possess gossipy elements—and it is certainly true for pure gossip. Open discussion of such hearsay in an official forum is not appropriate. Openly stating at a department meeting or publicly posting on the school district Web site that "Charlie is NOT having personal problems in his marriage!" would be strange indeed. A department meeting or Web site is not the right venue to discuss Charlie's personal life. Such an announcement would raise further questions and create greater uncertainty: "Why are we talking about Charlie's personal life at a department meeting?" "Is Charlie's marriage in trouble?" "I didn't know—I wonder if he drinks." "Perhaps he is having an affair with the manager." Also, dispelling uncertainty about why an employee was fired could be inappropriate and may be construed as defamation of character—and thus illegal. Managers are rightly hesitant to publicize such personnel matters and so rumors that the person was fired unfairly can flourish unhindered. In such circumstances, how can one effectively dispel or reduce uncertainty?

Fortune magazine advice columnist Anne Fisher reports one human resource manager's advice on this topic: "Get a few influential people and start your own rumors—accurate ones." In other words, develop a set of allies who are communication "hubs"— highly connected persons—and disperse the facts through this informal network. A study by communication researcher Keith Davis found that 20 percent of one office grapevine network consisted of highly connected hubs. Information can be disproportionately affected by them because messages tend to pass through them. The advantage of this approach is that the rumor can be dealt with through unofficial channels—a more appropriate forum for this type of hearsay. In addition, it may utilize more trusted sources than the individual who is the target of the rumor—and therefore be more persuasive to hearers. The disadvantage, of course, is that it takes time to develop such a network of allies. Another less direct way to dispel uncertainty is to provide pertinent, but not specific, information that will enable people to figure out the facts of a situation for themselves. In the case of rumors circulating just after an employee is fired, a savvy manager might send out a memo republishing the organization's policy on how terminations are conducted. For example, employees at one company were unaware that terminations involved repeated and documented negative performance appraisals. After a memo republishing the termination procedure, the employees inferred that there was good reason for the recent firing and rumors ceased about why the worker was sacked.

New experiences often give rise to fears that fuel rumors among children. Even a new librarian might be the object of a schoolchild's anxiety. Take the case of Mrs. Beamster, the fictional school librarian in the comical children's book *The Librarian from the Black Lagoon*. In this delightful story written by Mike Thaler and illustrated by Jared Lee, Mrs. Beamster was rumored to be a pretty tough bird. It was said that she laminated lads who talked or whispered—hence her nickname "the Laminator." She also glued antsy children to their seats to prevent movement and read card catalog indexes during story time. The library itself was thought to be a dangerous place—shelves were electrified to prevent students from touching the books, and these were bolted to the stacks anyway to keep kids from disordering them. The humorous tales grow more extreme—and funny—until the schoolchildren actually visit the library and meet Mrs. Beamster. She turns out to be much less fearsome than expected. In fact, she is warm and friendly—and invites them to freely explore the many funny books in the room.

Thaler's plot employs a long-known therapeutic technique for anxiety: talking about a fear, exaggerating it, and laughing at it. Simply exposing the fear to air and making it extreme and laughable helps us to cope with it. Thaler has written similar *Black Lagoon* books about rumors surrounding a new principal, cafeteria worker, teacher, class trip, and bus driver. These fun-to-read books serve a good purpose in reducing rumors by sapping the anxiety from which they spring.

New experiences also make adults anxious, and, as we know, often give rise to rumors. I've discussed many of the rumors that arise in contexts of change in organizations, such as mergers, takeovers, new technology, restructuring, layoffs, and new business strategies. Organizational consultant Larry Hirschhorn has suggested that many rumors can be reduced by systematically addressing legitimate anxieties. For example, managers can help to relieve fears by exploring the question "What is the worst-case scenario?" with those who could possibly face such scenarios. Confronting the worst that can happen often makes us realize what George Bailey attempted to convey: "Now, just remember that this thing isn't as black as it appears. . . ." Similarly, helping people prepare for the worst is anxiety relieving. Reminding people to back up their hard drives will reduce the fear of losing all of one's data from a supposed computer virus, and this reminder may actually reduce the spread of the rumor more than a statement that the rumor is false. Further, Hirschhorn suggests that members of the group through which a rumor is circulating can be enlisted in organized efforts to plan for any eventuality. Company employees facing layoffs, for example, can form committees that explore ways that the company can cut costs or can investigate possible employee retraining. Though this last idea is not often practiced and self-interest motivations would have to be overcome, it has always appealed to me as a way to productively harness the angst unleashed by dreaded potential consequences. Channeling anxiety in a constructive manner will lessen it; doing something is always more calming than doing nothing in such situations.

Of course, some anxieties are not rational. Therapists routinely deal with fears and phobias of objects and situations that are not in reality threatening, but which individuals are frightened by nonetheless. In fact, it's normal at times to unrealistically appraise a situation as threatening. Cognitive psychologists call such thinking "maladaptive" and attempt to help anxious persons understand the risks of the situation in a more rational manner. Irrational fears might simply be kiboshed with a *Black Lagoon*-type approach—that is, by making fun of them. Another method is to act in a manner that contradicts anxiety. People often don't know exactly how they should feel in a circumstance; seeing other people's behaviors often cues them about what emotion is appropriate. Seeing masses of people swarming toward a bank is likely to produce powerful feelings of anxiety, quite apart from any realistic fear one has about losing savings. When presented with a calm demeanor and smiles, however, people begin to feel that perhaps there is nothing to worry about. The point here is that a rumor manager should consider the various ways that anxiety—both legitimate and illegitimate—can be reduced.

The *Black Lagoon* series publisher provides a teacher's activity guide that not only helps students repel rumors about librarians, but also attempts to inoculate them from a variety of harmful hearsay. In this activity, students are first led in a discussion about rumors. They are defined as "a statement that people make about another person, place, or thing that is usually not founded in facts and is often untrue." Then students think of examples. Discussion questions guide pupils and point to the conclusion that rumors are usually negative and have harmful effects: "If you heard a bad rumor about someone, how would it make you treat that person?" "If you heard a bad rumor about a place, would you go there?" "How can rumors hurt people?" "What happens when rumors spread?" Students then brainstorm ways to stop rumors if they arise (an excellent teaching method). After this, they watch an animated version of the storybook. They then discuss how the rumors about Mrs. Beamster made the children in the story feel afraid of her and the library. Students also talk about experiences where they had been afraid of someone, something, or some place—and later learned that there was nothing to be frightened of. "Before I went to the (dentist, haunted house, school, school bus . . .) I felt _____. Afterward, I could see that the _____ was really _____." By comparing the rumors with reality, emphasis is laid upon the idea that the rumors turned out to be false—thus reducing the willingness of the children to trust in such rumors. All in all, the activity seeks to reduce the effects of harmful rumors by helping children cope with the fears expressed in them and by reducing their credulity.

Rumor workshops have similar goals—but usually for adults. Ralph Rosnow suggested these workshops as a way of training people about what rumors are, how they spread, and how they often harm people. Ralph thought that this type of training would help make people less credulous of rumors they heard. With repeated experience, for example, people can learn to suspend belief in the stories they hear and receive on the Internet. My own circle of family, friends, and colleagues has become increasingly skeptical as I have discussed the topic of rumor with them over time. In the rumor workshops I have conducted, participants are encouraged to establish a "checking norm": check the facts for all dubious statements that come your way. As more people in a group, team, or social network do this, the usefulness of checking becomes apparent and the practice spreads. A couple of years ago a friend called me to be sure that I viewed the night sky that evening. The story was that the planet Mars would be closer to Earth than it had been in 60,000 years (a true statement in 2003) and that it would appear as large as the Moon to the naked eye (a false statement that if true would have knocked Earth off its orbit around the sun). I was momentarily excited at the thought of two moons in the sky and the photographs I could take—when I realized that it might be false. A quick check of Snopes.com informed me that this false rumor has been circulating for quite some time. When I relayed this information to my friends, they saw the usefulness of checking. Now they tend to check themselves.

A checking norm could also be encouraged by sending a rumor-training e-mail to friends, family, employees, team members, and colleagues before rumors arise. The e-mail might run something like this (the reader should feel free to copy and send this message):

SUBJECT: Check the Facts

Hello. I learned something interesting recently: a lot of stuff you get on the Internet is garbage. Some of it might be spread by propaganda artists. Some of it is spread by well-meaning people, but it is false nonetheless.

I also learned how to check out those e-mail rumors and hoaxes that I receive all the time. Rumors can easily be checked by searching any of the following Web sites:

www.Snopes.com
www.TruthOrFiction.com
www.UrbanLegends.About.com
www.hoaxbusters.ciac.org

Each of these sites investigates a rumor, finds out if it is true or false, and then backs up the conclusion. I've pledged to first check my facts before I forward—I only want to pass along true information—and I encourage you to do so also.

PLEASE PASS THIS ON TO AS MANY PEOPLE AS YOU CAN AND YOU WILL RECEIVE $500 FROM A RICH BILLIONAIRE (JUST KIDDING☺).

A rumor manager can lessen the likelihood that potential and actual rumor participants will place faith in a rumor because they have fostered a checking norm and have helped people become more aware of how rumors can be false. The checking norm goes a long way to making rumor soil less fertile for rumor weeds.

One false rumor that has been around for more than a decade is that the fashion designer and clothing manufacturer Tommy Hilfiger was thrown off *The Oprah Winfrey Show* for making racist and anti-Semitic comments. The false story claims that Hilfiger stated, "If I had known African-Americans, Hispanics, Jews, and Asians would buy my clothes I would not have made them so nice. I wish these people would not buy my clothes, as they are made for upper-class white people." Whereupon—the false story alleges—Winfrey ejected him from the show and urged people to boycott the brand. A moment's thought will reveal that this rumor is absurd—a clothing manufacturer depends upon people purchasing his clothing—the more people who buy it, the better. Oprah has long posted a notice on her Web site about the falsity of this story, but it continued to dog Hilfiger and hurt sales. She refuted the rumor on air in 1999, and in 2007 Hilfiger actually appeared on the show to rebut the rumor in person:

OPRAH: Let's break this down. Tommy, in the twenty-one years that we've been on the air, have you ever been on the show before today?

TOMMY: Unfortunately, not.

OPRAH: And when you first heard it, Tommy, what did you think?

TOMMY: I didn't believe it. . . . Friends of mine said they heard the rumor. I said, 'That's crazy. That can't be. I was never on *The Oprah Show*. I would never say that.' And all my friends and family who know me and people who work with me and people who have grown up with me said that's crazy.

OPRAH: Well, did you ever say anything close to that? Where do you think this originated?

TOMMY: I have no idea. We hired FBI agents, I did an investigation, I paid investigators lots of money to go out and investigate, and they traced it back to a college campus but couldn't put their finger on it.

Hilfiger continued to explain how the rumor makes no economic sense: "I wanted to sell a lot of clothes to a lot of people." And that it had caused him heartache: "I have four children. My children would come home and say, 'Daddy, I go to school with a Jewish boy who says you don't like him.'" Ironically, Hilfiger founded a summer camp for inner-city children and helped raise funds for a Washington, D.C., monument to Martin Luther King Jr.—these actions render the rumor even more ludicrous. Oprah ended the interview with a strong instruction to listeners to help refute the rumor: "The next time somebody sends you an e-mail or somebody mentions this rumor to you, you know what you're supposed to say to them? You're supposed to say, 'That's a big fat lie.'"

As I discussed in Chapter 6, refutation will generally reduce belief in a rumor. Some refutations are better than others, however. A better refutation must first of all be based upon the truth. Don Quixote's maxim "Honesty is the best policy" applies here; it's the right thing to do. But in addition, it is futile to do otherwise.

Remember that people—when they want to and when they are able—are very good at eventually ferreting out the facts. Denying a true rumor is a dangerous strategy that may permanently impale your credibility. President Clinton's famous televised refutation of rumors about his affair with White House intern Monica Lewinsky—"I did not have sexual relations with that woman"—turned out to be a lie evident only weeks later. The denial of the facts eroded his credibility and contributed to his impeachment and the out-of-court settlement with Paula Jones.

Second, a better refutation is uttered by a source that is trusted. In research Prashant Bordia and I conducted, the refutation of a rumor that the undergraduate library would close down was more effective at dispelling uncertainty and anxiety when the source of the rebuttal was perceived as honest. Often the source of such a refutation is a trusted third party. Hilfiger's refutation is a great example of this. Oprah is not only a trusted source among groups through whom the rumor was likely to travel, but an authoritative one—if anyone would know whether or not she had ever thrown Hilfiger off the show, she would. Procter & Gamble's "truth kit" response to the false rumor that their company contributes to the Church of Satan includes letters from religious leaders and groups that the rumor was patently false; these included the late Rev. Jerry Falwell, the Rev. Billy Graham, the archbishop of Cincinnati, the Southern Baptist Convention, and the Church of the Nazarene. Among religious persons who might be interested in spreading that rumor, such refutations are almost impossible to discount. Religious authorities have also cooperated in denouncing the false rumor—circulating since 1975—that the late atheist Madalyn Murray O'Hair filed a petition with the Federal Communications Commission to ban religious broadcasting. The FCC has responded to millions of inquiries concerning this false story. And David

Dinkins—the African-American mayor of New York City—drank Tropical Fantasy Fruit Punch to aid Brooklyn Bottling's campaign against the story that its soda contained a substance that would cause sterility in black men. All of these refutations used trusted third-party spokespersons.

In a conflict, of course, trust is often hard to come by. This may explain the controversy surrounding the alleged events in the Hurriyah neighborhood of Baghdad in November 2006. According to the Associated Press, six Sunni Muslim worshippers were attacked, doused with kerosene, and burned alive by Shiite militiamen as they left Friday prayers—all while Iraqi Army soldiers looked on. These events allegedly occurred during the height of Iraqi sectarian violence, but, even so, constituted one of the most savage acts of brutality ever to occur in Baghdad. Iraqi Army officials and Iraq's interior minister, however, vigorously disputed the AP story, saying that they had dispatched forces to the neighborhood and had been unable to confirm the event. In addition—according to the interior minister—the nearby hospital received no burned dead bodies. One reported source of the story—a Captain Jamil Hussein—was not listed on the army or police staff rolls. According to the interior minister, the atrocity story was "a rumor," implying that it was part of the press's tendency to exaggerate sectarian tensions in Iraq. But the AP stuck to its story after revisiting the site, collecting further neighborhood eyewitness testimony, and photographing a burnt-out mosque graffitied with the words "blood wanted." The witnesses claimed that the bodies had been buried at a nearby cemetery. The incident and the issue of accuracy in reporting attracted a substantial amount of attention in the blogosphere. Did the atrocity occur or not? The answer to this depends in large part on which source you trust more: the Iraqi interior minister or the Associated Press.

Trust may indeed be the ingredient that prevents and reduces harmful rumors the most. It's also the most difficult asset to cultivate among conflicted parties. Trust is the belief that someone else has your best interests in mind. It is easily lost and hard to regain. Distrust toward others, official sources, and rival groups generally leads to more rumor activity. In a study of an organization undergoing a radical downsizing, distrust in management was a much better predictor of rumor spreading than feeling uncertain or anxious. Employees who distrusted management tended to participate in the rumor mill regardless of how much uncertainty or anxiety they were experiencing. For these employees, even a little uncertainty or anxiety was probably magnified by lack of trust. Conversely, those who trusted management seemed to participate in the rumor mill only when they were uncertain or anxious. Organizational management consultant Aubrey C. Daniels has stated that trust is what happens when you reliably pair what you say with what you do. This is not something that one can fake in the long term— if you utter lies they will eventually catch up to you. Remember that facts are stubborn things. Increasing trust, then, is one powerful way to prevent and manage harmful rumor—but it is a hard way.

Increased trust works in multiple ways. It should reduce the likelihood that self-enhancing wedge-driving rumors will latch onto the trusted individual or entity, if only because the "rival" group will be seen to be less of a rival. The "contact hypothesis" states that increased contact with members of rival groups— "reds" and "blues," white and black, Western and Middle Eastern— will decrease negative stereotyping, and it's likely that it will also decrease negative rumors. Perhaps this is one of the best reasons for exchange programs in which students from diverse lands change places for a year, giving two groups an opportunity to know one another a little better—and to develop trust. Increased trust is also an antidote to fear—greater trust in others will dampen the anxieties that so often spawn rumors. And increased trust reduces the believability of negative rumors. A rumor denigrating management becomes less believable when one has confidence that management is really looking out for employees. A rumor manager, then, should attempt to cultivate trust and to repair damaged trust, despite the difficulty of this task.

Third, a better refutation occurs earlier in the life of a rumor rather than later. Why? Like an epidemic of disease, after achieving a certain critical mass, the epidemic gets out of control. Early containment efforts will nip the rumor in the bud. I've mentioned how a sonar man might help detect rumors that have not yet been widely disseminated, and how hotlines, Web sites, and the development of a norm of transparency might aid also in this regard. For rumors that run rampant on the Internet, however, many companies have taken to monitoring Web sites, discussion groups, blogs, newsgroups, and chat rooms. Company personnel have been designated for this job, and many public relations firms perform this service. Monitoring can also be done on the cheap with robot Web crawler services such as BotSpot.com. Because a harmful rumor can propagate so rapidly on the Internet, early detection is crucial to heading off the false story before it reaches a critical mass. Once detected, the organization should be prepared to take swift action, by issuing a press release, announcement, or statement designed to clearly refute the rumor. Senator John McCain's campaign for president set up a "truth squad"—prominent individuals who were prepared to speak out quickly against any negative rumors that might have cropped up in the Republican primary election. McCain had been blindsided eight years earlier in South Carolina when a "whispering campaign" against him spread false tales that he had fathered an illegitimate black child. The rumor was patently false, but proliferated quickly in the Palmetto State, erasing his lead over George W. Bush. In 2008, the McCain campaign was prepared for such dirty politicking by recruiting prominent state Republican politicos beforehand—just in case.

Fourth, a better refutation comes with a context: explain why you are refuting. Merely issuing the denial of the rumor may raise uncertainty and lead hearers to wonder about your motives for delivering the statement. One conversational rule is that information should be appropriate or useful toward some purpose. The refutation "Bob Talbert is *not* part of the Mafia" introduced without warning will cause people to wonder if Talbert is trying to cover something up. Similarly, issuing the statement "PBR food products are not dangerous"—without any story about why PBR is making this statement—will raise questions about why this statement is necessary. Perhaps PBR has experienced cases of food poisoning lately or is involved in a cover-up. In the context of competition, one is often able to clearly state that malicious and false rumors are being circulated, perhaps by competitors, and thereby justify the need to set the record straight.

Fifth, a better refutation delivers a clear, detailed explanation with strong evidence for why the rumor is false. Sociologist Ralph H. Turner describes how rumors following earthquakes have been successfully rebutted in China by sending a credible team of experts to the area who collect rumors and issue clear, point-by-point responses. Such an explanation addresses uncertainty and reduces listener belief in the rumors. Thus, even in the midst of an anxious situation, rumors can be refuted successfully. Listing sources and evidence to support the refutation is a key element to hoax-busting Web sites such as Snopes.com. Hilfiger's refutation also contained elements of this by highlighting how the hearsay made no economic sense and how the clothing designer raised funds for the Martin

Luther King, Jr., National Memorial Project Foundation. The early Christian apologist Tertullian (160–225) strongly refuted false rumors that Christians ate babies and committed incest. In a work written to Roman authorities, Tertullian demonstrated how each of these rumors is impossible given Christian proscriptions against murder, infanticide, abortion, and even drinking the blood of animals.

Finally, a better refutation will convey to listeners clear directions about what they ought to do when encountering the rumor. It will seek to enlist hearers in not further propagating the rumor, and instead try to gain their help in spreading the refutation. Again, Oprah's instructions on this are clear: "You're supposed to say, 'That's a big fat lie.' "

In the week prior to the 2008 Democratic primary in South Carolina, Barack Obama stepped up his efforts to refute long-standing false rumors targeting him. According to Christian Broadcasting Network's David Brody, the rumors had been circulating freely within "evangelical circles" by e-mail for some time. They falsely alleged that Obama is (or was) a Muslim, joined the United Church of Christ only recently to downplay his Islamic faith, swore his oath of office on a Koran rather than the Bible, and refuses to recite the Pledge of Allegiance. In an interview with Brody on CBN, Obama first laid the context for his rebuttal by describing the rumors, then giving a point-by-point unequivocal refutation:

> I want to make sure that your viewers understand that I am a Christian who has belonged to the same church for almost twenty years now. It's where Michelle and I got married, it's where our kids were dedicated. I took my oath of office on our family Bible. I lead the Pledge of Allegiance when I open up the

Senate, I've been saying the Pledge of Allegiance since I was three years old.

The Obama campaign in South Carolina had also stepped up efforts to characterize him as a "committed Christian" who "felt the beckoning of the spirit and accepted Jesus Christ into his life." Such a religious faith, of course, is incompatible with rumors that he is a Muslim.

In the Brody interview, Obama then cast these rumors as part of a political smear campaign, and as personally offensive. By doing so, he laid to rest any possible uncertainty about why he was issuing these refutations:

> I think it's important for people *not* to buy into the kinds of dirty tricks that we've become so accustomed to in our politics. People need to understand so I'm unequivocal about this: I am not and never have been of the Muslim faith. I think that those who are of the Muslim faith are deserving of respect and dignity, but to try to feed into this fear-mongering and to try and question my faith commitments and my belief in Jesus Christ, I think is offensive.

Obama did not accuse any political rival of spreading these scurrilous tales but stated that "somehow they appear magically wherever the next primary or caucus is." Such a hint, of course, makes salient the possibility that a political competitor was promoting these falsehoods in order to damage him. The senator also indicated that the allegations offended him personally. It is perfectly natural, therefore, for him to respond in order to set the record straight.

Obama then specifically directed hearers of the rumor to delete the e-mail and spread the facts to their personal networks: "And I want to make absolutely clear about what's going on with this, and if they get another one of these e-mails that they're deleting it and letting their friends know that it's nonsense." This is a good refutation strategy. The candidate first of all spoke to the audience through which this rumor was most likely to be propagated. The refutation was a clear point-by-point response that gave strong evidence for why the rumors were false and gave clear reasons why the response itself was necessary. The refutation then asked for help. In studies of how people decide whether or not to intervene to help someone, bystanders who don't intervene fail to interpret the situation properly, fail to perceive their responsibility to help the person in need, or simply don't know what to do. Obama's statements address these concerns. He clearly conveys that the rumors should be interpreted as dirty politics, possibly spread by a rival camp. He then plainly tells people what to do in the event that they receive the rumor by e-mail: delete it and tell your friends that it is false. Persons hearing these refutation instructions are more likely to spread the facts.

Thus far I've explored how rumors may be managed by attempting to reduce the factors that give birth to them, such as uncertainty and anxiety, and by diminishing belief in them by reducing credulity, issuing good refutations, and fostering trust. Of course, they also have to circulate among people. Another time-honored strategy of managing rumor is therefore to attempt to decrease dissemination. One way of doing this is to bring your refutation messages to the networks where the rumor is spreading the most, as exemplified in the Obama example. Procter & Gamble sent "truth kits" to churches and religious groups. Hilfiger delivered his refutation on *The Oprah Winfrey Show*. Eric Miller's (Tropical Fantasy Fruit Punch) employees canvassed New York City's inner-city neighborhoods where the false rumor was spreading. All of these efforts brought the antidote message to "infected" populations.

A somewhat more forceful approach to tamping down dissemination is to punish spreaders. In India, it is a crime to start or spread false rumors that create panic after a disaster. Section 54 of the Disaster Management Act of 2005 states:

> Whoever makes or circulates a false alarm or warning as to disaster or its severity or magnitude, leading to panic, shall on conviction, be punishable with imprisonment which may extend to one year or fine.

Indian disaster-management personnel and police say that the chaos created by such rumors is dangerous and wastes an inordinate amount of resources. Speaking with news media in 2007, Prabhakar Deshmukh, chairman of the District Disaster Management Authority in the Pune district of the Maharashtra state, stated: "We have witnessed how false warnings circulating during flood situations in the past two monsoons created unnecessary panic." Deshmukh described how rumors of flooding and bursting dams circulating after the monsoons "had created unnecessary panic" and "immense chaos and confusion." He continued, "Strict action is needed against rumour mongers because such false alarms cause waste of time and energy." In general, the long arm of the law doesn't appreciate hoaxes and rumors that disrupt the common peace. After discovering that a rumor of a shoot-out and a bombing prior to the Hindu festival of Rath Yatra were hoaxes, Indian police in Ahmedabad vigorously attempted to discern the origin of these rumors and promised to punish the spreaders, whom they characterized as "miscreants who do not want the Rath Yatra to pass peacefully." The police commissioner promised that the rumor-mongers would "be dealt with very severely."

Even spreading rumors in high school—if they disrupt the normal flow of daily events—can invoke the wrath of authorities. Two Blackman High School students in Rutherford County, Tennessee, were suspended for three days following an investigation by school officials that they spread a rumor that another boy was about to bring a gun to school and shoot everyone. The rumor was false, but caused the school to close down. The rumor had disrupted and panicked the school community. The two students were suspended despite objections by their parents that the rumor was disseminated by numerous persons in the class at the same time. These examples should give one cause to pause a moment before spreading a story—it might be a hoax that the police—and your principal—don't look kindly on.

Corporations also don't like false rumors being spread about them, and sometimes they sue those who do the spreading. Recall that Procter & Gamble successfully sued four Amway distributors for $19.25 million because they had disseminated the false Satanism rumor. (The case may still be appealed.) This was not the first time that P&G had sued persons who had disbursed the falsehood. Companies are increasingly employing this type of strategy when confronted with "cybersmear" campaigns that harm their reputation or stock value. After anonymous postings to a Yahoo! message board that falsely denigrated the management of Phillips Services Corporation, the Canadian company filed suit for defamation. According to attorney Blake A. Bell of Simpson Thacher & Bartlett, LLP, the list of lawsuits against cyber rumormongers is growing and includes e*Trade Inc., Sunbeam Corp., National Semiconductor Corp., and Amplicon Inc. Lawsuits do not only emanate from large companies. Bell gives an example of a small Caribbean inn that filed suit after an anonymous posting on an America Online discussion site falsely claimed that the resort's scuba diving practices were unsafe.

Any rumor that harms a company, perhaps by revealing confidential corporate information, may become an occasion for a legal battle. In December 2004, thirteen-year-old Nick Ciarelli accurately predicted that the Apple Corporation would unveil the Mac mini, iPod shuffle, and iWork productivity suite at the Macworld Expo two weeks later. He was right. Evidently this youngster had inside sources. Claiming that Ciarelli had divulged trade secrets, Apple then slapped his site, ThinkSecret.com, with a lawsuit that eventually resulted in a settlement agreement. Ciarelli did not have to reveal his sources and in return agreed to shut down his Web site by February 2008. These examples should also give one pause before spreading a story that disparages or divulges—you may end up being the object of a lawsuit.

Though harmful rumors may still persist despite the best efforts to ameliorate them, the strategies I discussed in this chapter should go a long way toward taming and trimming them. They embody how we can help people make better sense together in a more positive, helpful, honest, and useful way.

Epilogue
Doing Rumor Well

*To admit that knowledge is intrinsically
erroneous is not to imply that we should
forgo it. The tragedy of knowledge is
not that it is inadequate but that,
inadequate as it is, it is indispensable.
Knowledge is a poor guide, but no
knowledge is no guide at all. That as
knowers we are condemned to do what
we cannot do well should lead not to
despair but to trying harder and having
more modest expectations.*

—WILLIAM J. McGUIRE, NOTED
SOCIAL PSYCHOLOGIST (1925–2007)

THIS BOOK IS ABOUT COLLECTIVE WISDOM in the midst of
uncertainty. Two paradoxical insights about humanity have
impressed themselves upon me more and more over the many
years that I've conducted research on rumor: Much of our experience is uncertain, and groups possess the capacity to overcome this
uncertainty.

On the one hand, I'm increasingly aware of the copious clouds
of uncertainty that occupy the airspace of our experience. My
daughter recently asked me why the facts of a particular topic did
not seem to be generally known among the many people that she

knew and in the media of the larger culture. I responded that knowledge is only awarded to those who really seek after it—and even then it is sometimes elusive. I was reminded of just how difficult it can be to make proper sense of any particular matter, even in our modern age of electronic interconnectedness, education, technology, and science. To *know* something, even in a favorable informational environment, requires effort, time, tenacity, interest, opportunity, and disciplined habits of the heart and mind. Psychologists have been mostly pessimistic on this topic and we have a right to be so; there are long and illustrious lines of research on errors and biases in individual and collective human perception and judgment. I've explored many of these in the pages of this book. I'm only too aware of the cognitive, motivational, emotional, situational, and social forces that seem to conspire against right knowledge, solid facts, and nuanced understandings. At the very least, knowing about these forces calls for an attitude of humility when we regard what we think we know, a ruthless assessment of how thin our understanding really is, and a sober appreciation for the hard work it will take to acquire wisdom.

On the other hand, I've been impressed with how communities working together can sometimes overcome uncertainty. At the moment I wrote this paragraph, I was also communicating by e-mail with two groups of people to resolve two different episodes of uncertainty. One incident concerned the use of Google Calendar by our department. It began when I recently scheduled a room using this online planning device, arrived to use the facility, and found it occupied by another professor. When I brought the problem up, she stated that she had indeed scheduled the room. This was perplexing, and I experienced a brief sense of uncertainty. Through discussion with a third faculty member, we discovered that when she made changes they didn't seem to register on the common calendar. I suggested that she might be editing her own rather than the common calendar, and the other professor concurred. This turned out to be the case and we happily made sense of the matter. A second episode concerned an anxious parent of a student who wanted to drop a course that she was not doing so well in. They were uncertain what to do because they had been given conflicting answers about what would happen if she dropped the class. It was of concern to them that such an action might make her a part-time student and adversely affect her financial aid. With some discussion and checking with people in the know, we were able to answer these questions. (Dropping the course would indeed reduce her to part-time status, but not her financial aid.) Though the parent and the student still have to make a decision, they are now more certain about what the consequences of the decision are.

Of course, these examples are the happy sort of resolution that occurs when people trust one another, ideas can be checked, parties can communicate freely, and everyone is primarily interested in ferreting out the facts. The process worked so smoothly that the "rumors" involved—the statements we passed around while trying to make sense of the situation—barely emerged as rumors per se. They hardly had a chance to circulate. Wouldn't it be nice—or at least involve less drama—if all of our uncertainties followed a similar life path? Our common experience, however, suggests that they often do not. It is all too easy to imagine how even these mundane situations could have gone awry. If the circumstances had involved distrust and infighting, a rumor of "calendar sabotage" might have gained currency and spread to other faculty. If the parent had been faced with the inability to communicate with me quickly, he might have relied on speculation circulating among other parents about financial aid to part-timers. Other life circumstances are even more intractable and powerful, and actively hamper our best efforts to make sense of the situation. But my point here is that, at times, good sensemaking is possible—and it often happens.

Theodore Caplow's wartime rumors were essentially 100 percent accurate and comprehensive in advance of official announcements. Like the fake statue itself, the truth about the Cardiff Giant was eventually uncovered. Thousands of rumors have been investigated, verified, and falsified by hoax busters Barbara and David P. Mikkelson on their Web site Snopes.com. News reporters from the *Times-Picayune*—operating under difficult postdisaster circumstances—corrected the false and grossly exaggerated rumors of rape, murder, and mayhem that flourished after Hurricane Katrina devastated New Orleans. Male New Yorkers of color purchase Tropical Fantasy Fruit Punch without fear of sterilization. Fewer and fewer people hear the false story of Satanism that dogged P&G over the years. The readers of this book will now continue to blink their lights as neighborly drivers should when seeing an oncoming vehicle without its headlights on at night, unafraid of being murdered as part of a gruesome gang initiation. My friends do not fear that their hard drives will be erased when they happen upon a teddy bear icon. My family does not schedule a midnight bout of sky gazing upon hearing that the planet Mars will appear in the sky as large as the Moon. Residents of the postwar community that Leon Festinger studied stopped believing that the volunteer leading the nursery school initiative was a Communist. Those who hear me lecture at length on rumor know that George W. Bush and John Kerry did not misquote the Bible. Oprah's many fans do not believe that Tommy Hilfiger was once ejected from her show. And the ancient Romans eventually abandoned their false belief that early Christians sacrificed babies. Ferreting out the facts is a distinct potential possibility for a community, especially if they know something about rumors.

What does it mean to understand rumors? It means appreciating how powerful rumors can be, and how they contribute to or cause many outcomes. It means being aware of the profoundly social processes involved in making sense of our world—for good and for bad. It means accepting the teamlike nature of ferreting out the facts of a situation. It means understanding the truth-seeking, social, propagandistic, self-serving, or artistic desires that can lay— and lie—beneath rumor discussions. It means possessing a degree of soberness when deciding what to believe, a modicum of humility when hearing what other people believe, and a pinch of playfulness when hearing stories of any variety. It means reading "between the lines" of a tale for the concerns, beliefs, fears, and precommitments of the humans through whom the narrative moves. It means a new appreciation for how threatening it is to hear your favorite rumor squashed. It means carefully checking. It means possessing the fortitude to refrain from passing something on. It means suspending belief in a story, especially in moments of fear and panic. It means extending the benefit of the doubt to someone, especially when trust is ebbing. It means seeking to help people express their best selves when engaged in making sense and coping with threat. Understanding rumors means becoming kinder, nobler, more discerning, more helpful, more humble, sharper in our thinking, and more charitable in our feeling. It means engaging in the basic human activity of making sense together in a way that is at once more difficult and more deeply gratifying. It means having a greater appreciation for truth.

Rumor is something that we do as humans together; my hope is this book will help us to rumor well.

Acknowledgments

I am indebted to my many bright and talented colleagues. The foremost of these, to whom I owe much, is Ralph L. Rosnow. Ralph continues to be an example of a diligent scholar, a man of his word, and an encouraging mentor. Another bright star in this regard is Prashant Bordia, my friend, frequent collaborator, and a gentle—yet penetrating—intellectual. I also wish to thank the many scholars that I have been fortunate to work with in my thinking about these topics over the years: Charles Walker, Eric Foster, Gary A. Fine, Jerry Suls, Marty Bourgeois, Bernard Brooks, Chris Homan, David Ross, John Yost, Jason Beckstead, Mark Pezzo, Chip Heath,

Jack Felton, Anthony Pratkanis, Frederick Koenig, Donald Hantula, and Holly Hom. I thank Theodore Caplow for his aid in understanding the background of his military rumors study; Jim Esposito for clarifying his 1986 SEPTA strike study to me; Daniel E. Phillips for leading me to Jewish ethical teaching on gossip; Anthony DiFonzo for his help in understanding military culture and terminology; and Chris DiFonzo for editorial assistance with regard to the Cardiff Giant story. I appreciate the help of many students in projects touching upon rumor: Lisa Burt, Jenna Crawford, Jennifer Taylor, Juliana Lehr, Scott Rabideau, Noah Stupak, Samuel Brougher, Meghan Frazee, Nicole Robinson, Andrew J. Younge, Alex Samachisa, Kate Walders, Erik Merriman, Deanna Olles, Rob Winterkorn, David Longo, Joel Harmon, Sumaiya Salim, Nick Schwab, Matt McKinlay, Diana McKee, David Weiss, Justin Blum, Melody Buchanan, Captain Stephanie Kelley, and Daniel Shuman.

I wish to especially thank my excellent editor, Jeff Galas, for his encouragement, assistance, vision, and persistence. This book was actually his brainchild; I could not ask for a finer editor. Special thanks also to the able staff at Avery Publishing, including Diane Hodges for superb copyediting and Gary Mailman, Esq., for careful vetting.

I acknowledge funding from the National Science Foundation (Grant No. BCS-0527371) for three recent studies whose preliminary results are described in this book.

Last but not least, this book would not have seen print without the unfailing encouragement and support of my wife, Margaret DiFonzo. Margaret has also been my close intellectual companion, offering many insights into human nature and discussing many ideas found in the pages of this book. She, along with Michele DiFonzo and Nick P. DiFonzo, were also willing sounding boards to portions of previous drafts.

Notes

1. To Rumor Is Human

The Paul of Tarsus quotation is taken from:

1 Corinthians 13:12 of the *New International Version* of the Bible.

Rumors about the Secretary of the Navy in 1876 were reported in:

"The rumors of Naval corruption" (1876, March 7). *The New York Times*. Retrieved March 7, 2008, from http://query.nytimes.com/gst/abstract.html?res=9D04EFD91E3FE73BBC4F53DFB56683 8D669FDE

Rumors of anti-sailor signs are documented in:

Mikkelson, B. (2005, November 8). "Keep off the grass." Retrieved March 7, 2008, from http://snopes.com/military/keepoff .asp

Melville's 1850 novel *White-Jacket* may be found at:

http://www.gutenberg.org/files/10712/10712.txt

Readers may learn about Alexander Litvinenko in the following news accounts:

"Pair tests positive for Polonium" (2006, December 1). BBC News UK. Retrieved February 3, 2008, from http://news.bbc.co.uk/ 1/hi/uk/6199464.stm

"Timeline: Litvinenko death case" (2007, July 27). BBC News UK. Retrieved February 3, 2008, from http://news.bbc.co.uk/2/ hi/uk_news/6179074.stm

Rumors in the aftermath of September 11, 2001, are described in:

Mikkelson, B. (2001, October 11). "Ryders of the storm." Retrieved December 2, 2005, from http://www.snopes.com/rumors/ ryder.htm

Mikkelson, B. (2001, October 26). "Dust in the wind." Retrieved December 2, 2005, from http://www.snopes.com/rumors/crop dust.htm

"Monday, Monday" (2002, October 1). Retrieved December 16, 2005, from http://www.snopes.com/rumors/fema.htm

Rumors surrounding the closing of the GM plant in Ypsilanti are reported in:

Rimer, S. (1992, September 7). "American dream put on hold at car plant doomed to shut." *The New York Times*, 1, 40.

Ralph Rosnow documented how his interest in rumor was piqued in:
Rosnow, R. L. (1991). "Inside rumor: A personal journey." *American Psychologist, 46,* 484–496.

An intriguing synopsis of the "Paul Is Dead" rumor is chronicled on the Beatles newsgroup site:
http://www.recmusicbeatles.com/public/files/faqs/pid.html

Ralph's contribution to the topic of rumor psychology has been reviewed in:
DiFonzo, N. & Bordia, P. (2006). "Rumor in organizational contexts." In D. A. Hantula (ed.), *Advances in Social and Organizational Psychology: A Tribute to Ralph Rosnow* (pp. 249–274). Mahwah, NJ: Lawrence Erlbaum Associates.

The study of rumors published in *The Wall Street Journal* can be found in:
Pound J., & Zeckhauser, R. (1990). "Clearly heard on the street: The effect of takeover rumors on stock prices." *Journal of Business, 63,* 291–308.

The experiment on how news affected individual trading behavior can be found in:
Andreassen, P. B. (1987). "On the social psychology of the stock market: Aggregate attributional effects and the regressiveness of prediction." *Journal of Personality and Social Psychology, 53,* 490–496.

My work showing that rumors affect stock-trading behavior in a similar manner as news—despite being regarded as less credible than news—is reported in:
DiFonzo, N., & Bordia, P. (1997). "Rumor and prediction: Making

sense (but losing dollars) in the stock market." *Organizational Behavior and Human Decision Processes, 71, 329–353.*

Susan T. Fiske's conviction that humans are fundamentally social beings is expressed fully in her excellent text:

Fiske, S. T. (2004). *Social Beings: A Core Motives Approach to Social Psychology.* Hoboken, NJ: John Wiley & Sons.

With Prashant Bordia, I have addressed many of the questions surrounding rumor in a more technical manner in:

DiFonzo, N., & Bordia, P. (2007). *Rumor Psychology: Social and Organizational Approaches.* Washington, D.C.: American Psychological Association.

A rumor survey may be taken at my Web site RumorExpert .com.

2. Swimming in Rumors

The Good Times virus hoax is falsified in:

"U.S. Dept. of Energy Computer Incident Advisory Capability" (1995, April 24). CIAC Notes Number 95–09. Retrieved February 25, 2008, from http://ciac.llnl.gov/ciac/notes/Notes09 .shtml

The searches using "rumor or rumour" were performed March 26, 2007.

The prevalence of rumors in organizations is investigated in:

DiFonzo, N., & Bordia, P. (2000). "How top PR professionals handle hearsay: Corporate rumors, their effects, and strategies to manage them." *Public Relations Review, 26, 173–190.*

The false rumor that most Americans are dehydrated is discussed in:
Mikkelson, B., & Mikkelson, D. P. (2005, December 31). "Eight glasses." Retrieved February 23, 2008, from http://www.snopes.com/medical/myths/8glasses.asp

Exaggerated Hurricane Katrina rumors were chronicled in:
Dwyer, J. C., & Drew, C. (2005, September 29). "Fear exceeded crime's reality in New Orleans." *The New York Times,* A1, A22.

Talk-show rumors about illegal aliens from Jamaica were reported in:
Feagans, B. (2007, March 25). "Foreign teachers test policy." *The Atlanta Journal-Constitution,* 1A.

Some evidence for our capacity for gullibility is found in:
Gilovitch, T. (1991). *How We Know What Isn't So: The Fallibility of Human Reason in Everyday Life.* New York: Free Press.
Standing, L. G., & Huber, H. (2003). "Do psychology courses reduce belief in psychological myths?" *Social Behavior and Personality, 31*(6), 585–592.
Langenderfer, J., & Shimp, T. A. (2001). "Consumer vulnerability to scams, swindles, and fraud: A new theory of visceral influences on persuasion." *Psychology & Marketing, 18*(7), 763–783.

The categorization of wish, dread, and wedge-driving rumors was set forth in:
Knapp, R. H. (1944). "A psychology of rumor." *Public Opinion Quarterly, 8,* 22–27.

VE and VJ wish rumors were documented in:
Allport, G. W., & Postman, L. J. (1947). *The Psychology of Rumor.* New York: Holt, Rinehart & Winston.

The spread of SARS rumors amid fears and uncertainty was explored in:

Jardin, X. (2003, April 21). "Text messaging feeds SARS rumors." *Wired.* Retrieved February 23, 2008, from http://www.wired .com/medtech/health/news/2003/04/58506

Stephanie Kelley's analysis of Baghdad rumors may be found in:

Kelley, S. R. (2004). "Rumors in Iraq: A guide to winning hearts and minds." Unpublished master's thesis, Naval Postgraduate School, Monterey, CA. Retrieved November 16, 2004, from http:// theses.nps.navy.mil/04Sep_Kelley.pdf

Rumors of exploding Indian cell phones are described in:

"Explosive rumor of killer mobile phone calls creates panic in Indian Kashmir" (2007, March 30). *International Herald Tribune* (Asia-Pacific). Retrieved February 23, 2008, from http://www .iht.com/articles/ap/2007/03/31/asia/AS-GEN-Kashmir -Explosive-Rumor.php

Rumors of Senator Obama's terrorist training were reported in:

Goldenberg, S. (2007, Jan. 26). "Candidate Obama attacks madrasa smear." *The Guardian,* London, 19.

Rumors of Senator Clinton's involvement in spreading these rumors was discussed in:

Beck, G., & Burguiere, S. (2007, January 19). "Is Hillary Clinton Spreading Rumors about Senator Obama?" *Glenn Beck Show,* CNN Transcript 011901cb.ho2.

Bush-Rice rumors were published in:

Layne, K., (2006, June 22). "The Bush-Condi rumors: An update." *Wonkette: The DC Gossip.* Washington, D.C. Retrieved February 23,

2008, from http://wonkette.com/politics/white-house/the-bush+
condi-rumors-an-update-182711.php

Internal, external, and organizational change rumors are investigated in:
DiFonzo, N., & Bordia, P. (2000). "How top PR professionals handle
   hearsay: Corporate rumors, their effects, and strategies to manage them." *Public Relations Review, 26,* 173–190.
DiFonzo, N., Bordia, P., & Rosnow, R. L. (1994). "Reining in
   Rumors." *Organizational Dynamics, 23*(1), 47–62.

Change rumors are studied in:
Bordia, P., Jones, E., Gallois, C., Callan, V., & DiFonzo, N. (2006).
   "Management are aliens! Rumors and stress during organiza-
   tional change." *Group & Organization Management, 31*(5), 601–621.

The Sheik restaurant rumor is detailed in:
Langlois, J. L. (2005). " 'Celebrating Arabs' ": Tracing legend and
   rumor labyrinths in post-9/11 Detroit." *Journal of American Folklore, 118*(468), 219–236.
Zaslow, J. (2002, March 13). "How a rumor spread by e-mail laid
   low an Arab's restaurant." *The Wall Street Journal,* New York,
   p. A1.

Product rumors are discussed in:
Koenig, F. W. (1985). *Rumor in the Marketplace: The Social Psychology of
   Commercial Hearsay.* Dover, MA: Auburn House.
Fine, G. A. (1992). *Manufacturing Tales: Sex and Money in Contemporary
   Legends.* Knoxville, TN: University of Tennessee Press.

The AIDS-infected melon rumor was reported in:
Nahmius, R. (2007, April 4). "Israeli melons have AIDS." Ynetnews,

Tel Aviv. Retrieved April 16, 2007, from http://www.ynetnews
.com/articles/0,7340,L-3387545,00.html

"Drop in fruit sales after rumours" (2007, April 14). *The Peninsula,*
Doha, Qatar. Retrieved April 16, 2007, from http://www.the
peninsulaqatar.com/Display_news.asp?section=local_news&mo
nth=april2007&file=local_news20070414803.xml

The relation between rumors and trust is investigated in:

DiFonzo, N., & Bordia, P. (1998). "A tale of two corporations: Managing uncertainty during organizational change." *Human Resource
Management,* 37(3&4), 295–303.

DiFonzo, N., & Bordia, P. (2007). *Rumor Psychology: Social and Organizational Approaches.* Washington, D.C.: American Psychological
Association, Chapter 8.

The shopping mall lavatory mutilation rumors were documented in:

Rosenthal, M. (1971). "Where rumor raged." *Trans-Action, 8*(4),
34–43.

The John 16:3 Kerry–Bush rumors are recorded in:

Mikkelson, B., & Mikkelson, D. P. (2004, August 23). "Verses, Foiled
Again." Retrieved November 25, 2005, from http://www.snopes
.com/politics/bush/bibleverse.asp

The relation between rumor and riots is studied in:

Kakar, S. (2005). "Rumors and religious riots." In G. A. Fine,
V. Campion-Vincent, & C. Heath (eds.), *Rumor Mills: The Social
Impact of Rumor and Legend* (pp. 53–59). NY: Aldine.

Knopf, T. A. (1975). *Rumors, Race and Riots.* New Brunswick, NJ:
Transaction Books.

The rumor that police chased an Aboriginal boy is reported in:

Chulov, M., Warne-Smith, D., & Colman, E. (2004, February 17). "Rumour the spark that fired racial tinderbox." *The Australian,* pp. 1, 6.

The statistic that 65 percent of civil rights–era riots were sparked by rumor may be found in:

Kerner, O., Lindsay, J. V., Harris, F. R., Abel, I. W., Brooke, E. W., Thornton, C. B., et al. (1968). *Report of the National Advisory Commission on Civil Disorders.* (Report No. 1968 O–291–729). Washington, D.C.: U.S. Government Printing Office.

Stock market rumor effects are investigated in:

Lazar, R. J. (1973). "Stock market price movements as collective behavior." *International Journal of Contemporary Sociology, 10,* 133–147.

Rose, A. M. (1951). "Rumor in the stock market." *Public Opinion Quarterly, 15,* 461–486.

Pound J., & Zeckhauser, R. (1990). "Clearly heard on the street: The effect of takeover rumors on stock prices." *Journal of Business, 63,* 291–308.

Schindler, M. (2007). *Rumors in Financial Markets: Insights into Behavioral Finance.* Chichester, England: John Wiley & Sons.

The March 2007 Iranian incident that boosted oil prices is reported in:

"Oil up $1 after brief spike on Iran rumor" (2007, March 28). *Budapest Business Journal.* Retrieved February 26, 2008, from http://www.bbj.hu/news/news_24567.html

Athanasiadis, I. (2007, March 28). "Blair warns Iran of next 'phase' in standoff." *The Washington Times,* A1.

The study investigating the effects of hearing negative organizational rumors is reported in Chapter 2 of:

DiFonzo, N., & Bordia, P. (2007). *Rumor Psychology: Social and Organizational Approaches.* Washington, D.C.: American Psychological Association.

Propaganda rumors are discussed in:

DiFonzo, N., & Bordia, P. (2007). "Rumors influence: Toward a dynamic social impact theory of rumor." In A. R. Pratkanis (ed.), *The Science of Social Influence: Advances and Future Progress.* (pp.271–296). Philadelphia, PA: Psychology Press.

Germany's use of rumor in World War II is presented in:

Knapp, R. H. (1944). "A psychology of rumor." *Public Opinion Quarterly, 8,* 22–27.

Rumors circulating in Grenoble, France, are discussed in:

Kapferer, J. N. (1990). *Rumors: Uses, Interpretations, and Images.* (B. Fink, trans.). New Brunswick, NJ: Transaction Publishers, 217. (Original work published 1987 as *Rumeurs: Le Plus Vieux Média du Monde* [Rumors: The world's oldest media]. Paris: Editions du Seuil.)

Whispering campaigns are discussed in:

Allport, G. W., & Postman, L. J. (1947). *The Psychology of Rumor.* New York: Holt, Rinehart & Winston.

The use of rumor by Saddam Hussein is detailed in:

Al-Marashi, I. (2002, September). "Iraq's security and intelligence network: A guide and analysis." *Middle East Review of International Affairs (MERIA) Journal, 6*(3), 1–13. Retrieved February 4, 2008, from http://meria.idc.ac.il/journal/2002/issue3/al-marashi.pdf

Slackman, M. (2003, June 5). "Ruled by rumors in Iraq." *Los Angeles Times,* A1.

The origin of rumors of weapons of mass destruction is discussed in:
Dwyer, J. (2004, July 9). "Defectors' reports on Iraq arms were embellished, exile asserts." *The New York Times,* A1.

Belief in cancer rumors is investigated in:
Gansler, T., Henley, S. J., Stein, K., Nehl, E. J., Smigal, C., & Slaugher, E. (2005, August 1). "Sociodemographic determinants of cancer treatment health literacy." *Cancer, 104*(3), 653–660.

The false Johns Hopkins Hospital e-mail is described in:
Mikkelson, B., & Mikkelson, D. P. (2007, April 3). "Cancer Update." Retrieved February 26, 2008, from http://www.snopes.com/medical/disease/cancerupdate.asp

The December 7, 2005, NPR *Talk of the Nation* radio program, "Anatomy of a Rumor," can be heard at:
http://www.npr.org/templates/story/story.php?storyId=5042756

The Visine rumor and prank by five Wisconsin high school students is recounted in:
Mikkelson, B. (2006, November 17). "Mickey Red Eyes." Retrieved July 18, 2007, from http://www.snopes.com/medical/myths/visine.asp.

The investigation of beliefs in conspiracy theories is reported in:
Abalakina-Paap, M., & Stephan, W. G. (1999). "Beliefs in conspiracies." *Journal of Political Psychology, 20*(3), 637–647.

The Indian Disaster Management Act of 2005 may be viewed at:
http://rajyasabha.nic.in/bills-ls-rs/2005/LV_2005.pdf

Rumors following Hurricane Andrew are reported in:
Rohter, L. (1992, September 5). "After the storm; rumors abound of storm deaths going untallied." *The New York Times,* 6.

The law of cognitive structure activation is theorized in:
Sedikides, C., & Skowronski, J. J. (1991). "The law of cognitive structure activation." *Psychological Inquiry, 2,* 169–184.

The study of rumors of mental illness is reported in:
Lehr, J. C. (2007). "The Effect of Negative Mental Health Rumors on College Students' Social Judgments: Psychology versus Non-Psychology Majors" [Unpublished Senior Project]. Department of Psychology, Rochester Institute of Technology, Rochester, NY. (As mentioned in the text, only results from the non-psychology student conditions are reported; psychology majors were unaffected by the rumors.)

The worm meat rumor study is published in:
Tybout, A. M., Calder, B. J., & Sternthal, B. (1981). "Using information processing theory to design marketing strategies." *Journal of Marketing Research, 18*(1), 73–79.

Conceiving rumors as explanations is explored in:
DiFonzo, N., & Bordia, P. (1997). "Rumor and prediction: Making sense (but losing dollars) in the stock market." *Organizational Behavior and Human Decision Processes, 71*(3), 329–353.
DiFonzo, N., & Bordia, P. (2002). "Rumor and stable-cause attribution in prediction and behavior." *Organizational Behavior and Human Decision Processes, 88,* 785–800.

The raison d'etre quotation is found on p. 121 of:

Allport, G. W., & Postman, L. J. (1947). *The Psychology of Rumor*. New York: Holt, Rinehart & Winston.

The view that stock price changes are random is set forth in:

Fama, E. F., Fisher, L., Jensen, M. C., & Roll, R. (1969). "The adjustment of stock prices to new information." *International Economic Review, 10,* 1–21.

The Arlington, Tennessee, school shooting rumor is reported in:

Kuebler, B. (2007). "School shooting rumor keeps many Arlington High School students home." WREG News Channel 3, Memphis, TN. Retrieved February 26, 2008, from http://www.wreg.com/Global/story.asp?s=6281781

Negativity bias is explored in:

Baumeister, R. F., Bratslavsky, E., Finkenauer, C., & Vohs, K. D. (2001). "Bad is stronger than good." *Review of General Psychology, 5,* 323–370.

Equity theory is outlined in:

Adams, J. S. (1965). "Inequity in social exchange." In L. Berkowitz (ed.), Advances in Experimental Social Psychology (vol. 2; pp. 267–296). New York: Academic Press.

The law of rumor is found in:

Allport, G. W., & Postman, L. J. (1947). *The Psychology of Rumor*. New York: Holt, Rinehart & Winston.

The Baghdad rumor is recorded in:

The Baghdad Mosquito, 6 July 2007, volume IV, edition, 1379, p. 6 (20070706_BM_Rumors.doc Received from bagskeet@yahoogroups.com on July 7, 2007).

Social learning theory is summarized in:

Lott, B. E., & Lott, A. J. (1985). "Learning theory in contemporary social psychology." In G. Lindzey & E. Aronson (eds.) *Handbook of Social Psychology* (3rd ed., vol. 1, pp. 109–135), New York: Random House.

Self-fulfilling prophecy is discussed in:

Rosenthal, R., & Jacobson, L. (1968). *Pygmalion in the Classroom: Teacher Expectation and Pupils' Intellectual Development.* New York: Holt, Rinehart & Winston.

The Continental Bank story is chronicled in:

Koenig, F. W. (1985). *Rumor in the Marketplace: The Social Psychology of Commercial Hearsay.* Dover, MA: Auburn House, pp. 150–151.

3. It's Clear That It's Unclear

The Nostradamus rumor is documented in:

Zorn, E. (2001, September 20). "Rush to cite Nostradamus too predictable." *Chicago Tribune,* 1.

Rumors in the aftermath of September 11, 2001, are described in:

Tucker, N. (2001, October 13). "All around, a chill in the air; FBI warnings, persistent rumors add to area's safety concerns." *The Washington Post,* A01.

Wallack, T. (2001, October 3). "A horde of hoaxes; The Internet has been rife with phony rumors related to Sept. 11 terrorist attacks." *San Francisco Chronicle,* D1.

Deener, B. (2001, September 20). "Rumors rattle market." *The Dallas Morning News.*

Recent definitions and descriptions of the contents, contexts, and functions of rumor may be found in:

DiFonzo, N. (2008). "Rumors." In William A. Darity Jr. (editor-in-chief), *International Encyclopedia of the Social Sciences* (vol. 7, 2nd ed., pp. 295–298). Detroit: Macmillan Reference USA (Thomson Gale).

DiFonzo, N., & Bordia, P. (2007). "Rumor, gossip, and urban legends." *Diogènes 213, 54*(1), 19–35.

The Harry Potter rumor is described in:

"Harry Potter worm claims teenage wizard is dead." (2007, June 28). *Sophos Inc.* Retrieved February 26, 2008, from http://www.sophos.com/pressoffice/news/articles/2007/06/hairy.html

The Tropical Fantasy rumor is described in:

Freedman, A. M. (1991, May 10). "Rumor turns fantasy into bad dream." *The Wall Street Journal,* B1, B5.

The headlights hoax is reported in:

Vigoda, R. (1993, Nov. 5). "Heard about the headlights? The big lie comes sweeping into town." *Philadelphia Inquirer,* B1, B8.

Michael Owen rumors are discussed in:

"Owen rejects Newcastle exit talk" (2007, July 12). ESPNsoccernet-England. Retrieved July 31, 2007, from http://soccernet.espn.go.com/news/story?id=445035&cc=5901

Ralph Rosnow's discussion of outcome relevance can be found in:

Rosnow, R. L. (1991). "Inside rumor: A personal journey." *American Psychologist, 46,* 484–496.

Saddam Hussein's use of rumor is detailed in:

Slackman, M. (2003, June 5). "Ruled by rumors in Iraq." *Los Angeles Times,* A1.

Hurricane Katrina rumors that turned out to be false are reported in:
Dwyer, J. C., & Drew, C. (2005, September 29). "Fear exceeded crime's reality in New Orleans." *The New York Times,* A1, A22.

The false Satanism rumor is related in:
Austin, M. J., & Brumfield, L. (1991). "P&G's run-in with the devil." *Business & Society Review, 78,* (summer), 16–19.

The study in which I interviewed a large consumer loan corporation is reported in:
DiFonzo, N., & Bordia, P. (1998). "A tale of two corporations: Managing uncertainty during organizational change." *Human Resource Management, 37,* 295–303.

The official report on the death of Martin Luther King Jr. is found in:
U.S. Department of Justice (2000, June). *Investigation of Recent Allegations Regarding the Assassination of Dr. Martin Luther King Jr.* Retrieved February 26, 2008, from http://www.usdoj.gov/crt/crim/mlk/part1.htm

A statement issued by the family of Martin Luther King Jr. expressing doubt about the official conclusions about his death is found at:
http://www.thekingcenter.org/news/trial.html#Statement

Dexter King's belief that his father was not assassinated by James Earl Ray is reported in:
James Earl Ray, "Convicted King assassin, dies" (1998, April 23). CNN Interactive. Retrieved February 26, 2008, from http://edition.cnn.com/US/9804/23/ray.obit/#top

A transcript of the wrongful death trial brought by Coretta Scott King against Lloyd Jowers may be found at:
http://www.thekingcenter.org/tkc/trial/Volume14.html

The Santander, Spain, arrest is reported in:
"Ferry firm rejects terror rumour" (2007, July 12). BBC News. Retrieved July 13, 2007, from http://news.bbc.co.uk/2/hi/uk_ news/england/devon/6896061.stm

The computer consultant interview was part of a study published in:
DiFonzo, N., Bordia, P., & Rosnow, R. L. (1994). "Reining in rumors." *Organizational Dynamics, 23*(1), 47–62.

The WorldPublicOpinion.org survey is found at:
Kull, S. (2007, April 24). *Muslim public opinion on US policy, attacks on civilians, and al Qaeda.* Retrieved February 26, 2008, from http://www.worldpublicopinion.org/pipa/pdf/apr07/START_Apr07_ rpt.pdf

The questionnaire and news conference associated with the WorldPublicOpinion.org report can be accessed at:
http://www.worldpublicopinion.org/pipa/articles/home_page/346 .php?nid=&id=&pnt=346&lb=hmpg2

The 4,000 Jews rumor is rebuffed at:
U.S. Department of State Bureau of International Information Programs (2005, January 14). "The 4,000 Jews rumor." Retrieved December 18, 2005, from http://usinfo.state.gov/media/ Archive/2005/Jan/14-260933.html

The head-on collision that killed five young women is reported in:

McDermott, M. M. (2007, July 14)." Teens' deaths linked to a chain of errors." *Rochester Democrat & Chronicle,* A1.

The "Avoid Boston on September 22nd" rumor is reported in:

Marks, A. (2001, October 23). "From survival tales to attack predictions, rumors fly." *The Christian Science Monitor,* 2.

The use of racial rumors to justify negative racial attitudes was explored in:

Allport, G. W., & Postman, L. J. (1947). *The Psychology of Rumor.* New York: Holt, Rinehart & Winston.

Rumors surrounding the aftermath of Hurricane Katrina are presented in:

Thevenot, B., & Russell, G. (2005, September 26). "Rumors of deaths greatly exaggerated." NOLA.com. Retrieved January 30, 2008, from http://www.nola.com/newslogs/tporleans/index.ssf?/mtlogs/nola_tporleans/archives/2005_09_26.html #082729

Mikkelson, B. (2005, September 23). "Rest Stop." Retrieved February 26, 2008, from http://snopes.com/katrina/personal/rest stop.asp

Explanation theory and cognitive structures are summarized in:

Krull, D. S., & Anderson, C. A. (1997). "The process of explanation." *Current Directions in Psychological Science, 6,* 1–5.

Anderson, C. A., Krull, D. S., & Weiner, B. (1996). "Explanations: Processes and consequences." In E. T. Higgins & A. W. Kruglanski (eds.), *Social Psychology: Handbook of Basic Principles* (pp. 271–296). New York: Guilford Press.

The Snapple rumor is debunked at:

Mikkelson, B. (2006, December 4). "Snapple Dragoon." Retrieved February 26, 2008, from http://www.snopes.com/business/alliance/snapple.asp

The American Home Mortgage rumor is discussed in:

"American Home Mortgage falls pulled facility rumor" (2007, July 19). Reuters. Retrieved July 23, 2007, from http://www.reuters.com/article/bondsNews/idUSN1923916120070719

The Prodigy rumor discussion was analyzed in:

Bordia, P., & Rosnow, R. L. (1998). "Rumor rest stops on the information superhighway: A naturalistic study of transmission patterns in a computer-mediated rumor chain." *Human Communication Research, 25,* 163–179.

The roles in rumor transmission were originally set forth in:

Shibutani, T. (1966). *Improvised News: A Sociological Study of Rumor.* Indianapolis, IN: Bobbs-Merrill.

Communicative postures are derived in:

Bordia, P., & DiFonzo, N. (2004). "Problem solving in social interactions on the Internet: Rumor as social cognition." *Social Psychology Quarterly, 67,* 33–49.

4. A **Family Resemblance**

Alice Roosevelt Longworth biographical data is contained in:

Quinn, S. (1980, February 20). "The Canny Candor of Alice Longworth." *The Washington Post,* D1.

Bingham, J. (1969, February). "Before the colors fade: Alice Roosevelt Longworth." *American Heritage Magazine, 20*(2). Retrieved

August 27, 2007, from http://www.americanheritage.com/articles/
magazine/ah/1969/2/1969_2_42.shtml

Cordery, S. A. (2007). *Alice: Alice Roosevelt Longworth, From White
House Princess to Washington Power Broker.* New York: Viking.

Knutson, L. L. (1999, June 7). "Alice Roosevelt Longworth, Wild
Thing." Retrieved August 27, 2007, from http://www.salon
.com/people/feature/1999/06/07/longworth/

Gossip, urban legend, and rumor are defined and differentiated in:

DiFonzo, N., & Bordia, P. (2007). "Rumor, gossip, and urban legends." *Diogènes 213, 54*(1), 19–35.

Shame and veneration gossip are investigated in:

Walker, C.J., & Struzyk, D. (1998). "Evidence for a social conduct
moderating function of common gossip." Paper presented to the
International Society for the Study of Close Relationships,
Saratoga Springs.

Talmudic and Jewish ethical teaching with regard to gossip is nicely
summarized in:

Telushkin, J. (1991). *Lashon Ha-Ra/* Gossip. In Rabbi Joseph Telushkin,
Jewish literacy: The Most Important Things to Know About the Jewish Religion, Its People, and Its History (pp. 522–524). New York: William
Morrow and Company. (I am indebted to Daniel E. Phillips for
this excellent text.)

Meir, A. (undated). "The Jewish Ethicist: Office Gossip. How to
protect yourself from listening to workplace gossip." Retrieved
September 1, 2007, from http://www.aish.com/societyWork/
work/The_Jewish_Ethicist_Office_Gossip.asp

Gossip's functions are explored in the following:

Foster, E. K. (2004). "Research on gossip: Taxonomy, methods, and future directions." *Review of General Psychology, 8,* 78–99.

Wert, S. R., & Salovey, P. (2004). "A social comparison account of gossip." *Review of General Psychology, 8,* 122–137.

Baumeister, R. F., Zhang, L., & Vohs, K. D. (2004). "Gossip as cultural learning." *Review of General Psychology, 8,* 111–121.

Dunbar, R. I. M. (1996). *Grooming, Gossip, and the Evolution of Language.* Cambridge: Harvard University Press.

Quotations of Curry's and Feverstone's gossip to Mark Studdock are taken from p. 17 and pp. 39–40, respectively, of:

Lewis, C. S. (1946). *That Hideous Strength: A Modern Fairy-Tale for Grown-ups.* New York: Collier Books.

Holly Hom's research was reported in:

Hom, H., & Haidt, J. (2002). "Psst, Did you hear? Exploring the gossip phenomenon." Poster presented at the Annual Meeting of the Society of Personality and Social Psychologists, Savannah, GA.

Rumor and gossip are contrasted in:

Rosnow, R. L., & Georgoudi, M. (1985). "Killed by idle gossip: The psychology of small talk." In B. Rubin (ed.), *When Information Counts: Grading the Media* (pp. 59–74). Lexington, MA: Lexington Books.

Rosnow, R. L., & Fine, G. A. (1976). *Rumor and Gossip: The Social Psychology of Hearsay.* New York: Elsevier.

The case of the Hooksett 4 is reported in:

Hayasaki, E. (2007, July 24). "4 go through the mill for rumor in N.H." *The Los Angeles Times,* A1.

Russell, J. (2007, May 21). "Rumor mill churns trouble in town." *The Boston Globe*. Retrieved September 5, 2007, from http://www.boston .com/news/local/articles/2007/05/21/rumor_mill_churns _trouble_in_town/?mode

The penguin urban legend, as well as its possible origin in rumor, is retold in:

Clark, R. (2007, July 1). "Penguin rumor stopped cold." Cincinnati.com. *The Enquirer*. Retrieved July 18, 2007, from http:// news.nky.com/apps/pbcs.dll/article?AID=/AB/20070701/ NEWS0103/707010428

Mikkelson, B. (2006, November 26). "Birdnapped." Retrieved February 28, 2007, from http://www.snopes.com/critters/farce/ smuggled.asp

Urban legends are described in:

Fine, G. A. (1992). *Manufacturing Tales: Sex and Money in Contemporary Legends*. Knoxville, TN: University of Tennessee Press.

Mullen, P. B. (1972). "Modern legend and rumor theory." *Journal of the Folklore Institute, 9*, 95–109.

"The Haitian Rat," "The Killer in the Back Seat," "Bosom Serpent," excessive tanning, "AIDS Mary," and "Concrete Cadillac" stories, analysis of urban legends, and many other interesting tales are delightfully recounted in:

Brunvand, J. H. (1981). *The Vanishing Hitchhiker: American Urban Legends and Their Meanings*. New York: Norton.

Brunvand, J. H. (1984). *The Choking Doberman and other "New" Urban Legends*. NY: Norton.

Brunvand, J. H. (1986). *The Mexican Pet: More "New" Urban Legends and Some Old Favorites*. New York: Norton.

Brunvand, J. H. (1999). *Too Good to Be True: The Colossal Book of Urban Legends*. New York: Norton.

Disgusting urban legends were investigated in:
Heath, C., Bell, C., & Sternberg, E. (2001). "Emotional selection in memes: The case of urban legends." *Journal of Personality and Social Psychology, 81,* 1028–1041.

5. It's a Small World Around the Watercooler

The Nancy Wyckoff episode is described in:
Shelton, J. L., & Sanders, R. S. (1973, April). "Mental health intervention in a campus homicide." *College Health, 21,* 346–350. (Quotations in this section originate from p. 347.)

Causes of rumor spread have been summarized in:
Rosnow, R. L. (1991). "Inside rumor: A personal journey." *American Psychologist, 46,* 484–496.

DiFonzo, N., & Bordia, P. (2007). "Rumors influence: Toward a dynamic social impact theory of rumor." In A. R. Pratkanis (ed.), *The Science of Social Influence: Advances and Future Progress* (pp. 271–296). Philadelphia, PA: Psychology Press.

Rumor as a response to an "undefined" situation is best explicated in:
Turner, R. H. (1964). "Collective behavior." In R. E. L. Faris (ed.) *Handbook of Modern Sociology* (pp. 382–425). Chicago: Rand McNally.

Shibutani, T. (1966). *Improvised News: A Sociological Study of Rumor.* Indianapolis, IN: Bobbs-Merrill.

Information on refugees is available from:
"U.S. Committee for Refugees and Immigrants." (2007). *World Refugee*

Survey 2007. Retreived February 29, 2008, from http://www
.refugees.org/article.aspx?id=1941

Rumors among asylum seekers are documented in:
Jawad (undated). "The destructive effect of rumors." *New Times* (a
magazine by Danish Red Cross asylum centers). Retrieved September 15, 2007, from http://newtimes.dk/index.php?option=
com_content&task=view&id=60&Itemid=9

Rumors in the former Soviet Union are investigated in:
Bauer, R. A., & Gleicher, D. B. (1953). "Word-of-mouth communication in the Soviet Union." *Public Opinion Quarterly, 17,* 297–310.

The St. Bonaventure study on rumor and anxiety is reported in:
Walker, C. J., & Beckerle, C. A. (1987). "The effect of anxiety on
rumor transmission." *Journal of Social Behavior and Personality, 2,*
353–360.

The role of the loss of sense of control in rumor transmission is investigated in:
DiFonzo, N., & Bordia, P. (2002). "Corporate rumor activity, belief,
and accuracy." *Public Relations Review, 150,* 1–19.
Bordia, P., Hunt, L., Paulsen, N., Tourish, D., & DiFonzo, N. (2004).
"Communication and uncertainty during organizational change:
Is it all about control?" *European Journal of Work & Organizational
Psychology, 13,* 345–365.

The study investigating infants' reactions to loss of control is
reported in:
Lewis, M., Allesandri, S. M., & Sullivan, M. W. (1990). "Violation of
expectancy, loss of control, and anger expressions in young
infants." *Developmental Psychology, 26*(5), 745–751.

Secondary control in stress management is discussed in:

Rothbaum, F., Weisz, J. R., & Snyder, S. S. (1982). "Changing the world and changing the self: A two-process model of perceived control." *Journal of Personality & Social Psychology, 42,* 5–37.

Primary and secondary control functions of rumor are investigated in:

Walker, C. J. (1996). "Perceived control in wish and dread rumors." Poster presented at the Eastern Psychological Association Meeting, Washington, D.C.

Walker, C. J., & Blaine, B. (1991). "The virulence of dread rumors: A field experiment." *Language and Communication, 11,* 291–297.

The study of rumors in a large Australian hospital is reported in:

Bordia, P., Jones, E., Gallois, C., Callan, V., & DiFonzo, N. (2006). "Management are aliens! Rumors and stress during organizational change." *Group & Organization Management, 31(5),* 601–621.

Rumors during the SEPTA strike are investigated in:

Esposito, J. L. (1986/1987). "Subjective factors and rumor transmission: A field investigation of the influence of anxiety, importance, and belief on rumormongering" (doctoral dissertation, Temple University, 1986). Dissertation Abstracts International, 48, 596B.

The definition of rumor stressing importance is taken from:

Rosnow, R. L., & Kimmel, A. J. (2000). "Rumor." In A. E. Kazdin (ed.), *Encyclopedia of Psychology* (vol. 7, pp. 122–123). New York: Oxford University Press & American Psychological Association, p. 122.

The headlights hoax is described in:

Vigoda, R. (1993, November 5). "Heard about the headlights? The big lie comes sweeping into town." *Philadelphia Inquirer,* B1, B8.

Mikkelson, B. (2004, September 23). "Lights out!" Retrieved November 2, 2004, from http://www.snopes.com/horrors/madmen/lightout.asp

Motives in rumor spread have been theorized in:
Bordia, P., & DiFonzo, N. (2005). "Psychological motivations in rumor spread." In G. A. Fine, C. Heath, & Campion-Vincent, V. (eds.), *Rumor Mills: The Social Impact of Rumor and Legend* (pp. 87–101), New York: Aldine Press.

Research on motives involved in social influence was reviewed in:
Wood, W. (1999). "Motives and modes of processing in the social influence of groups." In S. Chaiken & Y. Trope (eds.), *Dual Process Theories in Social Psychology* (pp. 547–570). New York: The Guilford Press.

The Plymouth High School shooting rumor was reported in:
"Principal: No threat in rumor student will bring gun to Plymouth High School" (2007, October 22). WSBT Channel 22. Retrieved February 29, 2008, from http://www.wsbt.com/news/1071 5596.html

The teddy-bear icon hoax is described in:
JDBGMGR.EXE (September, 2002). Retrieved June 7, 2004, from http://www.snopes.com/computer/virus/jdbgmgr.htm

Being "in the know" as a motive in preferring one rumor over another is described in:
Turner, R. H., & Killian, L. M. (1972). *Collective Behavior* (2nd ed.). Englewood Cliffs, NJ: Prentice-Hall.

The study about RIT and UR rankings is reported in Chapter 3 of:

DiFonzo, N., & Bordia, P. (2007). *Rumor Psychology: Social and Organizational Approaches.* Washington, D.C.: American Psychological Association.

The relationship enhancement motivation is explored in:

Baumeister, R. F., & Leary, M. R. (1995). "The need to belong: Desire for interpersonal attachments as a fundamental human motivation." *Psychological Bulletin, 117,* 497–529.

Leary, M. R. (1995). *Self-Presentation: Impression Management and Interpersonal Behavior.* Boulder, CO: Westview.

The rival school rumor study at the University of Arkansas is reported in:

Kamins, M. A., Folkes, V. S., & Perner, L. (1997). "Consumer responses to rumors: Good news, bad news." *Journal of Consumer Psychology, 6,* 165–187.

The motives behind racist rumors are explored in:

Allport, G. W., & Postman, L. J. (1947). *The Psychology of Rumor.* New York: Holt, Rinehart & Winston.

The tendency for rumors to flow along racial lines is investigated in:

Turner, P. A., & Fine, G. A. (2001). *Whispers on the Color Line: Rumor and Race in America.* Berkeley, CA: University of California Press.

Maines, D. R. (1999). "Information pools and racialized narrative structures." *The Sociological Quarterly, 40,* 317–326.

Sodium laureth sulfate rumors are described in:

Emory, D. (2001, April 8). "What is sodium laureth sulfate, and why are people saying those awful things about it?" Retrieved February 29, 2008, from http://urbanlegends.about.com/library/weekly/aa090998.htm

Jean Noel Kapferer's quotation about rumors during primaries may be found at:

Kapferer, J. N. (1990). *Rumors: Uses, Interpretations, and Images.* (B. Fink, trans.). New Brunswick, NJ: Transaction Publishers, p. 217. (Original work published 1987 as *Rumeurs: Le Plus Vieux Média du Monde* [Rumors: The world's oldest media]. Paris: Editions du Seuil.)

Push-poll rumors about Senator McCain in 2000 are described in this op-ed piece:

Davis, R. H. (2004, March 21). "The anatomy of a smear campaign." *The Boston Globe.* Retrieved December 21, 2007, from http://www.boston.com/news/globe/editorial_opinion/oped/articles/2004/03/21/the_anatomy_of_a_smear_campaign/

Rumors about Hillary Clinton's rumormongering are discussed in:

McCauliff, M., & Katz, C. (2007, November 18). "Hillary Clinton and Barack Obama battle over scandal rumor." *Daily News* (New York). Retrieved February 4, 2008, from http://www.nydailynews.com/news/politics/2007/11/18/2007-11-18_hillary_clinton_and_barack_obama_battle_.html

The many rumors about Barack Obama are described at:
http://snopes.com/politics/obama/obama.asp

Caplow's study of military rumors is reported in:
Caplow, T. (1947). "Rumors in war." *Social Forces, 25,* 298–302.

Cory Booker rumors are described in:

Jacobs, A. (2007, July 3). "Newark's mayor battles old guard and rumors." *The New York Times*. Retrieved July 18, 2007, from http://www.nytimes.com/2007/07/03/nyregion/03dissent.html?_r=1&pagewanted=print&oref=slogin

The role of network structure on rumor spread has been theorized in:

DiFonzo, N., & Bordia, P. (2007). "Rumors influence: Toward a dynamic social impact theory of rumor." In A. R. Pratkanis (ed.), *The Science of Social Influence: Advances and Future Progress* (pp. 271–296). Philadelphia, PA: Psychology Press.

Small worlds are described in:

Watts, D. J. (1999). *Small Worlds: The Dynamics of Networks between Order and Randomness.* Princeton, NJ: Princeton University Press.

Milgram's small world study is reported in:

Milgram, S. (1969). "Inter-disciplinary thinking and the small world problem." In M. Sherif & C. W. Sherif (eds.), *Interdisciplinary Relationships in the Social Sciences* (pp. 103–120). Chicago: Aldine.

The dead mouse rumor is reported in:

Powers, C. (2007, July 20). "Mice at the movies? An e-mail gets the rumor mill going." *The Bulletin*. Retrieved November 6, 2007, from http://www.bendbulletin.com/apps/pbcs.dll/article?AID=/20070720/NEWS0107/707200445/1002

American Internet usage is reported at:

Ho, S. (2007, November 5). "Poll finds nearly 80 percent of U.S. adults go online." *Reuters*. Retrieved February 29, 2008, from

http://www.reuters.com/article/internetNews/idUSN055982
8420071106?feedType=RSS&feedName=internetNews&rpc
=22&sp=true

Festinger's investigation is chronicled in:

Festinger, L., Cartwright, D., Barber, K., Fleischl, J., Gottsdanker, J., Keysen, A., & Leavitt, G. (1948). "A study of rumor: Its origin and spread." *Human Relations, 1,* 464–485. (The quotation on motivation is from p. 482.)

The mathematical simulation of rumor is reported in:

Brooks, B. P., DiFonzo, N., & Ross, D. S. (2006). "Empirically-based mathematical modeling of rumor transmission within social networks." Poster presented at the National Science Foundation Human and Social Dynamics 2006 Principal Investigators Meeting, September 13, 2006, Washington, D.C. (Funding for this research was provided by National Science Foundation Grant No. BCS-0527371.)

Differing shared realities regarding the O. J. Simpson trial are discussed in:

Hardin, C. D., & Conley, T. D. (2001). "A relational approach to cognition: Shared experience and relationship affirmation in social cognition." In Gordon B. Moskowitz (ed.), *Cognitive Social Psychology: The Princeton Symposium on the Legacy and Future of Social Cognition* (pp. 3–18). Mahwah, NJ: Lawrence Erlbaum Associates.

The computer-assisted studies using sixteen-person groups are reported in:

DiFonzo, N., Bourgeois, M. J., Homan, C., Suls, J. M., Brooks, B. P.,

Ross, D. S., Bordia, P., Stupak, N., Frazee, M., Brougher, S., Schwab, N., & McKinlay, M. (2008). "Dynamic social impact mechanisms in rumor propagation." Poster presented at the Group Processes and Intergroup Relations Meeting at the 2008 Annual Conference of the Society for Personality and Social Psychology, February 7, Albuquerque, NM. (Funding for this research was provided by National Science Foundation Grant No. BCS-0527371.)

6. Believe It, or Not

The Brooklyn Bottling story is recounted in:

Freedman, A. M. (1991, May 10). "Rumor turns fantasy into bad dream." *The Wall Street Journal,* B1, B5. (The quotations of the Harlem roofer are from this article.)

Harris, N. (1992, August 10). "Eric Miller is no soda jerk." *Business Week,* p. 28.

Farrell, B. (2003, January 3). "Bottler pops a cork: Buying Iberia Foods." *Daily News* (New York). Suburban, p. 1.

Efforts of the eugenics movement to reduce the birth rate among African-Americans is documented in:

Dula, A. (2007). "Yes, there are African-American perspectives on bioethics." In Nancy S. Jecker, Albert R. Jonsen, Robert A. Pearlman (eds.), *Bioethics: An Introduction to the History, Methods, and Practice* (2nd ed; pp. 252–258). Sudbury, MA: Jones & Bartlett Publishers. (The quotations of Guy Irving Burch and Margaret Sanger are found on p. 253.)

Dula, Annette (1994). "Bioethics: The need for a dialogue with African-Americans." In Annette Dula & Sara Goering (eds.) (1994), *"It Just Ain't Fair": The Ethics of Health Care for African Americans* (pp. 12–20). Westport, CT: Praeger.

The story of the Cardiff Giant is recounted in:

Sears, S. W. (1975, August). "The giant in the earth." *American Heritage Magazine, 26*(5), 94–99. Retrieved December 13, 2007, from http://www.americanheritage.com/articles/magazine/ah/1975/5/1975_5_94.shtml

Brown, R. J. (undated). "P. T. Barnum never did say 'There's a sucker born every minute.' " Retrieved November 21, 2007, from http://www.historybuff.com/library/refbarnum.html

Ross, I. (1968). "A giant of a hoax." *American History Illustrated, 3*(5), 38–41.

Franco, B. (1969). "The Cardiff Giant: A hundred-year-old hoax." *New York History, 50*(4). 420–440.

The world's tallest living man is reported in:

Harvey, L. (2007, August 24). "Leonid Stadnyk named world's tallest man." MSN Hotlist. Retrieved February 29, 2007, from http://hotlist.uk.msn.com/hotlist/leonid_stadnyk_finally_named_world's_tallest_man.aspx

The world's tallest man ever is reported in:

"Tallest Man" (undated). Guinness World Records.com. Retrieved February 29, 2007, from http://www.guinnessworldrecords.com/records/human_body/extreme_bodies/tallest_man.aspx

The strong link between media violence and aggressive behavior is meta-analytically reviewed in:

Niels, C. P., & Wood, W. (2007). "Effects of media violence on viewers' aggression in unconstrained social interaction." In Raymond W. Preiss, Barbara Mae Gayle, Nancy Burrell, Mike Allen, & Jennings Bryant (eds.). *Mass Media Effects Research: Advances Through Meta-Analysis.* (pp. 145–168). Mahwah, NJ: Lawrence Erlbaum Associates.

Bangladesh's early warning system success in the face of Tropical Cyclone Sidr is described in:

Batha, E. (2007, Nov. 16). "Cyclone Sidr would have killed 100,000 not long ago." Reuters Alert Net. Retrieved March 1, 2007, from http://www.alertnet.org/db/blogs/19216/2007/10/16-165438-1.htm

"BANGLADESH: Megaphones save thousands" (2007, November 23). IRIN Humanitarian News and Analysis, UN Office for the Coordination of Humanitarian Affairs. Retrieved March 1, 2008, from http://www.irinnews.org/Report.aspx?ReportId=75470

Dolnick, S. (2007, November 24). "Bangladesh's storm-warning system saved thousands." Star-Tribune.com, Minneapolis-St. Paul, MN. Retrieved November 26, 2007, from http://www.startribune.com/nation/11918861.html

Prasad's study is published in:

Prasad, J. (1935). "The psychology of rumour: A study relating to the great Indian earthquake of 1934." *British Journal of Psychology, 26,* 1–15.

Rumor panic following Tropical Cyclone Sidr is reported in:

Khan, A. W. (2007, November 23). "Tsunami rumour panic [*sic*] thousands." *The Daily Star,* p. 1. Retrieved November 24, 2007, from http://www.thedailystar.net/story.php?nid=12728

"Stampede after tidal surge rumour kills 7 in Barguna" (2007, November 24). *The New Nation*. Retrieved November 24, 2007, from http://nation.ittefaq.com/issues/2007/11/24/news0921.htm

Wartime rationing is described in:

Thorson, P. K. (2001). *Eleanor Roosevelt 1942–1945* (Camp David Diaries, vol. 1). Sterling-Miller Publishing Co.

"World War II Rationing" (undated). Ames Historical Society, Ames, Iowa. Retrieved November 29, 2007, from http://www .ameshistoricalsociety.org/exhibits/events/rationing.htm

The study of rumors of waste and special privilege is presented in:
Allport, F. H., & Lepkin, M. (1945). "Wartime rumors of waste and special privilege: Why some people believe them." *Journal of Abnormal and Social Psychology, 40,* 3–36. (The quotation on motivation is from p. 9.)

Knapp's rumor collection is presented in:
Knapp, R. H. (1944). "A psychology of rumor." *Public Opinion Quarterly, 8,* 22–27.

Declining prejudicial attitudes is documented in:
Quillian, L. (1996). "Group threat and regional change in attitudes toward African-Americans." *The American Journal of Sociology, 102,* (3), 816–860.

The nature and effects of source credibility on persuasion is investigated in:
Hovland, C. I., & Weiss, W. (1951). "The influence of source credibility on communication effectiveness." *Public Opinion Quarterly, 15,* 635–650.
Hovland, C. I., Janis, I. L., & Kelley, H. H. (1953). *Communication and Persuasion: Psychological Studies of Opinion Change.* New Haven: Yale University Press.

Birth control rumors in the Dominican Republic are investigated in:
Porter, E. G. (1984). "Birth control discontinuance as a diffusion process." *Studies in Family Planning, 15,* 20–29. (Porter's results refer to informal information heard from a friend or family and

she unfortunately differentiates informal information from "rumor"; she defines rumor as information "heard on the street." But this definition of rumor is too narrow; rumors also include what Porter referred to as informal information—see Chapter 3 of this book. My summary here is therefore based on Porter's findings pertinent to informal information heard from a friend or family and *not* on what she refers to as rumor.)

The appearance of an authoritative source in successful rumors is investigated in:

Blake, R. H., McFaul, T. R., & Porter, W. H. (1974). "Authority and mass media as variables in rumor transmission." Paper presented at the Western Speech Communication Association, Newport Beach, CA.

The report of the investigation of Foster's death by Whitewater counsel Kenneth Starr is available from *The Washington Post* at:

http://www.washingtonpost.com/wp-srv/politics/special/whitewater/docs/foster.htm

A summary of the above report is found at:

Schmidt, S. (1997, October 11). "Starr probe reaffirms Foster killed himself." *The Washington Post,* A04. Retrieved March 1, 2008, from http://www.washingtonpost.com/wp-srv/politics/special/whitewater/stories/wwtr971011.htm

Foster's depression and eventual suicide is described in:

Von Drehle, D., & Schneider, H. (1994, July 1). "Foster's death a suicide." *The Washington Post,* A01. Retrieved March 1, 2008, from http://www.washingtonpost.com/wp-srv/politics/special/whitewater/stories/wwtr940701.htm
Apple, R. W., Jr. (1993, August 11). "Note left by White House aide:

Accusation, anger and despair." *The New York Times.* Retrieved March 1, 2008, from http://query.nytimes.com/gst/fullpage .html?res=9F0CE7DC1E3AF932A2575BC0A965958260

Hillary Clinton's autobiography is published in:
Clinton, H. (2003). *Living History.* New York: Simon & Schuster.

Preliminary results of the belief-repetition study are reported in:
DiFonzo, N., Bordia, P. Bourgeois, M. J., Brooks, B. P., Ross, D. S., Homan, C., Suls, J. M., Beckstead, J. (2007). "Rumor Propagation: Modeling & Testing Dynamic Social Influence Mechanisms." Poster presented at the National Science Foundation Human and Social Dynamics 2007 Principal Investigators Meeting, October 1–2, 2007, Arlington, VA. (Funding for this research was provided by National Science Foundation Grant No. BCS-0527371.)

Studies of the illusory-truth effect include:
Begg, I. M., Anas, A., & Farinacci, S. (1992). "Dissociation of processes in belief: Source recollection, statement familiarity, and the illusion of truth." *Journal of Experimental Psychology: General, 121,* 446–458.
Boehm, L. E. (1994). "The validity effect—a search for mediating variables." *Personality and Social Psychology Bulletin, 20,* 285–293.
Hasher, L., Goldstein, D., & Toppino, T. (1977). "Frequency and the conference of referential validity." *Journal of Verbal Learning and Verbal Behavior, 16,* 107–112.

The effect of refutation on Pearl Harbor rumors is described in:
Allport, G. W., & Postman, L. J. (1947). *The Psychology of Rumor.* New York: Holt, Rinehart & Winston.

The effect of reading rumor clinic refutations on belief in rumors of waste and special privilege is reported in:

Allport, F. H., & Lepkin, M. (1945). "Wartime rumors of waste and special privilege: Why some people believe them." *Journal of Abnormal and Social Psychology, 40,* 3–36.

Studies on the effects of rumor denial are summarized in chapters 4 and 9 of:

DiFonzo, N., & Bordia, P. (2007). *Rumor Psychology: Social and Organizational Approaches.* Washington, D.C.: American Psychological Association.

Some research shows a "boomerang" effect for refutations (Skurniak, I., Yoon, C., Park, D. C., & Schwarz, N. [2005]. "How warnings about false claims become recommendations." *Journal of Consumer Research, 31,* 713–724). The idea is that refutations (especially if repeated) may make a false statement more familiar to the participant, while at the same time the "not true" tag is forgotten; this thereby leads people to misremember the statement as true. In the Skurniak et al. study, participants were given fifty-four statements that were labeled as either true or false, and then had to remember if they were true or false. Older people misremembered 28 percent as true thirty minutes later and 40 percent as true three days later. However, because this procedure taxed participants' memory capacities, they were more likely to rely on the familiarity heuristic (if it sounds familiar, it must be true) in making judgments of veracity. This study highlighted the importance of the familiarity heuristic, but has limited relevance to real-world refutation efforts in which persons typically hear one refutation at a time and are able to deeply process the denial. This is especially so if the refutation includes point-by-point arguments and evidence against the rumor.

The Broker studies are reported in:

DiFonzo, N., & Bordia, P. (1997). "Rumor and prediction: Making sense (but losing dollars) in the stock market." *Organizational Behavior and Human Decision Processes, 71,* 329–353.

"Watered down" belief is discussed in:

Prasad, J. (1935). "The psychology of rumour: A study relating to the great Indian earthquake of 1934." *British Journal of Psychology, 26,* 1–15.

Temple University strike rumors are investigated in:

Rosnow, R. L., Yost, J. H., & Esposito, J. L. (1986). "Belief in rumor and likelihood of rumor transmission." *Language and Communication, 6*(3), 189–194.

An introductory explanation of loss aversion is included in:

Plous, S. (1993). *The Psychology of Judgment and Decision Making.* New York: McGraw-Hill.

Motivated reasoning is explored in:

Kunda, Z. (1990). "The case for motivated reasoning." *Psychological Bulletin 108,* 480–498.

Trope, Y., & Liberman, A. (1996). "Social hypothesis testing: Cognitive and motivational mechanisms." In E. T. Higgins & A. W. Kruglanski (eds.), *Social Psychology: Handbook of Basic Principles* (pp. 239–270). NY: Guilford Press.

Trope, Y., & Thompson, E. P. (1997). "Looking for truth in all the wrong places? Asymmetric search of individuating information about stereotyped group members." *Journal of Personality and Social Psychology, 73,* 229–241.

7. Facts Are Stubborn Things

Michelle Cottle's advice may be found at:

Cottle, Michelle (1999, April 4). "Rumor might have it, but have it dead wrong." *The New York Times,* BU-7.

Base rates are discussed in:

Plous, S. (1993). *The Psychology of Judgment and Decision Making.* New York: McGraw-Hill.

Hammond, J. S., Keeney, R. L., & Raiffa, H. (1999). *Smart Choices: A Practical Guide to Making Better Decisions.* Boston, MA: Harvard Business School Press.

Rumor accuracy studies are summarized in Chapter 6 of:

DiFonzo, N., & Bordia, P. (2007). *Rumor Psychology: Social and Organizational Approaches.* Washington, D.C.: American Psychological Association.

The quotation from Caplow's study is on page 301 of:

Caplow, T. (1947). "Rumors in war." *Social Forces, 25,* 298–302.

Davis's review of grapevine accuracy is included in:

Davis, K. (1972). *Human Behavior at Work.* San Francisco: McGraw-Hill.

Davis, K. (1975, June). "Cut those rumors down to size." *Supervisory Management,* pp. 2–6.

Davis distinguishes rumor from grapevine information on p. 268 of *Human Behavior at Work:* "Rumor is grapevine information which is communicated without secure standards of evidence being present." He also states that rumors are false statements that circulate on the grapevine. This definition of rumor is too narrow. Rumor also includes most of the information that Davis labels "grapevine" information. A review of the kinds of information he studies confirms this. For example, on p. 263 of Davis [1972] the daughter of the manager marrying the welder is clearly a rumor—he calls it grapevine information. On p. 266, the story of a man having trouble with his computer taxes is a rumor from the point of view of "Smith." On p. 267: "company planning to move" is also a rumor. Thus, his results apply to rumor as I have defined it in Chapter 3 of this book.

Rudolph's study of telephone company employees is reported in:
Rudolph, E. (1971). "A study of informal communication patterns within a multi-shift public utility organizational unit." Unpublished doctoral dissertation, University of Denver.
Rudolph, E. (1973). "Informal human communication systems in a large organization." *Journal of Applied Communication Research, 1,* 7–23.

Published takeover rumor accuracy is reported in:
Pound J., & Zeckhauser, R. (1990). "Clearly heard on the street: The effect of takeover rumors on stock prices." *Journal of Business, 63,* 291–308.

Sinha's study of rumors after a landslide is reported in:
Sinha, D. (1952). Behaviour in a catastrophic situation: A psychological study of reports and rumours. *British Journal of Psychology, 43,* 200–209.

Rumor accuracy for rumors circulating in the wake of a graduate student strike is reported in:
Weinberg, S. B., & Eich, R. K. (1978). "Fighting fire with fire: Establishment of a rumor control center." *Communication Quarterly, 26,* 26–31.

Kyle Orland's analysis is found at:

Orland, K. (2007, January 11). "Rumor report ratings." *Game Daily.* Retrieved December 21, 2007, from http://www.gamedaily.com/articles/features/rumor-report-ratings/69916/?biz=1

The Matthew Accuracy Effect is explored in:

DiFonzo, N., & Bordia, P. (2007). *Rumor Psychology: Social and Organizational Approaches.* Washington, D.C.: American Psychological Association.

The Matthew Science Effect is explored in:

Merton, R. K. (1968). "The Matthew effect in science." *Science, 159,* 56–63.

The biblical quotation is taken from:

Matthew 25:29 in the *New International Version* of the Bible.

The teller-listener extremity effect is investigated in:

Baron, R. S., David, J. P., Brunsman, B. M., & Inman, M. (1997). "Why listeners hear less than they are told: Attentional load and the Teller-Listener Extremity effect." *Journal of Personality and Social Psychology, 72,* 826–838.

Allport and Postman's studies using serial transmission are documented in:

Allport, G. W., & Postman, L. J. (1947). *The Psychology of Rumor.* New York: Holt, Rinehart & Winston.

The extent to which serial transmission resembles real-life rumor transmission is discussed in:

Bordia, P. (1996). "Studying verbal interaction on the Internet: The case of rumor transmission research." *Behavior Research Methods, Instruments, and Computers, 28,* 149–151.

Buckner, H. T. (1965). A theory of rumor transmission. *Public Opinion Quarterly, 29,* 54–70.

The effect of discussion on accuracy in a serial transmission task is investigated in:
McAdam, J. R. (1962). "The effect of verbal interaction on the serial reproduction of rumor." Unpublished Doctoral Dissertation, Indiana University.

Allport and Postman explore leveling, sharpening, and assimilation in rumor transmission in:
Allport, G. W., & Postman, L. J. (1947). *The Psychology of Rumor.* New York: Holt, Rinehart & Winston.

The "Gary the Footballer" study is reported in:
Lyons, A., & Kashima, Y. (2001). "The reproduction of culture: Communication processes tend to maintain cultural stereotypes." *Social Cognition, 19,* 372–394.

The rumor that George W. Bush was nominated for the Nobel peace prize is true:
"Nobel Prize!" (2002, October 15). Retrieved March 1, 2008, from http://www.snopes.com/rumors/nobel.htm

Amway is described in:
"The largest private companies" (2006, November 9). *Forbes.* Retrieved December 31, 2007, from http://www.forbes.com/lists/2006/21/biz_06privates_The-Largest-Private-Companies_Rank_2.html
"About Amway" (undated). Amway.com. Retrieved January 1, 2008, from http://www.amway.com/en/General/About-Amway-10725.aspx

The transcript of the April 1995 rumor dissemination event is included in this complaint filed by P&G:

"Procter & Gamble Company vs. Randy L. Haugen" (1995, August 25). Civil No. 1:95CV 0094W. Retrieved December 9, 2007, from http://www.courttv.com/archive/legaldocs/misc/satan.html

Descriptions of the case and outcome of the trial are reported in:

Kirdahy, M. (2007, March 23). "The devil didn't make them do it." Forbes.com. Retrieved January 1, 2008, from http://www.forbes.com/facesinthenews/2007/03/22/procter-gamble-faces-markets-equity-cx_mk_0320autofacescano2.html

"Procter & Gamble awarded $19.25 million in Satanism lawsuit" (2007, March 20). FoxNews.com. Retrieved January 1, 2008, from http://www.foxnews.com/printer_friendly_story/0,356 6,259877,00.html

Fattah, G. (2007, March 20). "Amway distributors face $19 million judgment in suit." *Deseret Morning News*. Retrieved March 1, 2008, from http://deseretnews.com/dn/view/0,1249,6602 04650,00.html

Defendant's response to the award:

"Randy Haugen response to losing $19.25 million to Procter & Gamble" (2007, March 21). MLMblog. Retrieved March 1, 2008, from http://www.mlmblog.net/2007/03/randy_haugen_re .html

The false report of a child rape in Montgomery, Alabama, is reported in:

"Montgomery police debunk child rape rumor." (2007, July 10).

WSFA 12. Retrieved July 11, 2007, from http://www.wsfa.com/global/story.asp?s=6769212

Widespread prohibitions against lying are indicated by near universal cultural values of integrity as explained in:
Peterson, C., & Seligman, M. E. P. (2004). *Character Strengths and Virtues: A Handbook and Classification*. Oxford: Oxford University Press.

Accuracy motivation stemming from a desire to enhance relationships is theorized in:
Rosnow, R. L., Yost, J. H., & Esposito, J. L. (1986). "Belief in rumor and likelihood of rumor transmission." *Language and Communication, 6*(3), 189–194.

Conversational norms of truth-telling are described in:
Grice, H. P. (1975). "Logic and conversation." The William James Lectures. In P. Cole & J. L. Morgan (eds.), *Syntax and Semantics* (vol. 3, pp. 41–58). New York: Academic Press.
Higgins, E. T. (1981). "The 'communication game': Implications of social cognition." In E. T. Higgins, C. P. Herman, & M. P. Zanna (eds.), *Social Cognition: The Ontario Symposium* (vol. 1, pp. 343–392). Hillsdale, NJ: Lawrence Erlbaum Associates.

The murder rumors study is found in:
Rabideau, S. (2007). "The effect of impression and accuracy motivation on likelihood of rumor transmission" [Unpublished Senior Project]. Department of Psychology, Rochester Institute of Technology, Rochester, NY.

Evidence-based positive coping methods are described in:
Kleinke, C. L. (2002). *Coping with Life Challenges* (2nd ed.). Long Grove, IL: Waverly Press.

The study of a group undergoing radical downsizing is described in chapters 2 and 8 of:

DiFonzo, N., & Bordia, P. (2007). *Rumor Psychology: Social and Organizational Approaches.* Washington, D.C.: American Psychological Association.

The study in which students reported many more true than false workplace rumors is found in Chapter 6 of:

DiFonzo, N., & Bordia, P. (2007). *Rumor Psychology: Social and Organizational Approaches.* Washington, D.C.: American Psychological Association.

The Chinese dumpling story is reported in:

"Meat buns with cardboard fillings in Beijing is hoax" (2007, July 19). *China View.* Retrieved July 20, 2007, from http://news.xinhuanet.com/english/2007-07/19/content_6398168.htm

Message checking is exemplified in the accurate recovery of the details of a massacre during the Korean War many years earlier, as reported in:

Choe, S., Hanley, C. J., & Mendoza, M. (1999, October 17). "GIs admit murdering civilians in South Korea." *Rochester Democrat & Chronicle,* 1A, 3A.

Pete Wilson's death, rumored and real, is reported in:

Bell, D. (2007, July 21). "Pete Wilson is alive and well, thanks." *Union Tribune.* Retrieved July 23, 2007, from http://www.signonsandiego.com/news/metro/bell/20070721-9999-1m21bell.html

Nevius, C. W. (2007, July 22). Pete Wilson: 1945–2007. "TV news anchor was a straight shooter." SFGate.com. Retrieved July 23,

2007, from http://www.sfgate.com/cgi-bin/article.cgi?file=/
c/a/2007/07/22/MNGPCR500G1.DTL

Group characteristics and assets that foster checking were first
described in:
Buckner, H. T. (1965). "A theory of rumor transmission." *Public
Opinion Quarterly, 29,* 54–70.

The Prodigy rumor discussion was analyzed in:
Bordia, P., & Rosnow, R. L. (1998). "Rumor rest stops on the information superhighway: A naturalistic study of transmission
patterns in a computer-mediated rumor chain." *Human Communication Research, 25,* 163–179.

The accuracy achieved by newspapers as compared to nonmedia
Web sites in the aftermath of the events of September 11, 2001, is
analyzed in:
Lasora, D. (2003). "News media perpetuate few rumors about 9/11
crisis." *Newspaper Research Journal, 24*(1), 10–21.

Spread of the false Pop Rocks rumor among sixth-grade boys is ana-
lyzed in:
Fine, G. A. (1985). "Rumors and gossiping." In *Handbook of Discourse
Analysis,* vol. 3 (pp. 223–237). London: Academic Press.

Situations of high anxiety or threat where rumors are passed
indiscriminately are described as *extemporaneous* rumor spreading in:
Shibutani, T. (1966). *Improvised News: A Sociological Study of Rumor.* Indianapolis, IN: Bobbs-Merrill.

Conformity effects in rumor spreading are noted in:

Firth, R. (1956). "Rumor in a primitive society." *Journal of Abnormal and Social Psychology, 53,* 122–132.

Åckerström, M. (1988). "The social construction of snitches." *Deviant Behavior, 9,* 155–167.

Conditions for the emergence of collective intelligence are described in:

Surowiecki, J. (2005). *The Wisdom of Crowds.* New York: Anchor Publishing.

The vigorous debate over alleged Florida voting anomalies is reported in:

Zeller, T., Jr. (2004, November 12). "Voter fraud theories, spread by blogs, are quickly buried." *The New York Times.* Retrieved December 20, 2007, from http://www.nytimes.com/2004/11/12/politics/12theory.html?_r=3&ei=5070&en=da24076961c8d&oref=slogin

Liberal and conservative clustering on the World Wide Web is analyzed in:

Adamic, L., & Glance, N. (2005, March 4). "The political blogosphere and the 2004 election: Divided they blog." Retrieved March 1, 2008, from http://www.blogpulse.com/papers/2005/AdamicGlanceBlogWWW.pdf

The percolation model of rumor accuracy is presented in:

DiFonzo, N., & Bordia, P. (2002). "Corporate rumor activity, belief, and accuracy." *Public Relations Review, 150,* 1–19.

The percolation model builds upon an earlier model of rumor accuracy proposed in:

Buckner, H. T. (1965). "A theory of rumor transmission." *Public Opinion Quarterly, 29,* 54–70.

8. Managing the Rumor Mill

The screenplay for *It's a Wonderful Life* is available at:

Goodrich, F., Hackett, A., Capra, F., & Swerling, J. (1946). "It's a Wonderful Life. The Internet Movie Script Database." Retrieved January 14, 2008, from http://www.imsdb.com/scripts/It's-a-Wonderful-Life.html

Runs on Countrywide bank are reported in:

Reckhard, E. S., & Haddad, A. (2007, August 17). "A rush to pull out cash." *Los Angeles Times.* Retrieved January 14, 2008, from http://www.latimes.com/business/printedition/la-fi-country wide17aug17,0,5944637.story

The use of rumor as an independent information source in the Soviet Union is reported in:

Bauer, R. A., & Gleicher, D. B. (1953). "Word-of-mouth communication in the Soviet Union." *Public Opinion Quarterly, 17,* 297–310.

The press release for the report finding heavy reliance on rumors by European workers is found at:

"British businesses are buzzing with rumors" (2005, April 5). *ISR London.* Retrieved December 21, 2007, from http://www.isrinsight.com/pdf/media/UKRumour0405.pdf. (The suggestion that stock price is affected by internal company rumors should be viewed with caution; the causal sequence in this survey might be in the other direction [e.g., poor performance might lead to rumors], or might be due to a third factor [poor management leads to poor performance and many rumors].)

The role of communication in uncertainty reduction is investigated in:

DiFonzo, N., & Bordia, P. (1998). "A tale of two corporations: Managing uncertainty during organizational change." *Human Resource Management, 37*(3&4), 295–303.

DiFonzo, N., & Bordia, P. (2000). "How top PR professionals handle hearsay: Corporate rumors, their effects, and strategies to manage them." *Public Relations Review, 26,* 173–190.

DiFonzo, N., Bordia, P., & Rosnow, R. L. (1994). "Reining in Rumors." *Organizational Dynamics, 23*(1), 47–62.

Rumor control centers are described in:

Weinberg, S. B., & Eich, R. K. (1978). "Fighting fire with fire: Establishment of a rumor control center." *Communication Quarterly, 26,* 26–31.

"Rumors of war" (2001, September 26). *Baltimore City Paper.* Retrieved September 7, 2007, from http://www.citypaper.com/printStory.asp?id=3070

Allport, F. H., & Lepkin, M. (1945). "Wartime rumors of waste and special privilege: Why some people believe them." *Journal of Abnormal and Social Psychology, 40,* 3–36.

The Katy Independent School District rumor response Web site (Fact! or Fiction?) is located at:

http://www.katyisd.org/services/communications/fact_fiction.htm

The Charlotte County, Florida, rumor control Web site is described at:

"Charlotte County launches Rumor Central link on Web site" (2008, January 4). SunHerald.com. Retrieved January 7, 2008, from http://www.sun-herald.com/breakingnews.cfm?id=4357

The Charlotte County, Florida, rumor control Web site is located at: http://www.charlottecountyfl.com/

Research showing the ineffectiveness of a "no comment" response—without a context—is presented in Chapter 9 of:
DiFonzo, N., & Bordia, P. (2007). *Rumor Psychology: Social and Organizational Approaches.* Washington, DC: American Psychological Association.

Starbucks's "no comment" approach to rumors of free Wi-Fi is reported in:
"Starbucks mum on rumor it will offer free Wi-Fi" (2007, October 14). *Seattle Post-Intelligencer. The Insider.* Retrieved October 16, 2007, from http://seattlepi.nwsource.com/business/335456_theinsider15.html

Volvo's "no comment" response is reported in:
"Volvo no comment on MAN bid rumour, but notes 2 cos' high combined mkt share" (2007, July 19). Forbes.com. Retrieved July 20, 2007, from http://www.forbes.com/markets/feeds/afx/2007/07/19/afx3929736.html

Advice on handling gossip is found in:
Fisher, A. (2005, December 12). "Psst! Rumors can help at work." *Fortune.* Retrieved December 21, 2007, from http://money.cnn.com/magazines/fortune/fortune_archive/2005/12/12/8363102/index.htm

The finding that 20 percent of a grapevine network consisted of highly connected hubs (liaisons) is reported on p. 264 of:

Davis, K. (1972). *Human Behavior at Work*. San Francisco: McGraw-Hill.

You can read about Mrs. Beamster in:

Thaler, M., & Lee, J. (ill.) (1997). *The Librarian from the Black Lagoon*. New York: Scholastic.

Hirschhorn's methods focused on anxiety reduction can be read in:

Hirschhorn, L. (1983). *Cutting back: Retrenchment and Redevelopment in Human and Community Services*. San Francisco: Jossey-Bass.

Methods of coping with anxiety by making more rational appraisals are documented in:

Kleinke, C. L. (2002). *Coping with Life Challenges* (2nd ed.). Long Grove, IL: Waverly Press.

The *Black Lagoon* Teacher Activity Guide is available at:

http://teacher.scholastic.com/products/westonwoods/study_guides/librarian_from_black_lagoon.pdf

The Mars story is debunked at:

"Mars Spectacular" (2007, July 28). Retrieved March 1, 2008, from http://www.snopes.com/science/mars.asp

The Hilfiger rumor is debunked at:

Mikkelson, B. (2007, May 2). "Tommy Rot." Retrieved January 19, 2008, from http://www.snopes.com/racial/business/hilfiger.asp

A partial transcript of *The Oprah Winfrey Show* in which Tommy Hilfiger appeared to help debunk the rumor may be found at:

"Oprah and Tommy Hilfiger set the record straight" (2007, May 2). Retrieved January 19, 2008, from http://www2.oprah.com/tows/slide/200705/20070502/slide_20070502_350_101.jhtml

Rumor refutation is discussed in:

Bordia, P., DiFonzo, N., & Schulz, C. A. (2000). "Source characteristics in denying rumors of organizational closure: Honesty is the best policy." *Journal of Applied Social Psychology, 11,* 2301–2309.

Bordia, P., DiFonzo, N., & Travers, V. (1998). "Denying rumors of organizational change: A higher source is not always better." *Communications Research Reports, 15*(2). 189–198.

Bordia, P., DiFonzo, N., Haines, R., & Chaseling, L. (2005). "Rumor denials as persuasive messages: Effects of personal relevance, source, and message characteristics." *Journal of Applied Social Psychology 35,* 1301–1331.

Kimmel, A. J. (2004). *Rumors and Rumor Control: A Manager's Guide to Understanding and Combatting Rumors.* Mahwah, NJ: Lawrence Erlbaum Associates.

Parts of the Procter & Gamble "truth kit" have been documented in:

Koenig, F. W. (1985). *Rumor in the Marketplace: The Social Psychology of Commercial Hearsay.* Dover, MA: Auburn House.

The persistence of the Madalyn Murray O'Hair rumor is described in:

Noguchi, Y. (2001, December 26). "Fighting a myth of Biblical proportions." *The Washington Post,* D07. Retrieved March 2, 2008, from http://urbanlegends.about.com/gi/dynamic/offsite.htm?site=http://www.washingtonpost.com/ac2/wp%2Ddyn/A24664%2D2001Dec25%3Flanguage=printer

Mikkelson, B. (2008, February 21). "Petition to ban religious broadcasting." Retrieved March 2, 2008, from http://www.snopes.com/politics/religion/fcc.asp

The Hurriyah affair is reported in:
Memmott, M. (2006, November 30). "Iraqi official calls AP's atrocity story a 'rumor'; AP stands by its work." USAToday.com. Retrieved January 21, 2008, from http://blogs.usatoday.com/ondeadline/2006/11/iraqi_official_.html
"New savage twist to violence in Baghdad" (2006, November 24). USAToday.com. Retrieved January 21, 2008, from http://www.usatoday.com/news/world/iraq/2006-11-24-car-bomb_x.htm

The study of trust and rumor in an organization undergoing radical downsizing is presented in Chapter 8 of:
DiFonzo, N., & Bordia, P. (2007). *Rumor Psychology: Social and Organizational Approaches.* Washington, D.C.: American Psychological Association.

Building trust by reliably pairing words and deeds is discussed in:
Daniels, A. C. (2000). *Bringing Out the Best in People: How to Apply the Astonishing Power of Positive Reinforcement.* New York: McGraw-Hill.

Evidence supporting the contact hypothesis is summarized in:
Pettigrew, T. F., & Tropp, L. R. (2000). "Does intergroup contact reduce prejudice? Recent meta-analytic findings." In S. Oskamp (ed.), *Reducing Prejudice and Discrimination* (pp. 93–114). Mahwah, NJ: Lawrence Erlbaum Associates.

An analysis that recommends responding to rumors early is found at:
Van Hoffman, C. (2007, March 26). "News Analysis: Companies

have devil of a time denying rumors." Brandweek.com. Retrieved January 21, 2008, from http://www.brandweek.com/bw/ magazine/current/article_display.jsp?vnu_content_id=10035 62559

Combating rumors about one's company on the Internet is discussed in:
Bell, B. A. (1998). "Dealing with false Internet rumors: A primer." Retrieved January 19, 2008, from http://library.findlaw.com/ 1999/Aug/1/130891.html

John McCain's "truth squad" strategy is reported in:
Schnur, D. (2008, January 18). "McCain's anti-rumor strategy." *Los Angeles Times*. Retrieved January 18, 2008, from http://www .latimes.com/news/nationworld/nation/la-na-trail truth18jan18,1,699442.story?coll=la-headlines-nation&c track=1&cset=true
Eilperin, J. (2008, January 8). "McCain ready to truth squad." WashingtonPost.com. Retrieved January 21, 2008, from http://blog. washingtonpost.com/the-trail/2008/01/08/mccain_ready _to_truth_squad.html

The PBR study (a fictional corporation) is presented in Chapter 9 of:
DiFonzo, N., & Bordia, P. (2007). *Rumor Psychology: Social and Organizational Approaches.* Washington, D.C.: American Psychological Association.

Chinese earthquake rumor refutation is described in:
Turner, R. H. (1994). "Rumor as intensified information seeking: Earthquake rumors in China and the United States." In R. R. Dynes & K. J. Tierney (eds.), *Disasters, Collective Behavior, and*

Social Organization (pp. 244–256). Newark, DE: University of Delaware Press.

Tertullian's rumor refutation can be found in *The Apology,* available at:
http://www.tertullian.org/anf/anf03/anf03-05.htm

Senator Obama's efforts to squelch rumors are described in:
"Obama battles Muslim rumors head-on" (2008, January 23). CNNPolitics.com. Retrieved January 23, 2008, from http://politicalticker.blogs.cnn.com/2008/01/23/obama-battles-muslim-rumor-head-on/

Senator Obama's refutation during his interview with David Brody can be viewed at:
http://www.cnn.com/video/#/video/politics/2008/01/22/blitzer.david.brody.cnn

A model for deciding to help others is found in:
Darley, J. M., & Latane, B. (1968). "When will people help in a crisis?" *Psychology Today, 2*(7), 54–57, 70–71.

The Indian Disaster Management Act of 2005 may be viewed at:
http://rajyasabha.nic.in/bills-ls-rs/2005/LV_2005.pdf

Police attempts to imprison rumor spreaders in India are reported in:
One year imprisonment for rumour mongers" (2007, June 27). *Pune Newsline.*
Police to hunt for rumour mongers (2007, July 1). *The Times of India.* Retrieved July 18, 2007, from http://timesofindia.indiatimes.com/articleshow/msid-2164391,prtpage-1.cms

Student suspensions for spreading rumors are reported in:

Broden, S. (2007, November 17). "Parent says son is rumor scape-goat." *The Daily News Journal.* Murfreesboro, TN. Retrieved November 18, 2007, from http://dnj.midsouthnews.com/apps/pbcs.dll/article?AID=/20071117/NEWS01/711170315/1002

Lawsuits against cyber rumormongers are described in:

Bell, B. A. (1998). "Dealing with false Internet rumors: A primer." Retrieved January 19, 2008, from http://library.findlaw.com/1999/Aug/1/130891.html

The ThinkSecret.com agreement is reported in:

Boran, M. (2007, December 21). "Apple forces rumour sites to think twice." SiliconRepublic.com. Retrieved January 26, 2008, from http://www.siliconrepublic.com/news/news.nv?storyid=single9927

Epilogue

The opening quotation is from p. 274 of:

McGuire, W. J. (1986). "A perspectivist looks at contextualism and the future of behavioral science." In R. L. Rosnow and M. Georgoudi (eds.), *Contextualism and understanding in behavioral science* (pp. 271–301). New York: Praeger. (Thanks to Jim Esposito for drawing attention to this quotation.)

Index